Edgar Fawcett

Divided Lives

A Novel

.

Edgar Fawcett

Divided Lives
A Novel

ISBN/EAN: 9783337026363

Printed in Europe, USA, Canada, Australia, Japan

Cover: Foto ©Thomas Meinert / pixelio.de

More available books at **www.hansebooks.com**

DIVIDED LIVES.

DIVIDED LIVES

A Novel

BY

EDGAR FAWCETT

AUTHOR OF "AN AMBITIOUS WOMAN"; "THE CONFESSIONS OF CLAUD"; "A HOPE-
LESS CASE"; "THE HOUSE AT HIGH BRIDGE"; SOCIAL SILHOUETTES"; "THE
ADVENTURES OF A WIDOW"; "TINKLING CYMBALS," ETC.

NEW YORK

NATIONAL BOOK COMPANY

3, 4, 5 AND 6 MISSION PLACE

TO MY FRIEND,

GEORGE PARSONS LATHROP,

POET AND NOVELIST,

IN THE HOPE THAT MANY PROSPEROUS DAYS

MAY BE

APPORTIONED TO A WRITER

WHOM THE LETTERS OF HIS LAND

SO ILL CAN SPARE.

DIVIDED LIVES.

I.

THE world, for at least one man who lived in it, was hung with black. This man's name was Hubert Throckmorton.

He had taken the cars (a journey of about an hour or so) from New York to Ponchatuk. In this part of Long Island lay an estate of his, left him some years ago by his late father. The season was early June, and Locustwood (the name of Hubert's domain) was full of that peace, dream, and tender surprise which marks our belated American spring.

There had been times, with Hubert, when he had told himself that he detested Ponchatuk. Its name had always seemed to him the most aggressive array of bristling consonants. Then, too, the "South Side," as it is elliptically called, had been apt to bore him past words, except during the season of woodcock and quail. He hated fishing; it had, he thought, too much mean and sly craft in it to make a real sport of; and if you did not fish at Ponchatuk you hardly dwelt there. Take away its blue-fish, Hubert had long ago asserted, and the South Side had nothing left except its deadly pancake flatness and its sanguinary mosquitoes.

He was in error, here; it had its magnificent salty breezes, rushing straight across Fire Island from the ocean. This evening, at twilight, he felt one of them sweep his face and throat like the firm, cool fingers of a woman. The spring sky had got a translucent daffodil color, as though the sunken sun had dropped into some awful cauldron of ruin, and

7

this wild gold light were flung upward from its giant confla-
gration. A few of the locust-trees about the big, solemn old
house were pale with vernal flowers; as their boughs tossed
in the uncertain dusk they were not unlike hands that pleaded. Soon the stars began to come out in their sweet, reluctant way, and dotted the darkening heaven with globules of
white fire.

Hubert continued to walk about the grounds. The hour
suited him, with its melancholy and mystery. Notwithstanding the tender hint of promise that all nature gave,
there was a plaintiveness in the rise and fall of the wind, in
the loitering advent of gloom, in the glitter of dawning plan-
ets or far remoter orbs, that accorded with his own heart-
broken state.

That day had been the wedding-day of the woman whose
smile had once fed his being, whose glance had possessed
the power to dizzy him with a delicious vertigo, whose
touch had held for him the electric energy no wisdom can
explain and no rhapsody can fitly portray.

She had married, that afternoon, a man whom she could not
have loved, and toward whom her matrimonial motive must
have been sordid in the extreme. A few weeks ago, if Hubert had been told that Angela Laight would have stood at
the altar with any lover except himself, he would have felt inclined to rank such a prophecy at one with the mad babble
heard in cells of asylums. But fate had kept this poison-
tipped dart in her quiver, nevertheless, and had shot it at
him with a frightful abruptness. He had been like one who
at the same time is called on to stanch as best he may an
ugly and almost mortal wound and to realize that it has been
dealt him by the last person he has deemed capable of so
base an injury ... Angela had never cared for him? She
was incapable of a sincere passion? To answer these questions negatively was like denying gravitation or affirming
that two and two make five. And yet he had been forced to
face the anguish and irony of such a concession. Even now,

two good weeks after it had been made known to him, the
novelty of this truth appalled him no less than its nudity.

Still, it had become, in another sense, fatally familiar.
Hubert saw into his future, and found that it had about the
same sort of perspective as a prairie for one who roams
there. His life seemed to him like a tangle of torn and
bleeding vine-tendrils. " What shall I do with my days? "
he moaned in spirit to himself, again and again.

He and Angela had known each other just a year. Destiny had perpetrated one of her most poignant sarcasms in
making the occasion of the girl's marriage to Bleakly Voght
the anniversary of her first meeting with Hubert. Angela
had been the former school-mate and present friend of a
brilliant and admired young widow (in some rather far-
removed degree a kinswoman of Hubert's) named Mrs.
Prescott Averill.

At the dainty and ornate little Madison Avenue abode of
the latter lady, Miss Laight and Mr. Throckmorton had met
one another. There were those who liked to say that Alva
Averill was equal to almost any device for making Hubert
visit that pretty Madison Avenue house of hers oftener than
he already did. If such biting talk were based on fact,
Angela served as a most effective decoy.

" She's the sweetest and brightest of girls," Mrs. Averill
had told the man who had afterwards fallen passionately in
love with her expected guest. " Everybody loved her at
Madame Charnier's. She will be with me for a month, and
I do so hope you will help me to make things pleasant for
her."

These words had been spoken in Mrs. Averill's drawing-
room, one evening, while the rose-tinted beams from a near
lamp fell across her lucent silken dress, and a fitful fire on
the low hearth flung flashes of luxurious revelation over
pictured screen, tiger-skin rug, or big *email cloisonné* jar.

Hubert nodded amicably, and looked at his hostess. Being
a sort of distant cousin to her, and having received from her

many social courtesies, he had often asked himself why it
was that he cared for her so slightly. She had made a re-
pulsively cold-blooded marriage. He had always hated the
willingness that we find in some women to wed old men for
their money, and Alva's husband had been sixty if a day,
with red-lidded eyes, and a very senile rheumatism.

"I'll make things as pleasant as I can," he said. "I'll give
her a little Delmonico dinner, and a dance afterwards—you
to receive for me, of course."

"That will be ever so nice," answered Mrs. Averill. Her
voice had grown lower as she went on speaking, and into it
had crept a husky note which some men thought fascinating.
"I often wonder, Hu," she said, "why you *are* so good to
me always. It isn't because we're a kind of cousin to one
another; it can't be; for there's Effie Van Dam, who's your
first cousin, and yet whom you don't care a button for."

"And I care about the same for you," Hubert told himself. As he glanced, then, at Mrs. Averill, this quick and
harsh mental response dealt its own covert composer a sting
of conscience. There she sat, with keen-tinted cushions
piled for vivid background on the small sofa that held her,
looking lithe and delicate as a lily. But the semblance
went no further; in cheek and throat dwelt almost the olive
shade of a mulattress, and where her smooth, full arm lifted
a coil of snaky gold, its darkness of tinge turned nearly
swarthy. Her eyes had been pronounced, by those who win
repute as judges of such facial effects, too large for the visage they beamed from. But they were eyes that could flood
their night-black pupils with a rich and gentle splendor, and
one whose sorceries found few men so callous as Hubert.

It all came to this : she was very much in love with him,
and wanted him for her second husband; while he saw in her
only a pretty woman who made him reproach himself because of the vague and causeless repulsion that she sometimes
inspired. Meanwhile he had no idea that she aimed to be
his wife; he would have laughed loud disbelief at anybody

who had so affirmed to him. His friends had always said that he did not know how to behave uncivilly toward a soul on earth, and this was true past all doubt whenever it became a question of his receiving civil treatment from another. Indeed, the art of repelling people who approach us in a spirit of amity is never easy for a large and fine nature ; it is the *âme de laquais* that can both bend the knee and curl the lip with a most facile readiness. "If Hubert had not been a rich man, a good-looking man, and a Throckmorton as well," somebody had once said of him, "society would never have forgiven him for being a poet." To which the answer is possible, that if he had not been a poet he would perhaps never have seen anything to chill him in those sensuous ebon eyes of Mrs. Averill.

As it was, Angela Laight came to her friend's house, and for about two months all went wholly to the young widow's approbation. Hubert plainly admired Angela ; that was but nature, his hostess would argue, since the girl was both handsome and bright. She would serve her purpose admirably, if she only proved, for a month or so longer, enough of a mild drastic power to fix in Hubert's mind the habit of going at brief intervals to her own little bandbox of a dwelling. Angela could retire, then ; her services would have grown needless. Poor pauper that she was, she could post up into Ogdensburg again, where that shiftless father of hers had plunged into some new scheme with a smell of the worst risk about it. "I shall have been very good to her," Mrs. Averill mused. "She can't complain ; she had no claim upon me ; and I shall have let her stay here in town with me a small eternity."

Angela did not complain ; she would have held that a most thankless part to play. But a few days before the time of her departure she innocently made heaven and earth crash together for Mrs. Averill by saying, while a little haze of pink came hurrying along either pure-curved cheek to either sweet blue-gray eye.

"Mr. Throckmorton asked me last evening, Alva, if I'd

be his wife, and—and—though I was ever so surprised and
confused, and could hardly speak at all, still, I believe I—I
said 'yes.' "

The ground seemed swinging like the sea under Mrs.
Averill, and she felt as if her standing upright were a mira-
acle. At the same time she had begun to say, in cool
tones :

" My dear Angela, I'm so pleased ! I half suspected it
about a week ago. It's an engagement that will charm
everybody." And then she kissed the girl on each cheek.

Till Angela left her house it more than once struck the
young widow that she might go mad and do some dire thing.
Her secret, her pain, her infinite chagrin, were not to be
told in the hearing of any mortal ; she sometimes caught
herself wishing that she were a Catholic and could pour all
into the ear of a confessor. Then she would laugh with
scorn of such an impulse, though the laugh was one of those
terrible silences which the silence of a tortured soul can
alone echo back. This infatuate choice, in its eager trend,
meant the single sentiment of a woman who had never
known one gleam of similar feeling heretofore. She could
never have made the marriage for money and place that she
had made, if love like this had ruled her in the past. Since
her widowhood she had looked into the eyes of passion and
breathed its dizzying breath. In those other days she had
thought Hubert a mere *poseur* for literary distinction, a man
whose foreground (as the world pictorially saw it) was
assumed modesty, and whose sole background was the raw
flamboyance of wealth. One chance meeting had changed
her to the core. She had afterward read his two books of
verse and had told herself that they were factors in the al-
terative process. But this had already happened, and moreover hers was not a temperament that the rhythm and lilt of
poetry could stir ; she had no nerve-cells that vibrated to
such impression ; life and she were bound together only by
the hard cords of prose.

Angela went back to Ogdensburg, where her father had

by this time discovered that his scheme of quick self-enrich-
ment was air, and had begun to plan another which would
be earth itself for impregnable solidity. The girl had
begged Hubert to wait a little while before he followed
her. Shame was at the root of this entreaty; she invented
some excuse for the delay, but in reality it had been im-
posed because she was fearful lest affairs at home were
harshly embarrassed. This proved to be the case. Her
father, who had managed to educate his motherless child,
now lacked the means of decently supporting her. But he
had hopes; he was going to redeem the failure of one cnter-
prise by the splendid success of another. Angela smiled
drearily as she listened; she wondered, while she recollected his former hap-hazard career, how he had ever contrived to pay for her past tuition as a boarding pupil at
Madame Charnier's. But he had done so; perhaps he
would contrive to get on his feet again now, for the twen-
tieth time since she had known him and filially loved him.
A sense of commingled dread and dilicacy forbade her from
writing Hubert the word that would bring him at hot speed
to Ogdensburg. A like sense made her conceal from her
father the fact that she was engaged to a very rich man in
New York. If she told him now, at this epoch of financial
jeopardy, what mortifying attitude of debtor toward Hubert
might he not swiftly assume? "No, no," she said to her
own anxious heart. "I will wait until papa rights himself
once more. It would kill me to have Hubert come here
and find us almost at straits, like this, for our daily
food."

But even then she sent Mrs. Averill a full account of all
her sharp worriments. "I trust you in every way," her
letters ran. "Say nothing to *him*. We are getting along,
but oh, how different it all is from your sumptuous and
lovely little home!"

Mrs. Averill sent her the kindest of responses, and a gift
of money as well. The latter came opportunely indeed.

" What a generous heart Alva has ! " her friend thought.
" Thank Heaven, I can repay her soon.   There must be one,
of two ways, either papa's rise or my marriage."

But destiny had given the cards of Lottimer Laight a final
disastrous shuffle.   Far from rising again, he sank as his
child had never seen him sink before.   He had always had
the most exquisite manners ; he was the sort of man who
prides himself upon being a gentleman even while concerned in transactions of plebeian dinginess ; it was lucky
for Angela that she did not know just how the expenses of
her schooling had been defrayed, but had accepted " papa "
during girlhood with a reverence remote from the faintest
heresy.   She rarely saw him then without he had on a pair of
neat gloves and wore a flower or two in his button-hole.
But now it was quite different ; his dandyism had evapo-
rated ; his handsome face, with its gray, martial moustache
and hopeful blue eyes, had a drawn, scared look, as though
the ghosts of the three or four fortunes that he had made
away with were whispering uncanny rebukes in his mental
ear.   One day he spoke to Angela in sharp rage, and
without a shred of reason for doing so.   He walked from the
room muttering oddly to himself, and with the last glimpse
that she caught of his face her pain swiftly altered to alarm.
His brain was already rocking to its fall, and in a day or
two the collapse came.   It brought a helpless imbecility
and not the more cruel curse of dementia that Angela had
been dreading.   At the first tidings of the calamity Hubert
hurried to Ogdensburg.   The shame of Angela was swal-
lowed up in ecstasy as they fell into one another's arms.

She told him everything, then, without a shadow of
reserve. ˴ She let him see to just how shabby a pass poverty
had brought her father and herself.   Hubert, pierced with
disgust at what he rated as his own dulness, clamored for an
immediate marriage.   Afterward, he fervently told Angela,
they two could watch beside her father together, and he

would have the right to offer that glad assistance which his future wife now shrank from receiving.

But within the very hour that Hubert made his passionate plea, one who had learned of his departure for Ogdensburg and who had boldly decided on the step of following him, presented herself before Angela. This, it need hardly be recorded, was Alva Averill. The bewildered and hesitating girl sprang toward her sudden guest with a cry of grateful delight. Bewilderment and hesitation thenceforth ceased to be her own concern. " What shall I do, Alva ? " she broke forth forlornly. " Poor papa is dying, and yet it may take him weeks, months, to die. Hubert is here, and begs me to become his wife now—in a few hours, or at best a day. Ought I to consent? Advise me! I leave it all to you!"

" Don't think of such a step," said Mrs. Averill. " Wait ; I am here with you now. I will help you; it's right enough that I should. Wait, I say. Trust all to me. You and he have a lifetime before you. Think only of your father for the present. Settling a few unpaid bills can't mean much for me, Angela; why should it ? Besides, to appease your sensitiveness, I'll jot down a full account, which you can make good to me aferward if so disposed."

" Oh, Alva ! how sweet of you ! "

Angela's tears were flowing. She kissed the cheek of the new-comer again and again. She was clinging about her friend's neck in her gratitude, her misery. Mrs. Averill, though responding by little pats of her gloved hands to these caresses, had swept her gaze about the cheerless room. In another minute she had summoned her maid, whom she had brought with her and who stood in discreet retirement.

" Gilberte," she instructed, " go and tell the lady who keeps this house to come to me. You understand."

Gilberte understood and obeyed. She was one of those keen young Frenchwomen whose errors of service are few, and who can speak English with a lucidity that transcends idiom.

A little later Mrs. Averill held a talk with the keeper of
the house.   On one side, at least, it was a mollifying conference, and several new bank-notes crackled crisply before its
end.   Still later, Hubert and his cousin spoke together.
During their converse, new wraps and pillows and other
means of bringing comfort to a sick-room were being carried
past them to the near bedside of Mr. Laight.   " No," Mrs.
Averill was saying, " her place, Hubert, is where her father
lies.   You must bear that in mind.   Remember, she has
friends in New York, whatever they might say here in this
dull little settlement.   Let me prove her friend now; you
can be that, and more, to-morrow—whenever to-morrow
really comes."

Hubert acquiesced.   He had never liked Alva Averill so
much as at this period, when he watched her, intelligent,
patient, aidful, apparently thinking of his Angela's weal, and
that alone.   Mr. Laight lingered on between life and death;
to-day he rallied a little; the next day he was in the gloom
of deathly threat; again he would show signs of spurious
recovery.

It was now April.   Mrs. Averill had remained with the
sick man and the two lovers, a model of gentle fortitude and
sympathy.   Her purse was the support of Angela and the
dying man.   When Hubert and his *fiancée* had their tender
meetings, her conduct was that which a very goddess of discretion might have approved.   " I once believed that woman
had a cold heart," Hubert said to Angela; " I see how I
wronged her.   Friendship and self-sacrifice couldn't come
much closer to one another than they've come in her present
conduct."

" Indeed, no ! " Angela replied.   " There was never a
more devoted friend than Alva is.   To leave her charming
home and all her gay town-life for weeks, just that she may
be near me !   It is something to vibrate through one's entire
lifetime."

" It teaches me a lesson," said Hubert.   " What is easier

than to misjudge our fellow-creatures, and how wantonly we're forever doing it! We are all like a lot of mountebanks behind an illuminated sheet. The uncouth shadows we cast there are the world's misrepresentations of us."

"But we in turn are a part of that very world," smiled Angela. "Oh, yes; it's give and take."

During early April Mr. Laight painlessly breathed his last. He was a man who had outlived all except the coarser associations; he ranked with those untoward beings who appear to drop out of life as deserters from an army, and to take death in the form of punishment rather than reprieve. It would have been idle to bury him from the huge city where many a friend of his untarnished days would simply have had the option of refusing to attend his funeral. So he was quietly buried from Ogdensburg, and no doubt made more than a single such contemporary privately grateful for being spared the need of deciding whether to go or remain away.

As soon as the funeral was over, Angela and Mrs. Averill returned to New York, accompanied by Hubert. A marriage had been talked of for the last day of April. It would of course be very quiet. Hubert was tenderly imperative about waiting longer than the first of June at the furthest. But, as it turned out, he had been forced to wait on indefinitely, with an almost suicidal anguish at his heart in place of the hope that once nestled there, like a viper coiling in the same nest where a bird has brooded!

During her former stay in New York with Mrs. Averill, Angela had received an offer of marriage from Mr. Bleakly Voght, a gentleman almost thrice her years. Bleakly Voght had long ago been accepted as one whose bachelor-hood was a crystal fact that resisted all the undermining erosions of gossip. He was tall, gaunt, almost bloodlessly pale, with a beetling nose, a pair of small, restless gray eyes, and a temper of notorious violence. But the attribute just named would flash and flare like the ebullitions of a hidden fire that only now and then broke bounds. He

2

could be suave enough when he chose, and he chose very
often.   Notwithstanding his ugliness, which was distinct, he
had the repute of a man who could exert at will strong fasci-
nation over women.   It had been affirmed of him that his
unhappy exterior had formed his ablest means of amatory
attack; he was understood to have achieved the adroitest of
his memorable conquests chiefly through the tactics of surprise.   Excessively rich, and with a name that had in its
very sound the memory of past patrician leadership, he fre-
quented circles where caste throve at a degree of the hardi-
est insolence, feared by some people, truckled to by others,
disliked by many, and treated deferentially by all.   Those
who hated him with the most acute zest envied the gloss and
chic of his brougham; those who resented most stoutly the
autocracy and assumption of his bearing recognized the
dainty excellence of his dinners.   We would say of a London man placed as Voght was that he belonged to all the
best clubs; but in New York the best clubs mean only two
or three, and to these he not only belonged but was a gov-
ernor of one of them.   In every sense a spoiled child of
fortune, he bore himself at nearly all times with imperious
caprice.   If he had been less the slave of codes he might
have tried to set loud and quaint fashions in attire; but con-
ventionalism had him in too firm a grip for that.   As it was,
he dressed ill enough to have been the object of his tailor's
clandestine hate; you never saw his lank figure that its
angles were not accentuated by misfits; even his shirt-front,
when he was clad for the evening, made a salient, untidy
bulge; a feminine critic of him had once freezingly said that
there was comfort in knowing he drew the line at cleanliness.   Years ago he had persuaded himself that he was a
parti who could marry just as he pleased, and now, in the
grayness of declining lustihood, he preserved the same conviction.   It was by no means a baseless one.   Despite certain ugly tales of his irascibility, and others that bore upon

immoral escapades both here and in Europe, he remained a popular favorite of secure repute for wit, tact, and the art of amusing.

Only a little while before he had become acquainted with Angela it had been more than whispered that he might one day wed Mrs. Averill. This report had never possessed the least foundation. Mrs. Averill, with her copious income and her enviable visiting-book, would as soon have thought of marrying her footman as Bleakly Voght. She knew very well, however, that he would still have been deemed a judicious match for any woman, and when he told her, with anger making him rather ludicrous than pitiable, that Angela Laight had refused him, she was rendered speechless by the girl's incredible folly. There had always been something about Angela that had caused her friend to seem tiresomely cloud-wrapped, idealistic, and *puritaine.* But that Lottimer Laight's daughter should have refused a husband like Bleakly Voght passed Mrs. Averill's understanding. She understood a short while after, however, and but too clearly.

When Angela's engagement to Hubert Throckmorton was announced, Bleakly Voght's dismay and humiliation were no less intense than juvenile. He at once sailed for Europe, after having held an interview with Mrs. Averill that showed him in hues as comic as they were contemptible. He had always despised Hubert, to whom he would allude as "that poet," quite in a manner which indicated that he regarded poet and fool as interchangeable terms. And now that the girl he had honored by the offer of his hand should have refused him for a sentimental scribbler like this, who might, truly enough, be a few years younger than himself, but who had not so big a fortune by at least a million of dollars—it transcended credence !

The coarse and hard materialism of the man never made a fitter background for his vanity than when he said to Mrs. Averill, in prolonged splenetic snarl :

"Why, confound it, I struggled against offering myself to the girl, and only gave in because I thought it would be mean of me to punish her for faults that she hadn't committed. Still, family's family, and blood's blood. And I'm . . ." He shut both eyes for an instant and shook his head vehemently with a most unbecoming look of disgust and annoyance . . . "I 'm Bleakly Voght."

"Of course you are," said Mrs. Averill, abettingly. "You've a right to feel proud. I'm amazed at Angela. Still, you know how unambitious a girl will now and then surprise one by showing herself. Her eyes might yet be opened to the really splendid position you will give her."

Voght assumed a milder look. There was no kind of personal flattery that he found obnoxious. You could have told him that his nose was ancient Greek instead of mediæval Gothic, and he would have suspected neither satire nor mendacity. Mrs. Averill was well aware of this foible : to play upon it might not be at all difficult.

"I don't wish her to marry me for whom I am, but for what I am," he still tartly grumbled. "And her engagement's on, now, with the verse-maker. No, I'd better sail for Europe and try to forget the cut she's given me. If it hadn't come from the daughter of Lottimer Laight—if it had come from a woman more *des nôtres*, you understand —I might have stood it better."

He carried himself off to Europe without so much as a good-bye to Angela. What followed for quite a long while after that has already been chronicled. It chanced that on her return with Angela from Ogdensburg, Mrs. Averill made an immediate discovery which did not by any means annoy her. They learned that Bleakly Voght had been among the recent arrivals from Europe.

'Shall I send for him?' she thought, one evening, while seated in the first of her two pretty little drawing-rooms and hearing the low murmurs of the lovers float to her from beyond, through half-drawn tapestries. 'He may not come if I

do not send. And I want to see him, somehow, before . . . '
Even her musings became indefinite, just here. There
seemed no reason why she should either send for Bleakly
Voght or desire to see him before Angela and Hubert were
made one. She knew that any effort on Voght's part to
break their engagement would be futile in the extreme.
And she herself, to put the matter with all daring bluntness
amid the secrecy of her own soul—what lie could she tell
that would prove powerful enough really to be separative
in its consequences ?

She was a woman who had thus far chosen what is termed
the safe path. No one could point to any gross duplicity
or treachery of hers; no one could accuse her of either rank
imprudence or flimsy peccadillo. But her character had always been of the sort that would feebly resist any potent
stress of temptation; the medium of such influence would
have been a submissive one. Self had for years lifted its
head, like that of a little household Lar, somewhere in the
deepest recesses of her nature, and just how reverent a cult
the small god received she alone could have told you.

On the following day, without the least omen to have
warned her of its approach, she found herself confronted by
a severe temptation. So suddenly did this event make itself
and its trenchant significance felt to her, that when all was
over and past she had something of the same sensation
which might visit some wayfarer stricken by a terrible
tempest, who raises himself from the spot whereon it has
flung him, and watches it disappear with wrack and flash
and rumble from the heaven over which its wrath has so
fleetly swept.

II.

ANGELA came buoyantly into the house, on the afternoon
of this same day. She was in deep mourning for her father,
and the dark garb she wore meant no mere nominal tribute,
either; all the faults of Lottimer Laight had not weakened
her filial fondness. And yet, how can the gloom of death
prevail, though it should fight with battalions of shadows,
against the sunshine of youth and love? Angela was happy
in a way just as unreasoning as that mood of the boughs
which makes them bud: she could no more have explained
to you why the future spread before her one shining vista of
welcome than a stream in the spring could declare its
reason for unsheathing all its dulcet babble of trebles from
their winter bonds of ice.

No hint of ambitious feeling entered into the love that she
bore Hubert. It was a sentiment founded upon tenets that
she had long held, and to which, as she had told a few of
her best friends in the past, she would always most firmly
cling. "The man whom I marry," she had said, "must win
my respect for him in two ways: first, morally, and second,
mentally. I want to admire his character as noble and un-
stained, and to see in his intellect the superior of my own.
And until I have done both I can never feel as if I were
acting rightly even to love him, apart from consenting to become his wife."

It must be granted that a speech like this has an extremely priggish sound. Several times Angela had been
punished by the sarcastic replies of her school-mates after
she had thus expressed herself; and once a truly heartless
reference was made to the dingy reputation of her father,
that threw her into a paroxysm of half-rageful tears. Oddly

enough, that very father had been the origin of her rather grandiose girlish resolve. There are no parents who contrive to shine so brilliantly in precept and maxim before their children as those with careers that have shown a reverse of rectitude.

But Angela had persevered in the worship of her lofty matrimonial ideal. It is not maintained that she would have refused to marry Hubert if he had failed to conform with it. She had been in love with Hubert some time before he proposed to her, and we know how fierce an iconoclast of theories young love may become. But in spite of the appeal to fancy and imagination by which fashion with its pomps and pleasures will nearly always address one of her impressionable age, she had felt a shudder as involuntary as it was covert while telling Bleakly Voght that she could not be his wife. Hubert stood to her as the realization of all her most poetic previous visions. He was a poet himself, and a little while after meeting him she had come very close to the shedding of tears over some of his published verses. Possibly she had been that worst of critics, a person with a liking for the author of the work which asks judgment. No doubt her verdict upon the man and his poetry had been alike simultaneous and partisan. But she would not for an instant have admitted this, and her bright native intelligence was surely a fair reason why she should have resented any such sweeping charge.

She was deeply happy to-day. She was indeed so happy that self-reproach hurt and irked her, now and then, in her more meditative moments. It seemed, at these times, as if the exhilaration that was born of her coming marriage pressed with an insolent profanity upon the bereavement that was still so fresh amid experience. She could not see her father's image in the dusky framework that now appeared its rightful surrounding. Joy shed too strong a light upon it; anticipation opposed retrospect; grief was driven from its urn and willow, for the first had become a little bubbling fount of hope, and the last had begun to lose its funereal droop, as though at any minute some miracle of magic might change it into a bush, burning with half-opened rose-buds.

She passed upstairs through the modish and tasteful hall, towards her own apartments. Just as she reached the upper landing of the staircase, a door opened and Mrs. Averill came out upon the second hall. A somewhat ill-dressed woman at once followed her, leading a little child. The woman had a pale, tired, work-a-day sort of face, but she did not look as if she were a month older than Mrs. Averill herself. She had been pretty once, as you could tell at a glance ; but pain, or perhaps toil, had sharpened her features and sunken her cheeks, while the querulous, worried light in her dark eyes bore further proof of a lot in which peace did not abide. The child whose hand clung to hers was not more than three years old ; she had no beauty beyond that which childhood may nearly always be said to wear, and in the wide blue gaze of her uplifted eyes dwelt that innocence which seems either to convey the most gently magnificent frankness or else to hide the very secret of the Sphinx.

Angela loved children. "What great big eyes!" she said playfully to the little girl, having passed her hostess and dear friend with a nod and a smile. And then she paused in front of the tiny creature. "*Oh*, what big eyes!" she went on, with that sweet *camaraderie* which only those who are the born devotees of children know how to use toward them.

"My dear Angela!" exclaimed Mrs. Averill, slipping in a trice between herself and the child, "*please* don't! I—I *can't let you!*" Then she broke into a slight hysteric sort of laugh and pushed the girl further along the hall, away from both the woman and her child.

Angela's glance swept Mrs. Averill's face. She saw that it was agitated. "Why, Alva!" she broke forth, and caught her friend's wrist, looking at her intently. But still no ray of suspicion had pierced Angela's mind.

"Will you go into my dressing-room, dear, and—and wait there for me a few minutes?" Mrs. Averill asked. Her voice appeared to be full of tremors. The door was near at hand and she unclosed it while she thus spoke, and then motioned for Angela to enter. The girl did so; but, as she crossed the threshold she half turned toward Mrs. Averill.

"I'll wait for you here, of course, Alva. But you seem as if something dreadful had happened."

"Something dreadful *has* happened," was the reply.

"Oh, Alva! Tell me! Not *Hubert !* You don't mean—"

"I mean that he is alive, and well enough. Nothing has happened to him, except—"

"Except!" the alarmed girl once more shot in.

"That woman has come here with her child, Angela. She has found out that you and I are friends. She came to tell me that she . . . that the child . . . But no; I'll not say another syllable on the subject until I've talked a little more with her. Pray keep inside this room, dear, and wait till I rejoin you here; I'll do so as soon as I possibly can."

Left alone, Angela sank into a chair, and wondered how sudden attacks of madness came on, and whether Mrs. Averill were not incontestably mad, and whether she herself ought not to take other measures than these of a passive kind. To doubt Hubert was like doubting the sun in heaven . . . Still, what was this chilly, creeping sensation in the region of her heart? *Might* such a horrid thing, after all, be true? No, no! A million noes!. . And yet a pretty little clock on the mantel, with two gilt cupids that were quarrelling for the possession of time's hour-glass, began to tick: "Might it be true? Might it? Might it?" till Angela was on the verge, three or four times, of rushing from the room in which Mrs. Averill had left her.

A drop of ink will cloud a gobletful of the most crystalline

water. As yet Angela had heard scarcely anything against
the man she loved; but what she did hear had been an in-
nuendo just keen and subtle enough to waken the dormant
devil that has its lair deep down in every lover's heart.

At last Mrs. Averill came back. Her olive face was a
picture of misery, and for a little while all but the most
dejointed speech appeared to fail her.

"It—it *is* true, my poor Angela!" were the first cred-
itably coherent words that she spoke. "She came here in
the hope that I would do something to prevent the marriage
between you and Hubert."

"Ah—that was it?" murmured Angela, who had grown
deathly white to her lips.

"Yes. She thinks he . . he owes marriage to *her* . . on the
child's account, you know, if not for any other reason. She
does not seem at all like a hardened person. I dare say
that circumstance has had a great deal to do with her sinful behavior. She says that her father, whom she loved
dearly, was lost at sea while she needed his care and support, and that she never remembers having had a mother.
Oh, Angela, it looks as though *he* were far more blamable
than she. Forgive me for saying that, my dear, but—"

"Forgive you?" cried Angela, with a flash from the blue-
gray eyes that now seemed to burn black because of her
great pallor. "Why should I have any cause to *forgive* you,
Alva?" A shudder passed through her frame as she hurried on : "I—I feel as if there were no power in my heart
to do anything but despise *him*." She sank into a chair
after thus speaking; both hands fell at her sides and hung
down as if quite effortless. Her mouth quivered once or
twice, but her fixed eyes gathered no tears; they grew
glassy instead, and this change in them, blending with her
complete absence of color, gave her the look of one who
might at any instant either swoon or die.

"Angela," said Mrs. Averill, stooping over her, "will
you not see this woman?"

"No," she answered, with a slight negative motion of the head. "No, *you* have seen her. That is enough."

"But, Angela," urged her companion, "it will be best for you to speak with her, you know, and make perfectly sure that what she says is true."

The girl rose, then, and a new energy revealed itself in her manner. "You are right," she cried. "What a fool I have been! This woman may have lied in the most horrible way; we will go to her, Alva. I have heard of such impostors before now; have not you?"

"Yes. But *she* is not—" Here Mrs. Averill checked herself.

A great sigh left the other. "I see. You believe that she tells the truth."

The two were standing close together, now. Mrs. Averill had put one arm round Angela's waist. Suddenly she drew it away and seemed searching for something in the pocket of her dress. "Here" she said, "is a likeness of him which the poor creature had hidden in her bosom. You see, it is no proof that she is *not* an impostor; it is only a rather old-fashioned locket, with a common photograph set behind the inside glass. But she did not even produce it until I had asked her whether she could give me any real evidence of her assertions."

Angela scanned for a moment what the locket contained, and then handed it back to Mrs. Averill. Her tones were placid, but they breathed of despair. "No one should be convicted on such proof as this," she said. And now her voice slightly broke, her lips trembled, her head drooped. "If—if the woman could show a letter from him," she faltered.

"A letter?" replied Mrs. Averill. "She has a package of them, or says that she has."

Angela stifled a sob. They stood looking at one another for a few seconds; Mrs. Averill's eyes, as the half-distracted girl met them, seemed to brim with an exquisite sympathy.

"Oh, Alva," came the abrupt cry, "if you would get her to show you these letters, and—and then judge for yourself ! Will you do this much more to serve me, Alva ?—you, who have done so much already ? "

"I will do anything to serve you, my dear ! " exclaimed Mrs. Averill. "But suppose I go to this woman's home and see those letters ? Unless you have seen them with your own eyes, how can you feel certain I have not been in error ? I know that you trust me, and yet . . ."

"I trust you in all things ! " broke from Angela ; and she threw both arms about the neck of her friend. "Should I presume *not* to trust you after all that I owe you ?—all that you have done for me ? "

"Hush, darling ! that was nothing."

"It was devotion I should despise myself if I forgot ! And this will be devotion just as great, if you will only consent to show it."

"There is none, Angela, that I would *not* show, provided I had the power."

"Bless you for saying so, Alva ! . . . I leave all to you. The—the thought of going coldly to work, myself, and finding him guilty is so horrible a one ! It will be bad enough to know it hereafter—as perhaps I must ! . . ."

She did know it, in about two hours from then. She had promised Mrs. Averill that she would under no conditions permit Hubert to see her if he should present himself while her friend was away. But Hubert did not present himself hat afternoon ; he was looking forward to a long, divine *tête-à-tête* in the evening.

When he did make his appearance at Mrs. Averill's door, he was told that neither this lady nor Miss Laight was at home. "Not at home ! " he repeated, in pained amazement to the footman who had opened the door. "And no word was left for me if I called ? "

"No, sir."

Wanting to ask more questions, but fearing lest he might

appear ridiculously love-sick to the servant, he took his departure.

That same evening, on his return home, he found a letter from Angela awaiting him. He reeled as he read it. It broke their engagement, without giving the least reason for such action. It desired him never willingly to look on her face again, as she meant never willingly to look on his. She wished him all happiness hereafter. She brought no accusation against him. It was true, the change in her had been a sudden one; but on that account it was none the less radical. All was at an end. She begged him to remember this fact, and not permit the faintest doubt to disturb his complete certainty of it.

There are no such fools as lovers. If so sweeping and dumfounding a letter had been sent him in relation to any other question of his daily existence except that most vital one of his love for Angela Laight, Hubert would have striven to probe and dissipate the mystery by every common-sense means in his scope of search. But now he passed a night of wakeful agony and arose with only a vague intention of making direct, stringent appeal to her who had thus flung so abrupt and black a shadow across his life.

He compromised with his own bleeding pride, that next morning, and went again to the Madison Avenue house, asking for Mrs. Averill.

She was at home. "My unhappy Hubert," she said, as she entered the room where he waited for her.

"You—you know, then, about that letter?" he stammered, pale and forlorn of mien.

"Yes." She nodded several times in quick succession, gazing down at the carpet. Then she lifted her eyes, and it seemed to him that their dusk pupils (which he had once thought devoid of all the softer feminine beams) were melting with pitiful emotion.

"Angela told me she had written you," came the next words.

" Ah ! she told you ? " he sharply inquired.

" Yes."

" Pray, did she tell you the monstrous treachery that letter implied ? "

Alva Averill toyed with one of the front buttons of a dark-blue cloth dress that fitted her neat, *svelte* figure like a glove. "I wonder if you ever thought—you men are so stupid about thinking things, Hubert, where it concerns a woman you're fond of—that Angela is . . . ambitious."

" Ambitious ! "

She smiled, very sadly, yet with a smile full enough to show the white glisten of her even teeth. " My dear Hubert, I suppose you know that Bleakly Voght cared for her."

" Bleakly Voght ! Yes—well, and if he did, or does ? "

" Ah, that is just it ! He not only did, but does. He's back from Europe, and . . . "

" My God ! Alva, you don't mean—? "

Mrs. Averill gave a short, melancholy laugh. " I mean," she said, " that he's back from Europe."

" And . . and . . it's *he?* " Hubert gasped, recoiling, with his face full of horror.

Mrs. Averill laughed again—this time with a great gentleness and an equally great sombreness. " Bleakly Voght is a man who has always been *said* to possess a curious influence over women . . . And then he is an exceeedingly rich man . . a good deal richer than you are, Hubert . . Don't ask me for the real facts in the case ; I positively do not know them. But he has been here to see Angela since his return . . . "

" He has been here ! "

" Yes—two or three times. I think three times in all— Why, Hubert, you're ill ! "

" No, no," he said.

He had staggered backward and almost fallen into an arm-chair just behind him. He was wiping from his color-less face a few drops of sweat that had gathered there.

In another second, however, he had sprung to his feet again.

"I'm all right, Alva—it's nothing," he exclaimed, not knowing what a queer ring his voice had. "Bleakly Voght, eh? It's nothing . . . I'm quite myself, now. A shock, you know—a sharp shock . . We men have our nerves, at times, just as you women have . . . ." And then he laughed shortly. If the laugh had been a wild cry of grief, it would have had far less odd a sound.

A little while after that he had left the house and had never sought again to see Angela. He had felt no surprise on learning that she would marry Bleakly Voght. Mrs. Averill had prepared him for such tidings. They got abroad, and two or three of his friends came to him with eyes grown saucer-like from consternation. In the repressed delirium of that woful week, Hubert could ill prevent himself from insulting replies. "*Trop de zèle, mon vieux,*" he recalled murmuring on one occasion; and as he afterward walked away, no doubt the stern, strained look that he wore accentuated his irony. For seven days all sorts of mad ideas transiently ruled him. One was to find a means of forcing Voght into a duel; another was to sting his face with a horsewhip in the public street; and still another was even savage enough to take the form of dreaming about a double assassination. But after all, in spite of his excessive suffering, Hubert was a true child of his century; and that has not only given crime a scientific explanation, but has vulgarized it lamentably.

When the news of the marriage came to him, he experienced a certain relief. It was the same sensation as that which comes to mourners when their dead has been placed under ground, and all excitement and suspense have given place to the dreary anticipation of going home and staring at an empty chair.

Hubert, as we know, had taken the train for Ponchatuk. His house there was a homestead, rambling, spacious, and American enough to have been built years ago in the heart of New England, with her most beauteous hills at either hand, instead of here on the ugliest portion of a huge sandbank called Long Island. Still, on the lawns of breezy-Locustwood, twilight deepened into night with a lovely tenderness of gradation. When the stars had filled the heavens with their white throngs, Hubert looked up at them, and the thought came to him of what a mite our one little world is, and what lesser mites are we that fret and strut upon it. How did it matter to some of those gigantic and glorious creatures who may inhabit the splendid continents of Saturn, whether or no a particular female atom here on earth had jilted a second male atom for a third that had more mean, wee dollars to pride itself on? Feeling the poetry wake and stir in his heart, he wondered if he would ever write another line while he lived. Then he answered his own surmise with a no, that seemed solemn enough to be the sound of all mortal anguish since men began. And then, unconscious of his own egotism, even while he had just been bowing his spirit before the enormity of the infinite, he passed indoors with loitering steps and lowered head.

Some letters, newly-arrived by a late mail, were on a table in the hall. He had given orders that his letters should be sent here; and now, as he stood and glanced at them, he had not the energy to do more than pass his eye over their superscriptions. Just above the table gleamed a portrait of his dead father; at this moment he chanced to lift his head and meet the well-remembered face, gazing out at him through mellow lamplight from the canvas on which a skilled artist had painted it with Rembrandtesque power; there seemed to him an expression of earnest, brooding solicitude on those familiar features; he started backward al-

most in awe and dismay. Another instant had told him that
his impression had merely been wrought by some unusual
effect of the light. And yet a hundred times he had seen
his loved father look at him just like that!

"Not to mind who has written one's letters to one," shot
through his thought, "may mean the beginning of some
frightful mental apathy. . . . Well, I don't care. . . . Let it
come! Dear old father! . . . . he looked at me, there, as
if he meant to reproach me. Reproach me? For what?
Because I think my life is ended? It *is* ended. I've nothing more to live for—nothing!"

He glanced again at the portrait. Its eyes (following his
own as the eyes of portraits do when you observe them with
attention) seemed to indicate the letters on the table just
below it. Hubert glanced a second time over his correspondence, and discovered that one of the envelopes bore
every sign of containing a telegram. He opened it and
. read, with a thrill of sharper concern than he had believed
it possible for him to feel, these few yet pregnant lines:

"New York, *May,* 18 —.

"Mrs. Averill, my mistress, was thrown from her carriage
while driving in the Park this afternoon, and very dangerously hurt. The doctors do not think she can live more
than a day or two. She has asked several times to see you,
and as if there were something on her mind that she wanted
to have you know. Please try and get to her at once.
"Delia Lamb."

There was a train that left Ponchatuk for New York at
nine o'clock that evening. Hubert had just time to catch
it. This telegram from the servant of Mrs. Averill had
affected him in the most unforeseen way. It had swept a
galvanic current through his torpor, and quickened indifference into vivacity. After all, there was one person in the
world whose welfare or misfortune interested him. He had
learned of late to look on Alva Averill as the salt of the

3

earth. Angela's perfidy could not make him forget the devotion of her friend. In journeying from a gay metropolis where all sort of diversion was at her command, to help in vigils at the side of her old school-mate's dying father, had been a deed of the sweetest generosity. And to think that this good, true woman lay at the door of death, while she who had so steeped herself in the foulest guile might perhaps live on for years without a hint of disaster! It was one of destiny's many hideous injustices!

Hubert did not reach the Madison Avenue house until about eleven o'clock that night. Delia Lamb, an elderly woman, with gray streaks in her hair and a sedulous, responsible demeanor, met him immediately.

"She's very low, sir," said Delia. "It's her spine that was hurt, and the doctors are afraid she may go off any minute."

Hubert repressed a shudder. "Is she in much pain?" he asked.

"None, sir. She's just very weak—that's all."

"Thank God she doesn't suffer! The horses took fright, I suppose."

"Yes, sir. She was thrown out after they'd gone over two miles. They picked her up near the Webster statue. The poor coachman was killed, sir."

"Killed!"

"Yes, sir; and the footman, at his side on the box, escaped without a scratch. When they raised Mrs. Averill they thought she was dead; but before they got her home she'd come to."

"And you say that the doctors give no hope?"

"Oh, no, sir—none."

'Why the devil,' thought Hubert, 'does this woman talk about so horrid a calamity without shedding a tear? It doesn't seem as if she had human feelings. And she's lived with Alva for a century or so.'

Delia Lamb had indeed been for a long time in the service of Mrs. Averill. She had never been thought a cold woman; and yet so far she had not shown a trace of any strong sorrow since the calamity had occurred.

Hubert soon saw one of the physicians and learned from him that there need be no postponement of the interview which his kinswoman desired to hold. She might not live till morning, and she might linger on for a day or so; but her recovery was impossible, her speedy death certain. Already she lay quite paralyzed from the waist down. Still, her mind was clear as it had ever been, and since it had become set on holding a talk with Hubert, opposition to such a plan would be almost brutality.

Shortly after his talk with the physician, Hubert was shown into the chamber where Mrs. Averill lay. It was full of a soft, brooding light, high enough for him to discern how rich and effective were its appointments. The olive-tinted face that was visible on one of the pillows of the bed made his nerves tingle as he regarded it. Naturally it was untouched by the faintest ravage of emaciation, and yet it bore the plain and ghastly stamp of death.

"You came," she said, as Hubert dropped into a chair at her bedside. Her voice was feeble, and keyed so uncharacteristically that if he had not known it was she who spoke, he would not even have dreamed it to be hers. "You came," she repeated, while he stooped over one of her hands and fondled and kissed it. Then, to his astonishment, she drew the hand away and slipped it beneath the coverlid. "They told me," she now proceeded, "that you had gone out of town. I suspected that you had gone down there to the South Side. I made her telegraph you. I was right, wasn't I?"

"Yes," Hubert said. He let a slight pause ensue. "I'm so glad, Alva," he presently ventured, "that you are not in any pain."

"No; I don't suffer at all. I can only move my hands, and yet I have no restless feeling. I don't want to do anything but just lie still like this. It's lucky, isn't it?" And she smiled, almost in the same way that he had seen her smile numberless times before now.

"My poor Alva!" he said; and here he put forth his hand as if to take her own again; but she would not give it him, keeping it hidden.

"Hubert," she began, with her black eyes full on his face, "I'm afraid you will not pity me when you've heard what I sent for you that I might . . . confess."

"Confess?" he iterated. "Ah, my dear Alva, you've nothing to confess except good deeds!"

"Have I not?" She closed her eyes, and he saw her joined lips tighten. In another minute she was looking at him again.

"'Confess' is the only right word," she said. "I've wronged you horribly, Hubert. I did the most dastardly thing to you. If I were a man, alive and well, instead of a woman with only a little while to live, I believe you would try to kill me when you have heard the whole truth."

'She is raving,' he thought, as he sat and watched her. 'Poor Alva! what a forlorn end of a gay, innocent, unsullied life like hers!'

But she continued speaking, and a great horror seemed slowly turning his blood to ice as he listened.

III

"HUBERT," this dying woman said, "I am to blame for all that Angela Laight did. Yes, I. One day, not long since, a woman with a child came to me. She had heard some tale about my being on the verge of marrying Bleakly Voght. After I had told her that the report was wholly false she burst into tears, and declared to me—what I had already felt almost sure of—that Bleakly Voght was the father of her child. He had sworn to marry her and had not done so. The woman begged that I would force him to make her this long-promised reparation. . . . . That same day Angela Laight and my strange visitor chanced to meet in one of the halls here. I was tempted, and I committed a wicked crime. I told Angela that the child was yours, that the woman had been your paramour. I told her this, and she believed it. But she wanted further proof, and I affected to want it as well. She played into my hands by asking me to get such proof, and assuring me that she would think it a kind service if I did. This made my task of deception strangely easy. Angela and you, between you, put the whole wicked game into my own hands. I had let a devilish impulse rule me, and when I thought, just afterward, of how detection would be almost sure to follow my act of madness, I made up my mind that I would hurry off to Europe as soon as exposure came, and pass the remainder of my life there. Well, you know what course *you* chose to pursue. If you had forced yourself into her presence after receiving her letter (one which I had dictated to her almost word for word), you might have found out the scandalous truth in no time. But you simply became the slave of your own pride.

You and she had made puppets of yourselves, and I held the wires. Bleakly Voght's return from Europe was terribly opportune, and . . . "

"Stop. You need not go on. I see this whole vile thing."

He had risen, and stood quite near to where she lay. His hands hung at his sides, but a stronger light would have shown how they were clinched. She looked up, and marked his lips quiver and his eyes blaze.

"Still, you may not see what my motive has been," she returned. "I loved you. I can say it now without shame, since I . . . I'm dying. Long before Angela ever saw you I—I wanted to win the place that she secured. Perhaps you'll grant there's a shadow of excuse for me on this account."

"Excuse!"

He lifted one hand, and for an instant it seemed to him that he must strike her dead, woman and dying though she was. But this madness left him in a second or two; his hand dropped at his side again; he moved toward the door of the chamber.

"I wanted you to forgive me," her voice now rang wailfully. "Ah, won't you, Hubert? Think of how I am! So soon to die!"

He turned, pausing, and met her eyes again. His own appeared kindled with a scathing contempt, and he unconsciously so curled his lip that she could catch a flash of the white teeth below his scant gold moustache.

"The evil you've done will live after you," he shot back at her. "Be sure of that."

"But ah," she called, "won't you forgive me, Hubert? *Won't* you?"

He passed from the room, and got out into the street as soon as his dazed, whirling brain would let him find the way thither. One of the physicians met him in the upper hall and spoke to him certain words—doubtless of surprise at

his brief sojourn near Mrs. Averill's bedside. But he did
not remember what answer he made the physician—or
whether, indeed, he made any.

He went home. He had lived, ever since the death of his
parents, in the roomy old family-house down Fifth Avenue,
not far from Washington Square. As he ascended its stoop
a white face with black, eagerly-dilated eyes went floating
up too, just at his shoulder. He fancied he saw the lips
open, and heard a voice issue from them. "Won't you forgive me, Hubert?" cried the voice, that was like a silence
made weirdly audible.

In the big, lonely house it was still worse. The face
flitted from right to left, left to right, and so did the voice.

He thought of her incomparable deceit, of the misery and
folly it had engendered, and he told himself that he had
been right, beyond all refutation right, in treating her as he
had done. A menace of sudden death had thrown its
falsely piteous glamour over her sin. But that sin was no
less loathsome because death had followed it with speed
instead of delay. It was no more pardonable on this account.

'What,' he indignantly mused, 'will be the results of her
hateful deed? She has driven that poor girl into making a
marriage which must mean agony of the rack itself ; she has,
for me, crippled the action and shackled the freedom of all
my future life.'

He thought of Angela, whom he might have saved an
hour, a half-hour, ten minutes before that wild, silly matrimonial plunge of hers was taken, and he ground his teeth at
the doltish way in which he had let a lie snare him. Even
if he had called out to her at the very altar's foot, "You are
marrying the betrayer of the woman whom you thought I
had wronged," she would have turned and renounced Voght
on the instant. It might have been melodrama, but it would
have been salvation as well. And what a boon, if some precious entrance-cue had only come to him, that he might
have played the leading rôle in even so sensational a scene.

As matters now stood, all life was at a dead-lock with him. Beyond doubt, it gave him comfort to realize that Angela had not steeped herself in the worst worldly greed, and that her marriage to Bleakly Voght was one of passionate pique, supposably fed with all the fuel of persuasion on which, at short notice, alert duplicity could light. And yet wrath against her who had brought this abomination to pass, and contempt of self for having failed to believe any falsity in a love that he had till then trusted so devoutly, made even the recognition of Angela's less blameworthy behavior confer upon him only a tepid joy.

He avowed to himself that it would have been terrible if he had killed his cousin, and yet that for him to do so would have belonged less to barbarism than to simple justice. And now, as for giving her his pardon—ah, no; she must find some new way to die, before one word of the sort her guilt-drenched soul was craving should ever be wrung from his lips.

He began slowly to pace the floor of his library, a room full of dark woods, and books on low shelves, and heavy-folded tapestries. There were a few bronze and marble busts here and there, looming through the soft light. Presently he drew near his favorite desk. What a pang of memory shot through him as he saw the white writing-paper lying there, with the pen thrown down beside it, and some unfinished verses that now bore so frightful a sarcasm, and were the last he had written before the blow fell, and would be the last (so he had inflexibly decided) that he ever meant to write again.

But during that slow, monotonous walk of his Hubert began to feel, as he had never dreamed of feeling before, how much greatness may lie in the power to forgive. Here was he, not cruel or even unkind by nature, and yet with ferocity of revolt waiting at any instant to rise against the idea of giving a dying woman his pardon !

At last he sank into a chair and buried his face in his

hands. It was a beautiful face that he thus concealed, but one on whose clear, noble, poetic features already the imprint of supreme sorrow had fallen. The light of a near lamp was shed, at this moment, on his short, thick golden curls; and sitting thus, with hidden visage, he made a pict. ure of complete desolation and dejection to which every line of his tall and graceful figure lent its especial aid.

Alva's voice was yet ringing through his brain. Its echoes were ineludible; they had become as persistent as a remorse. Were they growing to resemble one? And yet how should he, Hubert Throckmorton, find reason for the slightest compunction in his desire to resent so traitorous and abhorrent an act? 'Would I not inflict a mighty punishment upon her if only I could,' he asked himself, 'and shall I recoil from dealing her now what is but justice in its most meagre sense?'

Still, she was dying, and she had begged him to forgive her. He could not, in spite of every effort, escape the haunting potency of this appeal. His ratiocination gave it just the neat, sure answer that seemed adequate beyond all hint of cavil. But his sensibilities, his emotional part, his irresistible impulse of pity for one stricken down by an untoward blow of fate, slowly yet steadily gained ground against his merciless if righteous logic.

She had loved him. Perhaps no man who ever lived has been quite without vanity, and Hubert had not much of it, but he possessed, after all, let us say, a distinct human share. Her infamy had been committed through love of himself. The more he brooded, the more clean-cut this consideration rose as an off-set against the implacable causes why he should neither compassionate nor condone. . . . .

At last he sprang from the chair into which he had sunk, and looked at his watch. It had become later than he had thought. He sped from his house, got into a stray cab, and had himself driven at severe speed to the house in Madison Avenue. •

The servant at the door told him that Mrs. Averill was very ill, and that there was hardly any chance of her living through the night. He pushed past this servant, who knew well enough who he was. The little reception-room just off the hall was full of anxious-faced people, men and ladies, nearly all of whom he knew: Mrs. Averill had been too definite a social power for this news of her unhappy accident not to have caused a sombre gathering of her particular gay-minded little clan. But Hubert hurried straight upstairs. No one who observed his precipitancy was in the least surprised by it. As the poor injured lady's kinsman, he had, of course, a right paramount over any which her mere acquaintances could assume.

When he reached the door of Mrs. Averill's chamber, the physician with whom he had talked earlier in the evening opened and slowly emerged from it.

" Doctor," began Hubert, using a voice louder than he was himself aware of, " how is Mrs.—? "

The physician raised one finger, and a look went with his gesture that could have but a single meaning, while he whispered, " *She has just died.*" Hubert felt as if he had already heard the words.

Not until two days after their marriage did Mr. and Mrs. Bleakly Voght learn of Alva Averill's death. On hearing the poignant news, Angela, for the first time in her life, fainted away. Perhaps her youth and strength could have withstood even a shock so dreadful had not the severest mental strain and pressure been at work for days preceding her wedding-day. The newly-joined pair were now in Washington. It was impossible to reach New York in time for the funeral, unless they spent all that night in travelling.

" And you must not think of anything so foolish," Voght said to Angela, just after she had recovered from her fainting-fit, and while the pallor in her face yet recalled it.

"Oh, yes," she exclaimed, with instant resolution, "I would not miss it for the world. She was my dearest friend."

Voght smiled a little grimly. Perhaps he had his suspicions as to just how dear a friend she had really been; and in any case it is sure that he long ago had guessed her love for Hubert Throckmorton.

"We're not going, however," he said, "and that ends it." He spoke with very kind tones, but with the air, nevertheless, of one who pronounces a final decision.

"That does not end it," said Angela, shaking her head; "at least, not so far as I am concerned. I must go alone if you will not go with me; but go I certainly shall."

Voght bit his lip as he looked at her, with her creamy skin, her low-growing auburn hair, and her black-lashed, blue-gray eyes. She was to him peculiarly and intoxicatingly fair—and they had been married only two days. He shrugged his shoulders, in another minute, went up to her, kissed her on the lips, and said:

"As you please, darling. It was only of yourself that I was thinking. Since you are so bent upon going, why, let it be just as you say."

He had not been accustomed to yield like this. For a good many years he had had his own way, tyrannically, in everything. Angela had already observed in him an imperiousness toward all servants and officials which he would perhaps have restrained in her presence if long habit had not made him unconscious that he employed it. He was still too much under the thrall of passion for the least sign of his real temper to betray itself. He would have got down upon the ground and kissed her feet if she had even suggested to him any such obsequious act. It is safe to say that he had never loved any woman until now, and possession of her whom he had for many months regarded as unattainable wrought in him a softness, a deference, a tender humility, which would have rendered him in her own eyes, provided she herself had loved and not merely tolerated him, winsome to an untold degree. As it was, she dared not think at all deliberatively upon the step that she had taken. She had somehow been whirled into taking it. Pique, pride, a tingling sense of outrage, had abetted the counsels of Mrs. Averill and the ardent resumption of a former suit, urged by Voght himself. She had awakened, as it were, to find herself irrevocably married. And now had come this horrifying intelligence about Alva. That took her thoughts away from her own lot—and perhaps (for the interval, at least) such distraction was the most merciful of reprieves.

They spent the third night after their union amid the clangors of a sleeping-car. Angela did not gain a second of slumber, and while she lay and knew herself being darted through the darkness toward the dead face of her trusted and treasured friend, despairing voices seemed to address her in the cacophony of the hurtling train. At one moment she fancied that she heard Alva calling to her, just as Hubert Throckmorton had heard not long since—and yet with how deep a difference! At another moment she imagined that Hubert's voice called, and then the fanciful and delirious words were tinged with an equal repentance and reproach. " Was my fault great enough, after all," her lost lover seemed to say, " for you to have punished it as you did? And in so punishing it, what calamitous term of misery may you not have brought upon your own life? At least you might have remained unwedded, out of respect for the love I know so well that you once bore me, even though that love had become one which your self-respect and your sense of justice forbade you openly to return."

But all these antic and grotesque appeals melted into a dreary, matter-of-fact silence as dawn brought with it the grimy suburbs of New York and the termination of poor Angela's most dolorous wedding-tour. The funeral was to be held at twelve o'clock that day. Her husband took her straight to his handsome home in Gramercy Park, of which many a New York maiden had longed through many a past year to become the mistress. Here surprised servants bowed to her as she entered at Voght's side, and in a trice she found that a rich-appointed bed-chamber had been made ready for her reception, with the light of the brilliant May morning outside tempered into the most sleep-wooing dusk.

Bleakly Voght would have been unrecognizable to his friends if they could have seen him as he now adjured Angela to try and get some real repose before the funeral took place.

" But I must *see* her," she murmured, while sinking upon the soft bed. " I must go to her house and see her, before they close the coffin !" It was still quite early in the morning, and Voght, in his fond desire for her physical welfare, had hopes that she might sleep late on into the day. Still, he gave her a promise that if she fell asleep she should be aroused in time to carry out her most earnest desire.

As it proved, she scarcely slept at all. . . . While Alva Averill's friends were gathering about her coffined face some time before the hearse bore its burden to Trinity Chapel, Angela appeared among the little awed and low-whispering throng. Not far away, through her blinding tears, she saw Hubert. She stooped and kissed the dead woman's forehead again and again, while her sobs rang through the still room. Once he heard " my best of friends " leave her lips in a choked, struggling way.

' If she but knew,' he thought, while he watched her.

Afterward, at the funeral, amid the great crowd that filled the church, their eyes met. ' My God,' swept through his mind, ' does she so soon stand at bay before the irreparable ?' For thus it had seemed to him, judging from the wild, sweet wistfulness of her gaze, transient though that had been.

The funeral was very large, and the flowers were one splendid memorial glory that many a great man or woman has gone to the grave without so much as a hint of ; but

those who went to Greenwood were rather few, though Angela insisted upon being one of them, and perhaps because
of the pardon that he had failed to extend the dying, Hubert now paid this last act of kinship and kindliness to the
dead.   .

The birds were chirping over the dumb, white head-stones
at Greenwood, and the blue brightness of the May sky, the
delicate greenery of innumerable buds and shoots, brought
death and life, thrift and decay, motion and repose, into actual violence of contrast. The occupants of the various
carriages alighted after their long journey across the river.
Somehow, as they were all pressing toward the open grave,
it chanced that Hubert and Angela found themselves close
together. The latter had already seen that her husband was
some little distance ahead. An irresistible impulse now
took possession of her.

" Our poor Alva," she broke forth, " whom we both knew
and—and loved so well ! Is it not terrible ? "

He gave a great start as it became clear to him that her
words were meant for his own ears. Then, as he turned
and looked into her face, with that enchanting sensitiveness
and womanliness about the mould of its lips and chin, a
fierce agony stormed and shook his spirit. With flashes of
the eye, but in a voice no less equable than low, he answered :

" It is terrible, certainly. But if we had neither of us
known her nor cared for her so well, we might both have
been spared some of the worst suffering that lives here on
earth can be cursed by."

Then he forced his eyes away from hers, and soon had
widened the distance between them. Angela did not see
him afterward. He so managed that she should not. The
burial was made, in that implacable way which belongs to
all burials, whether the great or the lowly, the rich or the
pauper pass back into that earth whence they came. The

clods fell; the mound was heaped; the friends dispersed,
and the eternal monotony of forgetfulness began. . . .

For days Hubert was bitterly sorry that he had spoken to
Angela as he did speak. But there was no revocation possible, now. He had meant to keep the whole story of the
dead woman's vile conduct a strict secret. Angela had
done a mad thing; she must atone for it horribly. Her
expiation in itself would be hard and harsh enough. Why
burden her with new torments? Why seek to justify himself
in her eyes? She was lost to him; what mattered it whether
or no she realized the enormity of her blunder?

'I realize the enormity of mine,' he told himself, 'and I
endure misery in consequence.' And then there came a reflection of whose magnanimity he was not conscious, although
it bespoke a finer fibre of moral strength than that which the
majority of lovers, in all our recorded annals of them, usually
can appeal to. 'If she was insensately rash,' his musings
continued, 'so was I. She might have saved herself, and
did not. But I might have saved us both, and did not.
She knew that I loved her and that even if I *had* committed
a fault such as the one Alva charged me with, it was something that I must have loathed myself for, hence to a degree
meriting her pardon. But I, in turn, knew that such a letter
as the one she wrote me could not have meant her genuine
self. . . . I had kissed her on the lips too often for that; I
had felt the perfume of her love too richly and intelligibly;
I had surveyed in all its priceless breadth the dear dominion
of her trust!'

All that his dead relation had told him about a certain
woman and her child he had proved to be incontestably
true. There are always means of bringing to light these
grim secrets, and he had assured himself, through the employment of professional detective aid, that the sin of Voght
had been no less a fact than the almost equal sin of Alva
Averill. Inevitably his wound healed a little. He was an
idealist, in the imaginative sense, and he could not look on

the beauty of the world about him—a beauty which even the
ugliness of New York at its most metropolitan hideous failed
quite to dispel—without finding in his youth and the health-
ful beat of his pulse incentive for some sort of patient determination.

He had been born in what are called the ranks of caste,
and his extraordinary felicity, sweetness, and gentleness of
demeanor had made numerous men and women seek and
court him. His easy wealth, too, had helped toward his
popularity. We have heard how Bleakly Voght despised
his turn for poetry; but few others in the class to which
inheritance had long ago admitted him shared this prejudice.
On the contrary, he was esteemed so unconsciously winning
and even princely in his every-day deportment that the
fact of his being a poet but added attraction to his company.
He had indeed achieved a certain fame for his verses.
There is no critical authority in our land by which the
literary man may either rise or fall; but those few judges
who mingle charity and acumen had already declared
him a poet of remarkable excellence.

But now he felt as if his Muse had departed from him
forever. He had not been stirred, in his most vehement
moods of composition, by any ambitious fervors. He had
desired to write—simply that—and had written. No spur
for the gain of bread had pricked him, and on this account
he had wrought his poems with a courage and serenity of
purpose that had roused the incidental rancor of professional detractors. His art, in earlier days, had kept him
from those gross excesses which are the haunting demons
of idleness. He had loved poetry *as* an art no less than
painters love their canvases and colors for the same vital
and exhilarating reason. No one in his set had just
understood him, but he had not cared enough for his set to
care whether it understood him or no. Women had always
sought him and made much of him; but they had never
spoiled him. Like many poets, he had no sense of the

subtler and loftier effects of music. His soul was all for
rhythm and not for tonic harmony or even melody. "In
Memoriam" or "The Princess" could move him more
deeply than any opera he had ever heard or ever would
hear. Words were both hue and sound to him, if rightly
placed. Yet he was not a mere lapidary of words, treating
them like choice or valueless gems. He gave to them their
secondary and rightful place in the metrical scheme; he
revered Hugo, Tennyson, and a few other contemporaries as
poets, but the nobility of their themes first delighted him,
and the perfection of their art had always seemed of
minor import. He had, for some time past, felt convinced
that any poet worth hearing at all must have a voice of his
own, spontaneous and characteristic—not a mannerism, but
a series of natural, native notes that breathed of unques-
tionable authenticity. 'Have I this endowment?' he had
repeatedly asked himself, with the restless introspection of
the true artist. Again and again he had said, in discour-
aging reply, 'No.' But there had been a few kind voices
that had insisted 'Yes.' And so he had gone on, doubting, half believing, and yet writing the verses that had given
him far more fame than his intrinsic modesty would let him
recognize.

But now . . . Well, all was chaos and night, now. He
would scarcely have known that May had fretted itself
into the heats of June if climatic changes had not thus
assured him. He could not write a line; he visited his
clubs but rarely, and then with a feeling of annoyance, for
everybody there seemed to be drinking some fiery stuff
or another, and he had always detested that mode of
making time fly when it seems to lag. Women had always
charmed him, but he could not look on a feminine face nowadays that pleased him without having it in some pathetic,
half-piercing way remind him of *her*.

"Sha'n't you go to Europe this year, Throckmorton?"
somebody asked him one day in one of his clubs.

4

He hardly knew what to answer. Europe? He had been so often. What was new to see there? He had seen everything, from the *banalités* of Paris to the crude *couleur locale* of St. Petersburg. He had even been into Asia a little, and as for Egypt, he had explored its Nile-threaded monochrome of sand as far as the third cataract.

The weather grew hot. He thought of his place at Ponchatuk, and remembered how he had got to hate it. It made him think of that night, when the breezes were flying briskly at dusk, and the white stars were globing themselves, and he had felt as if he could put a bullet through his head or slip a knife into his throat. Then there had come that telegram about Alva. No, he would not go to Ponchatuk. All the mosquitoes on the South Side (and their name was trillion) would swarm round him and buzz into his ears ironies about his blasted life. He had quite forgotten a certain point relative to his estate at Ponchatuk. It was destined before long sharply to assail him.

There came, in latter June, one of those scorching days which made the town an odious glare. Till then he had been comfortable enough at the big house in lower Fifth Avenue. His people there were mostly old servants, who knew his simple wants and ministered to them with faultless discretion. But to-day the heat was unbearable. He thought of cows under trees and daisies lifting their starry discs to chance breezes.

"I must go somewhere," he thought, and went into Washington Square, only a step or two away from where he dwelt.

Here the heat was blinding. A few dingy men sat on benches. The fountain played with a fatigued spirt. He paused under a tree that failed to shade him, and as he thus paused he saw a figure approach with strides vigorous enough to mean no one more definitely personal than Callahan O'Hara.

The great, virile, handsome Irishman extended a hand.

"You're the last person, Throckmorton, I dreamed of meeting. What are *you* doing in town this dirty day?"

"Nothing," said Hubert.

O'Hara laughed in his mellow way. He had hazel eyes, with a little diamond swimming in the pupil of each, a thick reddish moustache, a crop of coarse, wavy red hair, two fascinating dimples, and the sunniest smile out of his native Ireland.

"Nothing must be harder to do this weather than something," he said; "it gives you nothing but the heat to think about."

"Just what I have found," Hubert grimly acceded. "And you, O'Hara? what are your plans?"

"Oh, I'm going to take the Long Branch boat and pass certainly one night, perhaps two, at the West End Hotel."

"I've half a mind to go down there with you," said Hubert. "Will you have me?"

"Will I have you?" cried O'Hara, in the most jovial echo. "*Can* I have you, old fellow?" And he seized Hubert's hand again, wringing it as if no such mishap as hot weather had ever been heard of.

IV

It was an age since Hubert had been down at Long Branch. He recalled that he had then told himself no power should ever drag him there again, and had denounced the place as a nude stretch of sand, whose chief products were intense heat, larger and more piratical mosquitoes than even those of Ponchatuk, and an assemblage of the most vulgar-looking people on earth. He had counted five separate ladies who wore rings outside their gloves, and at a hotel " hop " he had seen a young " society-man " in full evening-dress, but with a neck-tie of pink silk. That pink neck-tie had a criminal look which one needed not to be too callous a snob for the purpose of fully recognizing. As he watched its wearer's radiant self-importance, Hubert had satirically told himself that surely, after all, on this earth at least, we can often make our own heaven and our own hell.

Still, in spite of such harrowing memories, it now suited his caprice to take the boat thither in Callahan O'Hara's company. There was something dimly agreeable in the realization to Hubert that he could be visited by a caprice definite enough to be called one. As for O'Hara, he was beaming with satisfaction when Hubert dashed up to the wharf, perhaps three-quarters of an hour later, and not hardly a minute too late to catch the bellowing steamboat.

The two men lit their cigars on the upper deck, and soon felt that unutterable relief which an outgoing vessel will confer when the docks it has left are smitten by a sun whose rays are swords. The boat was loaded with people, but in these neither Hubert nor his companion took the slightest concern. Here was a different world from either of their own, which, in turn, were so different from one another. There had been a time when Callahan O'Hara, with his beauty and his lustrous mental gifts, might have won a high social place. He was a man of good literary attainments, but as so meagre a literary society exists in New York, he could not have shone among the *salons* of blue-stockings. What he might have done with brilliant success was to have made himself a star of wit and taste among that luxurious, indolence-loving throng which more than one clever New York journalist has managed very effectually to amuse.

There had been a time, several years ago, when Hubert had thought of pushing O'Hara into just such an environment. Indeed, he had presented the young Irishman to numerous ladies and gentlemen whom he knew. But the pushing had soon proved impossible. O'Hara delighted, charmed, and even dazzled all his new acquaintances. But there it abruptly ended. In those times he had two besetting faults— drunkenness and a tendency to borrow money. To-day he would fascinate some lady of society, who would be willing to declare him the handsomest and most entertaining man she had met in years ; to-morrow he would appear tipsy in her presence and send yesterday's roseate illusion flying away on the four winds. His borrowing proclivities would perhaps already have made themselves felt with her father, husband, or brother. *Le monde ou l'on s'ennuye* soon woke to the fact that here was an impossible human means of diverting itself. Hubert, too, had frankly conceded his mistake, and had apologized with some mortification in various directions.

But O'Hara had not gone from bad to worse as regarded his intemperance. He had, indeed, drawn a rather tight rein upon it for two or three years, and afterward managed to drink with that species of moderation which limits itself chastely to only three or four orgies a year. But it struck Hubert (who knocked up against him every now and then, just as he had done this afternoon) that in a journalistic sense he had markedly deteriorated. He was now in a much

better financial condition; he stood as one of two or three
rulers over the destiny of a certain weekly journal, whose
tone and atmosphere were to Hubert no less repulsive than
distressing.   He had not wanted to talk with O'Hara about
his paper; there were so many other things that the engaging fellow could talk about much more attractively for his
present hearer.   But the subject seemed almost inevitable
when O'Hara began, for the third time since they had begun
their sail :

"Look here, my dear fellow, you haven't yet given me an
answer about your 'White Violets.'   I recollect you don't
like to print your verses in the magazines, but I do so wish
you'd let us have that enchanting sonnet.   As for price,
you know, whether you cared for anything or not, I would
make a point of promising to pay you—"

"Oh!" Hubert here broke in evasively, "I'm afraid that
if you should see 'White Violets' a second time you'd lose
all respect for it.   You were in a mood of sentiment the day
I read it to you; your own personal equation had a great
deal to do with your admiration; yes, I assure you it had."

"Pshaw, my boy; it's nothing of the sort, as you're
perfectly well aware."   A little silence followed now, as
O'Hara watched the brisk marine wind hurry away a
gossamer cloud of his own cigar-smoke.   "I think I see why
you rebuff me whenever I try to get hold of that sonnet."

"Rebuff you?" murmured Hubert, deprecatingly.

"We don't print verses often," O'Hara went on, with a
decisive touch of stiffness most unhabitual to him.   "A
good many poets would take it rather as a compliment than
otherwise that we should want any of their work.   But it's
very evident, Throckmorton, that you don't like our paper."

"Frankly, I don't," said Hubert, who felt himself driven
into a corner, and left with nothing to do except flash out
his blade.   Usually, as his listener very well knew, he was
the soul of gentleness and suavity; he had that instinctive
politeness which is the appanage of all true breeding.   It

was called "blood" not long ago, and in the arrogant, not the merely scientific sense ; it is now beginning to be recognized as an accompaniment and an essential of the ampler moral temperament. " For manners are not idle," sings the greatest English-speaking poet of the century; and then he goes on to tell us how they are the fruit borne by a loyal nature and a noble mind.

" Personality in journalism is most repellent to me," Hubert now went on. " I seldom read newspapers to any great extent, but I studiously keep away from those in which I can hear either my best friend praised or my worst foe reviled."

O'Hara laughed, leaning back in his camp-stool on the breezy deck. " How fine for us editors if all readers had the same tastes as yourself ! I can't tell you what a bore *we* find the whole vulgar necessity. But there's no resisting it."

" I should resist it if I were an editor," said Hubert.

O'Hara turned and looked at him for a moment. " By Jove ! " he exclaimed, with a ring in his voice that meant the most unstinted admiration, " I suppose *you* would ! " He was rather a cynic on the subject of his fellow-men, this Callahan O'Hara, and doubted if very many of them would stay their feet from dancing a reverential measure whenever the guineas once began really to jingle. But Hubert was one of his beliefs, and before the quiet gravity and strength of the latter, with his rich vein of poetry and his immobile yet unostentatious ideals, the Irishman's misanthropic theories would somehow courteously recoil.

" Money isn't always given, in this world," O'Hara went on, " to those who value it the most. I dare say you could live on a crust, Throckmorton, with ten times more grace than I could. You might go off into some waste place and have your *thébaïde* there, and make it delightfully picturesque with your pilgrim-staff and scallop-shell. I, on the other hand, would bore myself to death in such surroundings. I never touch bread; it's such monotonous eating. . . . and I haven't for years drank any water without at least a dash of claret in it. Now that's precisely the way in which I stand. I want my claret. I must have my claret, even if I'm driven to procure it at the price of my self-respect."

While his companion lit another cigar from the lurid ash of its predecessor, Hubert rather dryly said : " I'm glad that my own liking for red wine is in no danger of betraying me into any such extravagance."

He knew very well that what O'Hara had meant as half a joke was a true enough way of hitting off his ethical relations toward society at large. There was certainly very little satisfaction to be found in talking with such a man about the degeneration of the modern newspaper. O'Hara would never be able to get any further than this : the demand for "spiciness" had become imperious, and not to supply "spiciness" was to go without claret. Natures that are selfishly immoral are like the dweller in the midst of a field wholly surrounded by ditches ; his grasses and his trees may be green and delectable enough, but outsiders cannot possibly share his own enjoyment of them without besmirching their boots.

Long prior to the landing of the boat, Hubert had succeeded in getting O'Hara to talk of other things. When they reached the iron pier the sun's ball of molten, seething gold, that it would almost have been blindness to gaze on longer than a second, had just touched the rim of the horizon. They were driven straight to the West End Hotel, and after dining, were greeted with a magnificent moon, that flooded the vast expanses of treeless and cottage-thronged shore. The piazzas of the hotel were swarming with people, but in the copious pearly light every face that Hubert gazed upon was unfamiliar to him.

"No chance for any fashionable items here," observed O'Hara. " The children of Israel are having it all their own way."

"And what a superb time of it they seem to be having as well !" said Hubert.

Just then a loud, gay laugh rang out at his elbow from a girl of about twenty, luxuriously yet not gaudily dressed, with a face that would have served for a sultana in its olive loveliness, and eyes that were dark stars of glory.

"They're welcome to their good time," sneered O'Hara. "I'm told that in the old days here it was so different for a fellow. Then they kept away."

"Yes," said Hubert. "I saw the place then. It wasn't half so vivacious : it was full of New York Christians—and snobs."

O'Hara looked at him with a start, and then burst out laughing. "How like you that is !" he exclaimed. "You always *were* endorsing unpopular questions."

"Unpopular !" softly echoed Hubert, as he glanced to right and left, where many other handsome feminine faces of either a dusky or blond type were visible in the wan, penetrant moonlight. "Well, no doubt it all depends upon one's line of approach. For my part, I should say that this remarkable and very genial race had the upper hand of us in almost everything. My limited experience has told me that they are very apt to be highly educated. They are certainly quite often handsome to look upon ; and—"

"What ? The men, for instance ?"

"Yes ; not perhaps from a standpoint of taste that would be held noteworthy by some dude in a Fifth Avenue club-window. Our ugly clothes are ruinous to their men. You should see them in the East."

"Perhaps it would be a better plan if they all went there and staid," grumbled O'Hara, glancing about him.

"I fancy they would not think it a better plan," said Hubert. "Why, indeed, should they ? Here so many of them are rich, and so many more of them well-to-do."

"I shall expect soon to see you going about among them and having a fine time," O'Hara replied, with a sarcastic tang in his tones.

" That would be quite impossible," Hubert answered, in
his quiet way, which had become, of late, a somewhat sad
way also. " They are too exclusive, too fond of one another.
I don't deny that they have many excellent reasons to be ;
Heinrich Heine was one of these reasons, and Spinoza was
one, and Mendelssohn was a third . . ."

A little later, when they had strolled toward the ocean
and entered one of the small pavilions that skirt in such
numbers the whole Long Branch bluff, O'Hara declared to
Hubert :

" You've a style of saying things, at times, that leaves a
fellow in doubt as to whether you're just sincere or not.
And yet in all important things I've never met a more sincere man. I won't add that I envy you your inflexible
honesty, however. I'm one of those chaps who can admire
a virtue without wishing to imitate it."

" Just," smiled Hubert, " as you'd enjoy looking at something pretty in a shop, with 'hands off' fastened to it." He
drew a long, ruminative breath, and stared down at the
molten silver of the combing waves. " You speak as if you
were making a revolt against the venders of proverbs . . as
if you didn't think honesty was (how do they put it ?) the
best policy. For my part, I'm honest, most probably,
because it would bore me to be anything else. I should
feel . . . what sort of pungent simile can I hit on to express
just *how* I should feel ? Let us say as if I were forced to
wear a coat that was much too tight in the armholes."

" There it is again," laughed O'Hara. " You *speak* that
as if you were only half in earnest. And yet your code of
morals and mine are like strength beside weakness. You're
always despising me for not living the higher, nobler life. . .
Oh, yes, you are ; you needn't lift one hand in that politely
contradictory way, for I am quite certain you *are*. Well, I'm
free to confess it, I do *not* think honesty the best policy.
Of course by honesty I mean unswerving rectitude, not the
mere decent keeping of the eighth commandment, and all
that sort of rudimentary thing. I revere it theoretically ; but

as an affair of practice I've found that the man succeeds best
in this life who tramples ideals into the dust and strikes out
in his own selfish and often pitiless path."

"Perhaps he does," half assented Hubert, slowly nodding
his head. "That is, if he really values success."

O'Hara regarded him with steadiness for an instant. "I
don't believe you value it," he said.

"Success?" queried Hubert, returning his gaze. "Em-
phatically I do not. The conditions of life on this planet
make it really so absurd a failure, after all."

"But you write your poems."

"I *did* write . . . my verses."

"What! you've lost—" began O'Hara; and then he
suddenly recollected the story he had heard of how a certain
cool-headed girl had jilted Hubert to marry a richer man.
With neat tact, however, he soon proceeded, as swiftly as
possible : "But of course you *can't* have lost your inspiration.
It's too genuine for that. Oh, I know, my dear boy! Your
'White Violets' isn't the only piece of your work that I've
thrilled over. And yet I'm tempted to admit you *are* one of
the very few men who despise worldly success, when I actually think over your poems."

Hubert gave a little careless laugh. "Ah," he said,
"when you think them over you discover that they are failures."

"No. Not for me. I like them just as they are. But . .
well, if they don't sell I understand why they don't."

Hubert shrugged his shoulders. "I didn't print them,"
he said, "caring whether or no they would sell. I always
am my own publisher, in a certain way; I merely hire, as
it were, the *imprimatur* of Messrs. Prescott and Everett.
They put the books on the market, as they call it. But the
books do not sell; I happen to know that. They've been
well received in certain critical quarters, but neither here
nor in England is there the standard, the criterion of criticism, nowadays, that may crown an author with any distinc-

tive kind of laurel. Even the two or three English Saturday reviews that were once more or less authoritative have
completely lost caste as judicial organs. It would seem as
if there were no longer any real critics; *le moule en est
brisé.*"

" Still, the public is a critic, after its fashion."

" I don't like its fashion."

" It has golden opinions indeed for those whose books it
likes."

" No doubt. I'm not avaricious."

" You mean—you're prosperous already," smiled O'Hara.
" Well," he went on, " if you were not both prosperous and
indifferent I could tell you how you could make the public
love your poetry."

Hubert looked mildly interested. "The public is just
now understood to detest all poetry," he said.

" Never," affirmed O'Hara, with an antagonistic little
flourish of one hand, "was there a greater mistake. You
mean, the public is so *mis*understood. Look how the poems
that it loves go flying from newspaper to newspaper, all
over this vast country! No, my dear Throckmorton, the
fault is with our poets, not with our public."

" And what is the poor poets' fault?" asked Hubert.
" That they *are* poor poets? or that they write too many
rondeaux, triolets, and *vilanelles*—write, in other words, with a
lisp and a simper?"

" Oh, I wasn't thinking of those little metrical mountebanks," replied O'Hara. " I referred to the few virile
fellows like yourself who care to write verse nowadays."

" Oh, I see. Kind enough of you. Well?"

" This agnosticism, this modern scientific spirit, creeps
into all you do. It confuses the people; they don't understand it; they believe that poetry should be a kind of
religion. I saw, not long ago, that an eminent English
writer had just stated poetry to be fully three-fourths religion."

"Eminent writers of all periods and all nations have said foolish things," returned Hubert. "I never have been able to see why poetry is any more religion than it is gastronomy. Poetry is feeling and beauty expressed rhythmically."

"Not at all a bad definition. Only, the wide throngs of readers don't concern themselves with definitions; they want to have their hearts touched and their faiths quickened when they read a poem."

"I know; they want it to affect them like a camp-meeting, or something in that way. Well, I don't write such poems."

"But you could, my friend, if—"

"If I wanted to be untrue to myself. Yes, then I could."

"But I mean this: you could, by so writing, with your extraordinary gifts of presentment and embellishment, achieve a great fame."

"Thanks." Hubert fixed his eyes on the face of his companion. The light here in the pavilion shone dimmer than it did outside, but O'Hara saw very plainly how serious yet how tranquil was the look he wore as he answered: "There's not much difference, to me, between the hypocrite in life and the hypocrite in literature."

O'Hara felt those words keenly. He was a man who had endured hours of the harshest unrest because of that very ideal whose desecration he now counselled Hubert to commence. With him it had once been a beautiful shining lamp; its lustre had pierced every corner of his soul. But it burned feebly now, and with occasional signs of total extinction. Again and again he had drearily told himself that this change had not been wrought by himself alone. The world had not let him tend his lamp as he would have desired. Cares, vexations, disappointments had intervened to thwart and spoil the fulfilment of such holy office. There had been a time when he would have shuddered to realize that he was ever destined to become the Callahan O'Hara of the present. He had started out with noble aims—in journalism (odd as it may sound) as in everything else.

But it would not do for him to heap too much of the blame on circumstance, and his own covert admission that it would not do gave him some sharply repentant hours. He had always envied Hubert, and said to his own troublesome conscience that he too would have preserved himself the model of honor, of manliness, of gentlemanliness, with so stout a golden buckler against adversity as that which fate had given this most fortunate of young poets. On the other hand, however, he would sometimes be assailed by a little haunting whisper which assured him that Hubert, if poorer than the traditional churchwarden, would never have stooped the least fraction of an inch lower than self-respect would have warranted. Money gives independence, but there are some few spirits in the world from whom no poverty can wring the meaner sort of humiliation. O'Hara had some- how acquired the most secure confidence that Hubert was one of these.

Till now they had been alone in the little pavilion; but a moment after Hubert had finished speaking, two new- comers, a lady and a gentleman, entered. The former had on her bonnet, and bore herself with a somewhat reluctant air, as though she wanted to receive a transient impression of how the glittering and sobbing ocean would appear from this dusky little coign of shelter on one of its bluffs. Her motions indicated that she was in a hurry. She stood at the gentleman's side for a very brief interval, during which both of their backs were turned to Hubert and O'Hara.

"Oh, *what* a lovely night!" she softly exclaimed. And then she slipped an arm familiarly within the gentleman's. "But come along, Jack," she continued; "we can look at the ocean by moonlight just as well over in Elberon as here."

"But you can't have *me* over at Elberon," said Hubert, rising.

The lady veered round and recognized him with a merry little cry. "Oh, it's really you!" she said. "Where *have* you been keeping yourself this age?" And then they both shook hands with Hubert.

A little later all three walked out of the pavilion together. After perhaps a quarter of an hour Hubert rejoined O'Hara.

"Your friend is vivacious," said the latter. "I mean the lady, of course."

"Mrs. Van Schaick? Yes; she's a jolly little body. But she has the funniest reputation as an entertainer. Perhaps, by the way, you've heard what it is."

"I? no."

"She's forever making mistakes; and so is he, for that matter. They live in an atmosphere of social solecisms and blunders. Somebody once said of Jack Van Schaick that it was dangerous to get a divorce in the same city with him, because he would be sure to have the two separated persons at dinner sooner or later. It is really very odd what a sinister fame this couple have secured for doing the wrong thing quite unintentionally. I think that as a rule the world miserably misjudges us; but I fear that for once it is right in what it says of Mr. and Mrs. Jack Van Schaick. They're both the dearest, kindest of people. Nobody has ever called Van Schaick anything but 'Jack' since he began to spend his forty or fifty thousand a year in charming entertainments for his myriad friends. And ever since Emma Van Alstyne married him she's been 'Mrs. Jack Van Schaick.' A good-hearted, true-souled woman as ever lived. *I've* never been present at the commission of any of their extraordinary *faux pas*. But it seems to be an irrefutable fact that they do commit them. And by the way, she and Jack have pressed me to dine with them at their Elberon cottage to-morrow night."

"You accepted?"

"Yes . . . I wasn't just sure whether I would stop over to-morrow or not. But . . . well, yes, I've accepted."

"Let us hope," said O'Hara, jocosely, "that you wont be the victim of their celebrated *malapropos* behavior."

"I?" said Hubert, starting a little, and then shaking his head. "I? Oh, no. I've nothing to feel afraid of in *that* connection."

Those words of his afterward came back to him . . . He went to Elberon on the following day. The dinner-party of Mr. and Mrs. Jack Van Schaick was a rather large one. About fifteen guests were assembled in the drawing-room of their exquisite cottage, just a stone's-throw from the sea. Among these guests were Mr. and Mrs. Bleakly Voght.

But this was not all. Hubert took into dinner a lady whom he had known for years in New York society, and after the assemblage was seated at the brilliant dinner-table, with its gay-shaded candelabra and its gorgeous effects of flowers, he discovered that on his left was—Angela.

The intensity of the mistake threw a chill over the entire throng. Hubert passed through several distinct moods. At first he thought of rushing from the table. Then he determined upon self-control as his only sensible and dignified course. Then he assured himself that self-control was impossible. After a little while he became aware that he had exchanged several words with Angela. Had she spoken to him first, or had he been the primary cause of their brief, formal, forlorn little episode of conversation?

'I shall go mad,' Hubert thought, a few minutes later. Angela was talking to the gentleman at her other side. The lady at *his* other side was being voluble, yet nervously and consciously so, as he could not help observing. He scarcely had the power to follow a word that she said. He was aware that the eyes of the entire company were fixed upon himself and Angela. To make matters worse, the eyes of Bleakly Voght, who sat just opposite, were fixed jealously, inexorably, vigilantly upon himself alone.

Never was a more awkward dinner. Luckily, Elberon afforded Hubert a kind of safely practicable topic. He had seen it by daylight, and had admired the numberless bright tinted cottages that verged its low, bare sweep of coast,

"It's like a more familiar and companionable Newport," he remembered that he said. Did he say it to Angela? He was not sure. A perfume of roses floated to him from her breast. Once their eyes met in a full, direct mutual gaze. He dared not speak to her except in the most threadbare commonplaces, and yet, toward the end of the repast he was conscious that he had said something by no means commonplace. What had it been? His pulses were at too unsteady a gallop for him to determine.

"How have I frightfully wronged you? Will you explain to me? Will you find a chance, later on, to do so?"

Who had spoken those words? Had it been Angela? Yes, it must have been she . . . And now the ladies were quitting the dining-room. Perhaps it would soon be necessary for him to exchange a few words with Bleakly Voght; already the two men had coldly bowed to one another.

Yet, no. Van Schaick was now but too poignantly aware of his own and his wife's last infelicitous deed. He continued to keep Hubert and Voght separated, and without showing either that the least effort had been made to produce this result—an impulse, by-the-bye, in the direction of pure tact such as he had not shown for many months.

Hubert smoked his cigar and talked with the two or three men nearest him. It grew warm, and their host flung back the broad panes of a window that opened upon a piazza. Straightway the sweet sea-breeze flowed into the candle-lit chamber, but only with impetus enough to make the delicate yellow points of flame waver slightly below their rich-hued little shades. You could see some high-hanging festoons and tangles of vine sharp-cut against the crystal blue beyond them, and still farther away, in its fairy tenderness and beauty, the spangled path of the moon across the ocean.

Hubert was thinking: 'I must see her alone; I must find the chance that she spoke of. But how shall I find it? .. How? .. how?'

5

This question began to make a sort of clock-stroke in his brain, mingling with the brisk hum of after-dinner converse about the Monmouth races and the last fortunate *coup* "over at the Club House," in roulette.

V.

THE Van Schaicks' abode was one of the largest and most beautiful in Elberon. Its piazza surrounded it on all sides, and though it rose, like nearly every residence there, from the centre of a rather meagre domain, cultivation had nevertheless poured some of her fairest favors upon this limited tract. No other lawn wore grass of such velvet richness or of so living an emerald, and in none other were the *parterres* radiant with blooms of such blended rarity and exuberance. When the gentlemen at length joined the ladies, these latter were found dispersed in groups, here and there, along the piazza, some of whose nooks were filled with the densest shadow. Suddenly it seemed to Hubert as if Angela glided out of the lucid air itself and paused not far away from him. She immediately spoke, and her voice was vibrant, but quite low.

"Can you say now," she murmured, "whatever there is to be said?"

Then, without waiting for him to respond, she moved away toward a part of the piazza that was much dimmer than this, either because of some sloping variation in the fanciful build of the roof above it, or through some special opulence and implication of its vines. Hubert looked about him. A few people were near, but even at slight distance their faces had become just recognizable and no more. Perhaps nobody had seen Angela address him. He now perceived that there was a large, low window not far from where he had been standing, and that this window was wide open, like the one in the dining-room. No doubt Angela had slipped through that from the faint-lit apartment beyond. His brain felt clearer now. It seemed to him as if he had been drunk

67

(though he had merely quaffed a few sips of champagne at dinner) and that he was now awakening from semi-stupor.

He passed along the piazza in the direction that she had taken.   Knowing now, as he did know, just how and why she had given herself to Bleakly Voght, would it not be cruelty to tell her the unflinching truth?

'Yes,' his conscience answered him; 'and all the more cruelty if she still loves you, as you have every reason to believe that she still does love you?'

But that last thought, 'she still does love you,' drowned conscience.   Besides, it seemed so hard for him to forgive her that mad matrimonial step.   Having yielded to Alva Averill's horrid counselling was one thing; having actually married Bleakly Voght was indeed another!

In a short time he found himself quite separated from all the other guests.   The light came very vaguely to this part of the piazza.   Off amid the shadow was another shadow.

It approached him.   He waited for it.   He knew it would be Angela.   It soon proved to be.

Her voice, as she now addressed him, was one subdued tumult of excitement.   The moment that he looked upon her face again, obscure yet passionately eager and question_ing in every lineament, he was certain that he would tell her all she might desire to hear.

"You accused me," she began; "there was something about your eyes, your tones, that made me imagine you—you thought yourself justified in doing so."

" Justified!" he repeated.

"And then those words you spoke at Alva's funeral. I—I don't know that I should have sought this meeting, even after what you said to-night, if you had not said what you did say *there*.   You accused *her*—Alva!   She was my trusted friend.   I had always believed her yours."

" She was."

" Was?   You mean that—"

"I mean that I thought her so until I found out that she was the worst, the cruellest, the falsest of women."

"Alva! Good Heavens! What did she do?"

"What did she *not* do?" answered Hubert, with his accent, faintly though each sentence rang, betraying the anguish that was now goading him into unrestrained utterance of the truth. "She sent for me to come to her after that accident happened. She was dying, and knew it. She .. well, she had cared for me."

"Cared for you?" He could see his companion's face much more clearly now, and there was no mistaking the woebegone naturalness of its innocent expression as she repeated: "Cared for you? Why, how could we mistake, either you or I, that she cared for us both?"

Hubert stood pressing his lips together in the dimness for a few seconds. "I mean—she loved me," he soon said. "That was what she had to confess when she sent for me on her death-bed."

"Loved you!" shot from Angela, in a wild whisper. A moment later she recoiled several steps, and her gaze flashed towards him in the dreamy gloom that engirt them both. "She's dead, and can't answer that charge!"

He clenched his hands .. It seemed to him, for a little while, that he hated the woman who stood before him as much as he had ever loved her. "So," he returned, "you don't believe me? Well, I've no proof. None, that is, unless you'll credit the monstrous treachery she practised."

"What treachery?" Angela asked. She was searching his face, now, as well as the dusk would let her. His old adoration of her rushed upon him, thrilling every vein, as he saw an involuntary credence of what he might impart to her light and melt the sweet, vague ovals of her eyes.

"A woman came one day to Alva Averill," he said; "a woman and a child."

"Yes—I understand you."

"That woman knew nothing of *me*," he went on. "I

doubt if she has ever even heard of my existence. Alva told you very differently, did she not?"

"Differently? Yes, she said . . ."

"I know; she said that the child was mine. It was a lie."

"A lie!"

"Yes; the child was your husband's, and that woman was its mother. Do you wish proof of this? Alva Averill told it me an hour or two before her death, and I believed her. But that did not prevent my searching it all out afterward. I held a consultation with the best detective I could secure, and at length he brought me a detailed account of the woman's life."

"One . . that incriminated . . my husband?"

"Yes; you may verify this for yourself. If you desire it at any future time, I will send you the name and address of my assistant, and will instruct him to answer all your questions without reserve."

She was staring at him with pain and terror blent on her colorless face; she had clasped her hands together very tightly and was holding them just on a line with her bosom, which he could see rise and fall in agitated way beneath its laces and roses.

"Perhaps I—I may ask you, some day, to give me such proof," she stammered. "Doubts *may* come to me hereafter . . I don't know. But now—now, as I look at you and hear you voice, I feel as if every syllable you speak were stamped with truth . . ."

He smiled, and made a little despairing gesture.

"If you had only believed in me a short while ago!"

"You—you forget," she faltered.

"I forget nothing," he said. The words hardly rose above a whisper, but in spite of that there was a knell in them.

She began to move her hands, one over the other, while not discontinuing their clasp; it was a gesture that betrayed depths of perturbation, notwithstanding the slowness of its motions.

"You—you knew more of the world than I," she recommenced. "It should have been less easy to deceive you than me. If, as you say, Alva did this sickening thing, you had experience as a guard against her; I had not. And so . . I—I am not *alone* culpable."

"Granted," he replied. "But that the guile of this woman should have got between you and me, to push us apart, is one thing. That it ever should or would have driven you to the marriage you made—to any marriage, in fact—is another."

She bowed-her head, and as she did so one of the jewels in her hair darted a spiteful enough flash at him to have come straight from the eyes of Bleakly Voght.

"And that child was *his*," now broke from her; "that woman was . . ." There she lifted her head again and looked at Hubert. "Oh, my God," she gasped, "what a snare has been set for me!"

"Say set for us both!" here fell from Hubert. He took several steps nearer to her without knowing what he did. And now a note of compassion pierced his tones; the great woe in her mien had addressed him with such potency that he had no more reproaches left. "Angela!" he softly exclaimed; "we have both been horribly wronged! Perhaps in a way we are both to blame; but neither has been so very culpable, after all. It was she—it was that arch-hypocrite, for whom the grave that she now lies in is too decent a resting-place!"

Angela looked at him with eyes that had suddenly become flooded in tears.

"Ah, but that letter I wrote you!" she faltered.

He bit his lip. "I should have torn it in shreds, and rushed to you afterward. I should have said: 'Angela, you do not mean that you are cold or ambitious—*you!* There is some devilish pique—some aching wound, behind every line that you have written! Tell me what this mystery means!' I should have spoken so to you—and in a trice all *her* villany would have been laid bare to us. We would have found it out by the light of our own love—by . . ."

He had caught her hand, but she said to him quickly and with a tremor of untold sorrow in the two little words : " No —no !" And then she almost flung his hand away; yet before she had made up her mind whether to hurry from him or to remain at his side a brief while longer, his response had come, contrite, touched with dignity, breathing to the ears that heard it of a familiar gentle chivalry and high-strung control over self.

" You are right. I think we had best leave one another. Send me a line, at any time, if you want a personal meeting with the man who investigated all that forlorn affair . . . God bless you ; may each year of your future life gain in peace and joy ! Remember that I hold myself, in the main, as rashly faulty as you were. If it were not for the marriage you made I would concede ten times more that that—I would admit that I had been the only culprit, and that you were even guiltless by comparison."

His sudden composure seemed to augment her tears. They half stifled her as she raised both hands toward him with timid yet fervent deprecation.

" Do not ever think of me hereafter as guiltless ! And as for my being happy again, that—that is beyond the most daring hope ! . . Ah, you don't know what my punishment has already become !" . . . . She threw back her head for an instant, and there was a desperate defiance glittering from her tear-besieged eyes that made her look of suffering all the more pathetic to him. " I never had a meek nature— you know that," she swiftly pursued. " But I've married a tyrant whom the meekness of a slave would not satisfy. . . The future ! I grow almost mad when I let my thoughts dwell on it ! And now you've turned the past into even a worse horror !—You've . . . "

She paused, listened for a second, and then dashed a handkerchief over her face, in wild effort to wipe away the compromising evidence of her tears. Hubert, like herself, had heard the sound of an approaching step; it was firm, deliberative, yet rapid. He discerned the lighted doorway of a hall at some little distance beyond them, and in a direction opposite to that whence the step proceeded.

"Come with me this way," he whispered, and moved forward as he spoke, expecting that she would at once accompany him.

But the injunction was given too late. "Are you there, Angela?" said a perfectly cool voice which they both recognized as Voght's.

"Yes," she managed to answer.

In another instant he was close beside them. Hubert saw that his naturally white face had got a chalky tint. He addressed his wife first. "I was wondering where you'd disappeared," he said.

"Neither of us had gone very far," Hubert struck in, with the utmost calm and nonchalance of manner. He aimed to convey a double meaning, yet one which this husband, whom he had just heard called a tyrant, might find reassuring and even consolatory, while it was by no means too pointed.

But Bleakly Voght, as we know, had but a weak sway over his own temper. Once it got control of him, the chances were strong that he would make himself either obnoxious or droll. Still, in the present case it must be chronicled to his credit that he did neither. The merciless mockery and amusement of two or three women who were seated, at that moment, not by any means far off, would not have spared him hereafter, he well knew, if he had afforded them any firm *point d'appui* for a "racy" dinner-party scandal.

He showed Hubert that he was inwardly furious, however, as he now answered in curt, frigid tones:

"This night-air is treacherous; there has been a change

during the past hour. I think it will be more prudent if my wife waits for our carriage indoors."

He offered Angela his arm, and as she took it he so stood that she was forced to turn her back upon Hubert. Whether or not she succeeded in hiding her tears and the traces of them as she bade good-night to their host and hostess and the other guests, Hubert afterward had no knowledge. The carriages were all arriving and being announced when he joined Mrs. Van Schaick, for the purpose of saying a quiet good-night and then slipping away. But the Van Schaicks did not merely commit blunders; they sometimes made them worse by would-be extenuation, reparation, and apology.

"Oh, I m *so* sorry it happened!" Mrs. Jack murmured to him, clasping his hand in her own gloved one. She was a plump little creature, and her beady black eyes glistened from a plump face, over which the glossy black hair was lifted high and tipped with little curving feathers, not unlike the crest of a guinea-fowl. "Oh, yes, *yes,* Jack and I are *both* so sorry! But it was *his* fault. Of course he should never have asked you, when he knew of how they were surely coming and of how you and *she* were once engaged! I declare, it makes me sick when I think of all the horrid things Jack does out of pure forgetfulness. And then, half the time, people blame *me.* If you recollect, when we saw you over at the Branch, *he* asked you, and not I. Still, *I* should have remembered about . . about *it,* you know. But it somehow escaped *my* mind too, although there's some excuse for a woman with a family, and one who's head of two or three establishments, like me . . . . whereas Jack, there, he has nothing on earth to do from morning till night except go to clubs and drive and bet and amuse himself."

"There's really nothing for you to feel distressed by," said Hubert, with all his best air of repose and polish; "nothing, I assure you."

"It's quite horrible!" Mrs. Jack gently wailed, however,

still detaining him. " Jack's mistakes are constantly being traced to me. We do, both of us, commit them ; there seems a grim fatality in it. But then his list is three times as long as mine. I'm sure this whole affair of to-night will get abroad and be called *Mrs.* Jack's latest ; you just see if it doesn't. The other day *I* was accused of asking Willy Wotherspoon whether he'd left that sweet little wife of his quite well at Bar Harbor, when everybody knew she'd just begun a suit for divorce against him in Newport. But this was Jack, not I. . . And I'm beginning to suspect that *he* is the one who turns the tables on me in that horrid way. If he does, woe to him ! . . And now I'm *so* glad you don't mind what has happened. It's so like you not to mind ; you always did have such a sweetly amiable disposition."

Hubert felt a dread lest Mr. Jack might make an attempt to smooth matters over with the same volubility that Mrs. Jack had just employed ; so, without seeking for that gentleman, he got into the hired wagon that had been sent for him from the hotel and was speedily driven back to Long Branch.

One big star, as Hubert watched it during his drive, appeared to sparkle over the immense pallor of the moonlit sea with scorn and irony in its beams. The film had been torn from his wound again ; it almost seemed to him that he could feel it bleeding, and with his best heart's blood.

On reaching the hotel again, he was met by O'Hara, who had been awaiting his return rather impatiently.

" There is hardly a soul here whom I know," began the Irishman, as soon as Hubert had consented to light a cigar in his company ; " and the few that I do know are of a sort that I can't abide."

" Of what sort ? " asked Hubert.

" Oh, the half-professional gambler. I suppose the Club House will be packed to-night, on account of the races this afternoon. A few sore-headed gamesters have come over here to salve their hurts at the card-tables, and a few tri-

umphant ones have been led to exploit their vein of luck still
further."

" That is nearly always the way with the winning dealer
in hazards ; he turns his own worst foe the moment fortune
makes him her friend."

The cottage-like structure of the Club House, white, graceful, airily filagreed about its roofs and porches, rose in the
moonlight, not many yards away. It had all the outside
innocence of some rather unpretending villa. But in another
minute a gallant equipage stopped before its front gateway.
The inmates had been singing a kind of rowdy song in a
semi-bacchanal manner; they were all young men, and a
little closer view than that which the hotel-piazza afforded
would have shown that most of them were tipsy.

Hubert was in a mood for any morbid excitement, just
then. " I haven't gambled," he said, "for over four years ;
and that last time was one night at Monte Carlo, when I won
six thousand francs and almost swore that I would never
court the vulgar and vitiating pastime again. But to-night I
—well, suppose we walk over and see what the interior of
the place is like . . . ."

Bleakly Voght had meanwhile lost no time in getting
Angela away from the Van Schaicks'. She had rallied with
a speed that surprised him and would have produced the
sharpest consternation if he could have seen the interior
workings of her tortured spirit. But she was by no means the
first woman who has known how to mask agony. Doubtless the thought that her name and Hubert's must be already
in process of covert discussion nerved her toward new rigors
of self-governance.

But she drew a great fluttering breath of relief as the
carriage rolled away from the Van Schaicks' door, bearing
herself and her husband. It was a heavy family-carriage,
and its appearance amid all the light, gay, brilliant modernity
of Elberon had evoked not a little derisive comment. But

Mr. and Mrs. Bleakly Voght were not at present the heads of their own household; they had come to Elberon as the guests of Bleakly Voght's maiden aunt, Miss Betsey Lexington. The latter, who possessed several millions, had for some years been expected to die and leave her only nephew at least half of her great property. But she had not died; instead of that she had built, at a considerable distance back from the sea-shore, what had been called the single really ugly house in all Elberon. Hither each year she would ask her nephew, Bleakly; and now that he was married she held it her duty to include his wife in the invitation. But Angela had not pleased this gaunt, gray old woman as a bride for one of her own kin. She was over seventy years old, and she remembered New York society fifty years ago. It was true that there had been Laights fifty years ago. Ah, yes, she admitted that. But a Laight had once married his cook. Miss Betsey recollected it so well! It had shocked the whole town, from Bowling Green to Canal street. That cook, though not in the immediate line of Angela's grandparents, had been, notwithstanding, an uncomfortably near ancestress, and Bleakly ought to have remembered it.

Curiously enough, when some friend, rather free of speech, pointed out to Miss Betsey the fact that Angela's father had been a gentleman of precarious repute, that lady gave the information hardly any heed. Scampishness in a family was one thing, this logical product of so-called American aristocracy declared. Where could you find a good old family that had been without at least two or three scamps? They were just as certain to crop out as drunkards. But a cook! No; depravity was one thing—plebeianism was another!

"You'll find Aunt Betsey a type," Voght had said to his wife, "and a rather odd one. It's fast dying out; it belongs to the little old provincial New York of the past. But she's a lady, and knows how to be nicely hospitable. We sha'n't

see much of her; she's nearly always in her room, with gout
or something of that sort. And these yearly visits, you
know, must be paid."

As the carriage moved to-night along the breezy, sea-
scented road, Voght was the first to speak. The coachman,
like the carriage, was an ancient family-affair, and known to
be almost wholly deaf.

"Do you think you showed good taste this evening?" he
asked.

Angela looked at his vague face, always so pale, with its
hawk-like nose and its two little twinkling eyes. She repeated his words, "Good taste?" questioningly, yet in a far
more stupid way than he suspected. They were words that
to her forlorn and shuddering soul conveyed at that moment
scarcely a shadow of real meaning.

"Oh," he re-commenced sneeringly, "I dare say you'll
lay the whole matter at the door of those blundering
Van Schaicks. But I'm not speaking of that. I'm speaking of
your going off to a lonely part of the piazza, after dinner was
over, and holding a meeting with *him* there. It was certainly
the most horrible taste. A year or two hence your former
engagement to him might almost be forgotten. But I don't
propose that my wife shall cheapen me, like that, before the
world at large. God knows what you talked about together,
but it was something that had made you as white as a sheet
and had set you crying like a baby."

He paused, with the intent of giving her a chance to
reply. But she remained Silent—exasperatingly so, as he
now hotly told himself. After a little while he again
addressed her.

"I must insist," he urged, "upon your telling me what it
was that Throckmorton said which caused such agitation in
you."

Angela started. She had always endeavored to keep
clearly before her mind a conception of the courtesy and
allegiance due this man whose wife she had become. For

weeks past he had done much to make her forget both ; nor
did a sense of her own exorbitant folly in having married
him at all serve by any means cogently as a reminder.

"There was something which it was best for me to know,"
she answered, "and he granted my own request by letting
me know it."

"Ah . . . he met you, then, at your own request."

Angela tossed her head a little. "Yes. I am not at all
ashamed to make that admission ; why should I be ? "

"You're better able to answer the question than I," he
retorted acridly.

"This anger of yours is quite without cause," she protested. "I have done nothing whatever to deserve it."
She thought of what *he* had done to deserve her disgust
(unless Hubert's entire story had been a false one) and
leaned back, softly shivering, against the cushions of the
carriage.

"I see," he exclaimed ; "you wish to avoid answering my
question. You haven't done so yet. Do you intend to do
so ? "

A very bitter smile crossed Angela's face, now. "If I
did answer it," she said, sternly and below her breath, "you
might regret that you'd ever asked it."

"What do you mean ? " he cried, so shrilly that the deaf
coachman thought he heard himself called and looked
round, waiting for a still louder appeal to relieve his doubts.

Knowing (as by this time she had had reason to know) the
violence of his temper, Angela regretted the utterance of
those last words. But it was too late now ; she had
unloosed a hurricane.

"You *shall* tell me what you said together about me—
against me," rang his next wrathful sentence. He leaned
his face close to hers, and suddenly gripped her wrist.
"You *shall* tell me," he repeated. "Do you hear? you've
let slip more than you meant—you've given yourself away
. . . I'll make you tell me what that was—I—"

Just then the carriage stopped before Miss Lexington's residence. Realizing that the end of the brief drive had been reached, Voght let his fingers fall from Angela's wrist. He sprang out of the vehicle, and stood at its door, waiting for her to alight.

But it seemed to her, then, as if all movement were impossible. These bursts of ire in him smote her with greater terror every time that she witnessed one of them. She had begun to hold him in physical fear, distressing though such attitude appeared to her own ideas of feminine dignity. But it was of no use; the old childish horror as of ogre and ghoul weighed upon her; she had had more than one dream, of late, in which he had tried to kill her, and from which she had wakened in a cold sweat of actual horror.

Her sensations were not far from that just now. He soon thrust his head into the carriage and peered at her.

" Are you coming?" he asked, with each word dropping from his lips as though it were leaden.

" I—I—can't," she murmured; and then, as he reached out his hand toward her, though not at all in a hostile manner, she suddenly uttered a little scream of fear and fainted completely away.

She awoke to find him bending over her where she lay on one of the drawing-room lounges. He had carried her into the house himself; those lean, long arms of his were powerful, at a necessitous pitch. He had summoned no help whatever, though if her swoon had continued longer than the brief interval it really occupied, he would no doubt have done so. The moment that Angela opened her eyes she saw the glad relief on his face.

" My darling!" he said, kissing her more than once; " are you better? It was nothing; it was the merest nervousness. I behaved too harshly; forgive me, my Angela! Don't let us think of it any more, dearest! I was a fool and a brute—both. But love made me so. That's no excuse, is it? But forgive me just this once! You shall never tell me a syllable that passed between you and *him*—never, that is, unless you choose. I want so to have you happy . . happy always, my love, my dear, dear wife ! . . ."

This was certainly an altered mood, and as such it repelled Angela no less than the antecedent mood had alarmed her. As soon as she could rise she struggled up from the lounge in spite of his penitential embraces. It was pleasant to think that this one storm of tyranny was over, but when might not the next appear with its rush and flare? She had begun to understand that there was no exemption from the persecutions of such an ill-governed being as he with whom she had linked her earthly fate. At any moment he might dart upon her like an inflamed tiger. And his love only gave a more tropic, hectic, even baneful character to his whole personality. It was like being loved by something uncanny and inhuman.

She knew that she keenly hurt him by going up-stairs without the least tender response to his remorseful protestations. But if it had been the saving of her own life (as she afterward rather exaggeratedly told herself) she could not have addressed him in any loving or even wifely way. Apart from the affright which he had roused in her during the homeward drive, there now rose up, as a fresh, miserable reason why she should never have committed the wild act of marrying him at all, that mother and that child whose wrongs she had laid at the door of the man whom she devotedly loved.

Meanwhile Bleakly Voght lingered down-stairs. He was now even more angry at himself than he had lately been at Angela.

6

VI.

His wife's apathetic treatment of him after his own rather hysterical prayers for pardon had wounded him in a most sensitive and expanded portion of his moral anatomy. We all know of what vagaries a really stalwart vanity is capable. Voght had taught his to believe that Angela loved him. The feline agency exerted by Alva Averill had, it is true, wrought distinct effect. After she had set in motion by her fatal duplicity that disjunctive force which pressed poor Hubert and Angela so sadly if so absurdly away from one another, she seized the chance to utter certain counsels in the ear of Bleakly Voght which not a few men of less vivid self-esteem would have regarded with indecision if not positive belief. She had told him that Angela had never truly cared for Hubert ; that the girl's heart had for months been given in secret to himself, yet that she shrank bashfully from all his great social grandeur. "Try her again," the smooth-voiced plotter had pursued. "You think she repulsed you before ; it may have been merely what I have endeavored to explain ; and we women know one another better than men know us. Try her again . . you have been in Europe since you asked her the last time, and she has watched by a dying father's bedside—an experience not apt to increase any girl's coquetry. See if I do not prove right ; you're in love with her still—you concede it ; this time you will win her ; it will be *reculer pour mieux sauter* with you."

So it had been ; and yet not even the illusory veil of self-importance could quite transform Angela's chill and grave acquiescence into the timidity of concealed adoration. Then there had been that hasty rupture of the engagement

between the girl and young Throckmorton. Had she really
grown tired of him, as Alva Averill insisted? When Voght
had mentioned the matter to his *fiancée* during the very brief
term of their engagement, she had a parrying and even veto-
ing little group of responses ready at hand. Then, soon
afterward, had come the marriage, and after that there had
been with Bleakly Voght a gradual confirmation of those
doubts and suspicions which had slept a little while but
never died. Perhaps it was because he guessed in Angela
the repulsion which his presence exercised upon her that he
strove to make himself (in fits of perverse and imperious
wilfulness) more antipathetic than ever. But in any case he
would have been hard to get along with; his temper had
been a savage one for years; he had already quarrelled
with almost every blood-relation he possessed except his
Aunt Betsey Lexington—and a substantial golden reason, as
some people avowed, alone kept him from long ago having
added her to the grim list of his foes.

But however he had thus far behaved to Angela, his love
for her was intense. The explosions of his anger were
always followed by episodes of tenderness and contrition,
but never had this result occurred with such an accent of
complete self-abandonment as to-night.

"I've made an infernal ass of myself," he said, standing
in his aunt's rich but prim drawing-room. "She cares no
more for me than for one of the buttons on her glove. She
married me out of pique—nothing more, and I was fool
enough to let her. She's in love with that verse-scribbler
still, and I don't doubt they were having some sort of an
explanation when I went round the edge of the piazza, there,
and caught her bathed in tears."

He gnawed his lips, and thrust both hands into the
pockets of his baggy, ill-fitting trousers, that had known the
scissors of a renowned Piccadilly tailor, but looked, like
everything he wore, as if they had come out of the Bowery.
All the latter part of his by no means youthful life he had

been what is termed a gentlemanly gambler. Cards were
his only vice, just as it might be said that shooting had once
been his only real amusement; for although he liked a good
horse and owned several, he nowadays rarely rode, and did
not drive half as often as he was driven. Wine he took in
very sparing quantities; it brought on a neuralgia which he
accounted for by reckless drinking in his youth. Tobacco
he seldom touched, as it made him, in its mildest forms,
painfully nervous. But cards had for years been his solace
and delight—when stakes of an appreciable kind were
played for.

Since his marriage he had striven, and with some success,
to control his master-passion. When he played at the club
in his bachelor days, it would frequently be dawn before he
departed for home. This form of diversion in a married
man he had not considered reputable, however indulgently
it might be condoned in a bachelor; and so he had put
gyves, as it were, on his own wrists, and had worn them, too,
with much stoic resolve. Now and then he had played, but
with a curb on his lust, permitting none of that old self-sur-
render which treats time as the slave all thorough-paced
gamblers regard him, and plucks its poppies from the brow
of night to find a wakeful and not soporific intoxicant in the
dusk eyes that burn below them.

But now, at this hour, stung, cut to the quick, feeling that
he had been duped by the dead as much as mocked by the
living, he felt a desire for that one sort of excitement which
would have power to soothe his fevered state. It was still
hardly eleven; the Elberon hotel was but a short distance
away; he could easily get a conveyance there and have himself taken to the Club House at Long Branch, where, no
doubt, cards would be procurable as an amusement in the
form of one game or another.

He soon set forth from his aunt's house with this determination in view, having first notified one of the servants
that he would probably not be home until quite a late hour.

He succeeded in procuring the desired vehicle, and had himself transported to the Club House in a brief space of time. He did not know one of the people assembled in the room where roulette was being played, but lingered there for quite a little while in rapt observation of those who were winning and losing at this game. It was one which had always fascinated him; his record with regard to it, years ago, while he was abroad, had been picturesquely disastrous. He was surprised to find it going on here in this establishment. Before long he determined to try his own luck. In five minutes the old gaming madness was upon him. He never once forgot his trouble while he continued to play, but the effect of the excitement he underwent was that of some potent nervine. No liquor could possibly have given him the same kind of exhilaration as now came to him from merely watching the red or black figures on those bits of pasteboard turn up in the hands of the dealer.

Few men of large intellect have ever been gamblers. In a manner Voght showed the narrowness of his mentality and the resourceless nature of it. Gaming is nothing but a diseased state of avarice, and appeals to qualities that broadminded beings rarely possess. The idlers through life are those whom its dangers chiefly threaten, and when its grip has once become relentless, the drunkard's doom is hardly a worse one to contemplate. Voght had long ago saved himself from that dire self-forgetfulness which brings ruin in its wake. But you saw to-night, if you watched him with any closeness of attention, that his relations toward the vice had just grazed those of minion toward master.

One person, who had entered the room since he began to play, did watch him with just such accentuated scrutiny. This was Hubert. Both he and O'Hara had strolled hither from one of the other rooms. After a little while Hubert commenced playing. There was quite a crowd about the table, and although he was stationed directly opposite Voght it was by no means remarkable that the latter did not immediately perceive his presence. Rather carelessly, and in his quick, nervous way, Voght flung four or five checks upon a certain card. At the same moment Hubert placed three checks there. Voght glanced across the table unconcernedly enough, and then gave a severe start as he saw Hubert. The latter met his irate eye tranquilly. Voght's hand hovered over the checks he had just deposited on the card. Then, with a scowl, he snatched them away. But in doing so he took one of Hubert's checks, though unwittingly. Just afterward the card won.

The dealer paid Hubert, whom Voght's action had keenly annoyed by the spirit of school-boy impertinence that i betrayed. But the payment was insufficient, and Hubert said so. The dealer shrugged his shoulders. " I paid on two checks—all the card had," he replied.

" I put three checks on the card," declared Hubert.

" I only saw two," replied the dealer, civilly but a little curtly.

" But there were three," insisted Hubert.

Several other voices now made affirmation that pointed directly to the heedless mistake of Voght. And then the eyes of Hubert and Voght met once more.

" True," Hubert proceeded, with firmness and calmness in equal measure. " That gentleman " (as he indicated the husband of Angela by a slight motion of the head) " *has* one of my checks. It was unintentionally taken, of course, and will be returned to me at once, as I can't help feeling quite certain."

Voght's frown grew blacker. He bit his lip and stared downward for an instant, while everybody intently watched him. Meanwhile Hubert's gaze was fixed upon his face; it was a gaze no less demanding than gentlemanly. Suddenly Voght's encountered it again. He was too much a man of the world not to realize perfectly that he had now but one proper course. But his devilish temper had quite got the best of him. If almost anyone else on earth except Hubert had confronted him with the polite yet resolute avowal which he had just heard, his restitution and apology would have been immediate. As it was, he now retorted, in tones of trenchant insolence :

"Oh, you claim the check, do you? Well, there it is. I don't believe in making a fuss about such trifles." And then he tossed a check across the table, with such violence that its ivory disc struck Hubert's hand.

"Still, it seems that you *do* make a fuss about trifles," leapt from Hubert, as he allowed the white round to roll past him and drop on the floor.

O'Hara's hazel eyes glittered as he stooped and picked up the check, handing it to Hubert. Voght had cut him superciliously a year or two before ; his remembrance of the cut may or may not have intensified his attitude of championship toward his friend just now.

"Right," he said to Hubert. "The check is your property. A civil way of restoring it would have been more advisable."

"It's no concern of yours," exclaimed Voght, who had recognized O'Hara as a "newspaper fellow" whom he had met somewhere an age ago and not thought worth bowing to afterward.

"No ; it is a concern of mine," said Hubert placidly.

"Gentlemen," called the dealer, with a flourish of one hand over his cards ; "the game, if you please."

Hubert at once presented his checks to the dealer and had them redeemed in money. As soon as this was effected, he strolled out of the room at O'Hara's side. Meanwhile the Irishman had recalled what he would have had no difficulty in recalling if his later life had not drifted so far away from the deeds and misdeeds of the so-named patrician world. He recollected that this Bleakly Voght was the man who had married, abruptly and peculiarly, the former sweetheart of his friend, Hubert. The two men reached the outside porch and stood there, for a few moments, in silence.

" What a devilish rowdy that fellow behaved like," O'Hara presently remarked.

" Yes," said Hubert. He took out a cigarette and began to roll it between leisurely fingers. " He has never known how to govern his temper. It has come near getting him into trouble several times."

" It came near doing so to-night," said O'Hara, with a pull at his reddish moustache. " But *you* spoke up very squarely to him ;" and a gleam of that affectionate admiration which the editor had long felt for Hubert was now manifest in his look. " You showed yourself his better both in wit and coolness . . But I'm a little sorry that you left the room as soon as you did. I can't help wishing you'd remained a short time longer."

" Perhaps it might have appeared best," answered Hubert, in a low voice. And then, for the first time, it flashed upon his companion that underneath his calm the hottest indignation might be smoldering.

This was indeed true. Hubert was one of the few men who believe in that consistent self-discipline which is not only the secret of inward repose but the talisman of good-breeding as well. Still, there are bounds to human patience. If he had not quitted the room when he did, Hubert was by no means positive that his powers of restraint would not have been most roughly over-taxed. And his philosophy admitted no cheapening meekness ; he was quick to resent insult, when it really came, as he was tolerant of rudeness until it had passed those limits beyond which charity wars with self-respect.

" You had the last word, however," said O'Hara, with a boyish note of triumph in his voice, "and a quiet but effective last word it was."

Hubert had lit his cigarette, now. He stood gazing across the garden at the immense hotel, shadowy in the opal air, with its vacated galleries and its diminished lights.

"Still," he said, "I think that if I had remained it would not have been the last word."

"Well, perhaps not," assented O'Hara. "The fellow is such a cad, you know."

Meanwhile Voght had gone on playing with a recklessness that he very seldom showed, and in quite a short space of time had lost several hundreds of dollars. He suddenly decided that he would play no further; the absorbing effects of the game were no longer dominant with him; his rage against Hubert grew as he recalled how serenely the latter had behaved and how entirely in the right he had been. With such a man as Bleakly Voght such a fury as his present one was wholly explainable. Never having been crossed in anything, he had found himself crossed in a matter which was of the most vital concern to him. He had been more than once *abattu*, of late, at the thought that Angela never had loved him and never would love him. But to feel the growing conviction that Hubert had formerly held her heart and still retained it, was for one whose passions had through years been as ill-ruled as his, a goad of the most savage torment. He had a restless craving to meet Hubert again and say or do something that would show the full scope of his hate. But he was better than this impulse, and it would perhaps be but pure justice to state that he had curbed it when he came forth on the little piazza where Hubert stood at O'Hara's side.

The truth was, he had made up his mind to go straight home. He had thought of walking, as the distance was not far and the facilities for such a mode of return were about as perfect as a macadamized pathway bordering a breezy sea could render them. He had his overcoat thrown over one arm, and his hat tipped slightly sideways on the bushy gray of his hair. The usual bulge was in his shirt-bosom, and his white cravat showed the usual rumpled laxity. He strode across the piazza toward the steps, and had almost begun to descend when he saw and recognized Hubert.

In some way it had been found out that Hubert had not quitted the building; and now, when Voght left the roulette table and went forth into the open air, his movements were stealthily watched by certain inquisitive eyes.

He stopped short on seeing Hubert. His lips twitched for a second before he spoke. It here occurred to Hubert that embarrassment rather than anger might just then have him in its clutch.

But no; the mere sight of Hubert had inflamed him once more. It had brought with it a vision of himself kneeling by the lounge on which lay Angela—his wife in name yet not in spirit; it brought with it, too, the echoes of those pleadingly contrite words that he had spoken, only to have them treated with the dead, indifferent silence that was worse than the iciest disdain.

"I hope," he said, quite bluntly and offensively to Hubert, "that you have made up your mind I didn't intend to rob you."

His demeanor was aggression itself. And for this reason Hubert felt wholly justified in replying, while his composed and stirless eyes were fixed full upon the glittering little gray ones before him :

"Pray, is that meant for an impertinence or an apology?"

"The first if you choose," said Voght. "Certainly not the last."

"Do you wish to quarrel with me?" asked Hubert.

Voght scanned him insultingly from head to foot. "It seems," he replied, "as if you wished to quarrel with _me_."

Forms had now gathered at the doorway leading onto the piazza. Some swift messengership must have prevailed during the next few seconds, for in a trice the four or five observers had multiplied themselves into twenty or possibly thirty.

"I've no wish to quarrel with you," Hubert replied. "But I can't permit you to address me with that look and tone, unless you account for both."

"Account? How?" queried Voght, as he came several steps nearer to Hubert.

The latter swept his eyes toward the near hallway and saw the throng that had gathered there. He hated publicity of all kind; he greatly deplored the chance of a public brawl like this; nevertheless, he was unflinching in his posture of calm defiance.

O'Hara, before he could make his answer, slipped to his side and stood there. Hubert felt the touch of the journalist's hand upon his arm as he responded:

"You must account to me as a gentleman for your ungentlemanly behavior, or—"

Here O'Hara's voice sounded: "Or lose a good deal of the caste you pride yourself on!"

"Is this fellow your friend?" inquired Voght, with an accent of extreme sarcasm.

"Yes," Hubert's retort sped. He instantly pushed O'Hara away from him, and at the same time rapidly whispered: "Leave this to me. Leave it to me—I beg of you, my dear fellow."

O'Hara obeyed him, though glowering with discomfiture, and not retiring at all far from his monitor.

"That gentleman is my friend," Hubert now said to Voght. "Tell me," he suddenly went on, with a fiery dart or two leaving his usually kind and mild eyes; "are you bent on making a ruffian of yourself? Or pray what *are* you bent on doing?"

Voght had not seen the clustered men in the near doorway. "You and I have met each other to-night before now," he hoarsely said.

"True," Hubert returned.

"At . . at the Van Schaicks'," came Voght's next words, thickly and with clear effort.

"Yes," said Hubert. He added: "Your mode of address is still not that of one gentleman to another."

"I don't mean it to be," foolishly, wildly responded Voght.

Hubert took a deep breath and knotted both hands. "You wish to insult me, then?" he questioned.

"I—I wish to tell you," said Voght, intimidated in spite of himself, "that—that you behaved. . . " And there he stopped, glaring at Hubert.

"Well?" came the challenging voice of the pale, collected man who faced him.

"You . . you and my wife," flurriedly continued Voght. "You know what I saw there at the Van Schaicks'. What were you saying to her? What right had you to say it, whatever it was?"

This puerility, uttered so low that no listener could possibly have heard it, brought a smile of satire to Hubert's lips. In the bitterness of his soul, with an ungovernable sense of his own excessive misfortune, he responded:

"I was telling her that *you* were the father of Jane Heath's child, not *I.* I was telling her that the falsehood Alva Averill told about *my* being the father of this child and not *you*, had caused our separation—had caused her to marry you instead of myself."

As Hubert spoke the last three or four words Voght recoiled.

"It was a lie," he faltered.

Hubert advanced toward him. "You scoundrel!" he answered. And then he struck Voght a strong, sudden blow between the eyes, that sent him sprawling wretchedly upon the planks of the moonlit piazza.

"I'm glad you did it," Hubert heard O'Hara say; and then he squared himself for a new attack from Voght, who had leapt up again and was dashing toward him. But the usual thing happened: people rushed in between the combatants and kept them separated.

"I shall be over at the hotel if I am wanted," Hubert said to one of the excited throng in a very unexcited way. Then he took O'Hara's arm and the two sauntered off together. Perhaps even by this time Voght would infuriatedly have pursued them. As it was, however, he had no choice in this matter, being surrounded by six or seven determined peacemakers.

"I don't see how I could have done anything else," said Hubert to O'Hara as they walked along. "Do you?"

"No, indeed—though I will admit that I didn't hear the words which caused you to strike him."

"He gave me the lie."

"Yes? And before that?"

"Before that?" repeated Hubert, in a peculiar voice. "Well, I said something he didn't like, very probably."

"That's answering me *tout bref*, with a vengeance," laughed the journalist. "Well, forgive me, Throckmorton; I didn't mean to be curious."

In a few minutes more they had reached the hotel. "Shall you wait here?" O'Hara asked, as they paused on the long, dim front piazza. "Wait here? Wait for what?" returned Hubert.

"Why, for some message from him."

Hubert shrugged his shoulders. "Oh, I don't think he will send any."

"But if he does?"

"I should take no notice of it."

"No notice?" O'Hara repeated. "Why, he's a man who might, sooner or later, send you a challenge—unless I'm a good deal mistaken in him."

"A challenge!" softly ejaculated Hubert. "He would be a precious fool to do that!"

"Still, he might do it," persisted O'Hara.

"If he did," Hubert gravely announced, "I should have but one course to take."

"You mean—fight?" inquired O'Hara, thinking that he could of course mean nothing else.

"Indeed, no," said Hubert with emphasis. "Quite the

opposite. I should place any challenge that I received from a fellow-citizen promptly in the hands of the authorities."

"You would do that!" exclaimed O'Hara. "No, no," he went on; "it isn't like you; I can't believe it."

"Ah, you don't know me yet," answered Hubert, shaking his head with a smile. "I serve my country by obeying her laws, not by defying them. Besides, I loathe duelling as much as I loathe murder."

"But there are times," protested O'Hara, "when its practise becomes a necessity among gentlemen. Take, for example, this affair of yours with Voght—granting that Voght *is* a gentleman, which I admit to be a rather high flight of the fancy. You struck him; it is not either his or your wish, most probably, to stand up and play the shoulder-hitter. There is a more serious and surely a more dignified way of settling your difference."

"By trying to kill each other? I should hardly call it more dignified."

"But you don't want to pound the fellow with your fists, and be pounded in return, for the space of an hour or two?"

"Decidedly not. I was wrong to strike Voght as I did. I committed a punishable offence. He has the power to obtain full redress if so inclined."

O'Hara lifted both hands amazedly. "You *can't* be referring, my dear boy," he burst forth, "to a suit for assault!"

"I am so referring."

"But what satisfaction can the law possibly give any man under such circumstances?"

"If it does not give him all the satisfaction that he ought to secure," replied Hubert, with a fleet, unwonted vehemence, "then it must be a very poor law and a very needless one."

"But good heavens, man!" exclaimed O'Hara. "How is a gentleman going to call on the law to aid him where it's a question of personal honor!"

" He should be proud to have in that law a faithful yet impartial friend. He rushes to it if he wishes to break his father's will—if he wishes to procure a divorce from his wife—if he is maimed by an accident—if he has been swindled by his neighbor. As it is both his friend and guardian, he owes it the duty of respecting one of its most just and moral commands. The exquisite nerves of his ' personal honor ' should be made to undergo a little of the pain that comes from sacrifice. And by the way, I have always observed that ' personal honor ' is nowadays found in a most flourishing state where the subject is just such a spoiled, selfish, tyrannical, arrogant person as Bleakly Voght."

" Still," O'Hara said, " you don't expect a challenge from him ? "

" No," returned Hubert. " I think there are reasons for his not sending me a challenge. Except for these reasons I can readily imagine his doing so."

Hubert meant that guilty incident of Voght's life which Mrs. Averill had made a means of separating Angela from the man she loved. And as it turned out, he judged wisely. Voght did shrink, and solely on this account, from the publicity of an attempted duel. That name, Jane Heath, wrought its paralyzing effect even upon a rancor as bitter as was his own. He knew the dastard character of his conduct, in previous years, to an unfriended and innocent girl. He knew that the world, lenient as it sometimes was to crying faults, would not pardon his share in that bitter little history.

He had never dreamed of the real measures Mrs. Averill had taken, and now, when Hubert's few words told him the whole hideous truth, it was like having the earth split under his feet. Some of those who had prevented him from returning Hubert's blow, said afterward among one another, in sarcastic criticism, that a good deal of their force had been thrown away on a rather peaceful individual. But

Voght's tractability had been simply the result of his growing dismay and dread.   The mark of Hubert's knuckles
would linger on his face for days to come ; pain was already
assuring him of that.   But the pain was also an incessant
reminder not only that his gross fault of the past had somehow transpired, but that it was now to rise up and mock him,
in his relations toward Angela, as with a devil's laugh.

He hardly remembered the walk back to Elberon.   On
arriving at his aunt's house, he passed straight up-stairs to
the large suite of apartments which Mrs. Lexington had
given himself and his wife, not omitting to lock and bolt the
main hall-door below.   But he had no clear perception of
anything until he stood within his wife's chamber.   The
traces of Hubert's clenched hand had already wrought
havoc with his face ; an ugly bluish bruise had begun to
show itself under either eye ; haggard, dishevelled, betraying acute mental perturbation, he presented so alarming
an appearance that Angela almost shrieked as she saw
him.

She had not yet gone to bed.   Feeling that sleep was impossible for at least two or three hours to come, she had
clad herself in a loose flannel gown whose pliant white folds
became her better than she either guessed or cared, and had
seated herself at a small table on which a lamp was still
burning.   Here she found two or three books, and had been
for a long time absently turning over the leaves of one after
another, when the sudden apparition of her husband set
every nerve in her body wildly tingling.

VII.

"You are up late," he said, approaching her.

"Yes," she murmured. "I—I could not sleep."

He drew a long sigh, that had for her a phantasmal sound in the big, still room. "And I," he said, with a lonely solemnity in his voice—"I feel as if I should never sleep again!"

She looked up at him. His face had always been to her a repelling one, but now it almost made her start with horror,

"You have been hurt, have you not?" she questioned peering at him.

"Yes," he said. "I was struck. Throckmorton struck me."

"Throckmorton!" she cried, starting to her feet, all color flying from her face in a second and leaving it ghastly.

Voght smiled; that smile seemed to her like an exclamation of sneering triumph. But she felt immense relief after he had spoken a few more words.

"Ah, you need not be so wildly distressed," he said. "I didn't harm him in the least. There were people who came in between us and prevented my returning his blow. But afterward I felt as if I could hardly blame him for having given it to me." He smiled again, pressing his thin white lips together with a sardonic tensity.

Angela sank back into her seat, and he drew a little closer to her. "I accused Throckmorton of lying," he continued, "but I now feel that I hadn't the shadow of a right to do so. What do you think he said to me?"

"I—I have no idea," she replied.

"I will tell you;" and then he repeated, almost word for

7   97

word, the two sentences that had left Hubert's lips on the piazza of the Club House. Angela listened eagerly. Afterward she bowed her head very low, and sat thus, with her gaze fixed on the floor.

"This is true?" Voght asked. "This is what he *did* say to you?"

"Yes."

"And you? . . . Did you believe him?"

"Yes," she half whispered, after a little pause.

"But suppose I should assert that it is all a falsehood?" he flashed, yet with a certain insecurity in his very sternness that betrayed it as a spurious outburst. "Did—did any woman come to Alva Averill?"

She made him no answer. He stood watching her for some little time, but she still kept her head drooped. An expression of the most passionate cruelty and jealousy crossed his face. He went very close indeed to her, then, and said, with the well-known ring of rage in his husky voice:

"It's all perfectly apparent, now, just why you married me. Alva Averill behaved like a demon, and you, because the man you loved seemed to you villanous, married some-one else from motives of punishment, of revenge. I was the someone else, and you showed me no more pity than if my peace of mind had been made for you to wreck. Now you learn that you visited *my* fault on Throckmorton—that I was the real culprit, not he—and it serves you right. You've only received your proper dues." At this point he hurried to the door of the chamber, waving one hand above his head. "It's all like a sort of devilish comedy, but you're booked for your part, and you must play it out. Let Throckmorton give everything away if he likes. Other men have been foolish as well as I. It was a good while ago. You've something to hate me for, now you know it. Almost anything's better than your dead indifference. Come, hate me —abominate me—as much as you please. But you must

stop there ; do you understand ?   No matter what *I've* done,
there are things I'd kill you for if I thought you'd more than
think them! . ."

He passed from the room, and left her trembling there in
her seat beside the lamp-lit table.

The next few days were full of the severest trial for her.
His disfigured visage not merely forced him to remain
indoors and refuse all the numerous visitors who called
upon him, but it produced a condition of irritability that
eclipsed even his valet's former experiences. Angela was
compelled to see certain of the visitors, though at times
their voices would sound far away to her, and a sensation
of deadly faintness would mingle with the throbbing pain
that scarcely ever quitted her temples.   Old Miss Lexington
was deceived by some story of a bad, dangerous fall, and as
she knew her nephew to be of abstemious habits, asked no
questions of the sort that bring ruin on loosely-wrought
fictions.   There were times when Angela felt as if she
should go mad ; there were times when she almost regretted
that she did not.   Her nature was what might be named the
romantic sort ; she had the clearest sense of abstract duty,
but after all, when it came to the test, emotion ruled her.
We have seen how physical fear now and then influenced
her dealings with Voght. Since Hubert's disclosure and her
husband's corroboration of it, physical loathing had taken
the mastery even over fear. Angela's purity and love of
purity in others had no pharisaic touch ; it was perhaps the
chief reason why she had loved what seemed to her this
element at its whitest, most poetic, and most spiritual in
Hubert. He had been to her not merely an idealist ; she
was old enough, she was enough of an American girl, to
understand that there are men who can be idealists in their
professions, their assumptions, their demands, and yet fail
miserably of any practical correspondence to these as regards
their material, sublunar lives. But in Hubert she had seen,
or had seemed to see, no vestige of either lip-service, hypoc-

risy, or cant. His religion had been to keep himself un-
spotted from the world, not proudly and pretentiously, but
because of an innate aspiration for the finer, wiser, and
sweeter life. . . It can hardly be thought strange that the
damnable falsehood of Mrs. Averill, once believed in, should
have confused, dizzied, and benumbed poor Angela. But
now that she knew the magnitude of that deception and of
her own misfortune she could not blame herself too harshly
for having let any rash, mad agency of pique push her
toward the marriage that she had made.

'Ah,' she would sometimes wofully ask herself, 'was it
not, after all, only that Alva Averill held me weak and
wounded in her grasp? There were times, during those
few days, when I had no power to think for myself—when I
believe that Alva might have led me to do almost anything
(even to commit some crime) if she had only spoken to me
vigorously enough, and used her own will upon me without
stint!'

From the night when he openly acknowledged the sin
that she had laid at Hubert's door, Angela's husband
appeared before her in a new and far more odious light. He
had no longer anything to conceal. He recognized the
situation, so to speak, and flung off his last remnant of
disguise. Angela loved another man, and had married him
because she had held that other man to be guilty of precisely the same fault which he himself had committed. "A
sort of devilish comedy" he had called it; and such it
indeed was, he now concluded, as he paced his chamber
overlooking the brilliant-tinted cottages of Elberon, whose
red, blue, or yellow tiles and shingles burned out against the
vivid sea. He was fond of his wife—yes, passionately,
jealously so. He had got her, and he meant to keep her.
He said this aloud to Angela, in so many words, while she
sat or stood beside him—sometimes while she was changing
the cloths that he kept almost incessantly spread upon his
injured face. She had made her bed and she must lie in it.

It wouldn't be exactly a couch of eider-down, either. She would have his temper to contend with. Oh, yes; he knew he had a temper. If any fellow came fooling about *his* wife, as he had so often seen happen to the wives of his friends, he would say *passez votre chemin* in no time. As for that woman, Jane Heath, her having dared to appear at all was a brazen outrage. He had settled two thousand a year on her, and had agreed to give the child an education, as well. He wasn't at all sure as to whether the child *was* his or no. It had been a rather generous thing for him to behave as he had done, any way, and her popping up like that had been a piece of abominable mischief and spite. Still, he couldn't regret it (could he?) since it had been the means of his securing the wife he wanted.

'Oh, this is torture!' thought Angela; and perhaps her eyes were wholly blinded to what lay beneath Voght's brutality and vulgarity. A sharp, goading pain lay beneath. The insufficiencies of his early education, the indulgences that his own wealth had showered on him, the manifold failures to live by any better law of conduct than that of selfish caprice, were all forces which he felt now, and which seemed blending themselves together in one scorpion whip of torment. He did not choose to show Angela that he was keenly ashamed or that he deeply suffered; instead of doing either, he employed a bravado which came in a certain sense natural to him, and which accounted for his apparent attitude of detestable candor. It would have been greater candor in him, after all, if he had begged Angela on his knees to love him, and caught her hand between both his own, bathing it with his impetuous tears. But no; he had humiliated himself once in that way and he would not do so again. It was better that she should fear him than despise him, he covertly argued. And if the full truth had been disclosed with regard to this poor young wife's feelings, he would most probably have discovered that she did both.

Hubert had asked O'Hara not to let a word of the Club

House quarrel to transpire in the weekly journal of the latter, and O'Hara would have lost his editorial place rather than have allowed the least line of disclosure to appear there. But the daily journals were quite another matter. No friendly editors existed on those whom Hubert could control. And in a day or two their commentaries appeared, copious and unsparing. Both men were of the kind that the modern newspaper loves to make a "story" about. And here was *such* a "story," all ready to be made! The real facts were twisted into twenty different effects of com bination. One or two newspapers gave Hubert a pair of black eyes and sent Voght back to Elberon unscathed, victorious, and superb. The occurrence was just what Long Branch had been wanting to "wake it up." The resident journalistic letter-writers dashed for it as a starving dog dashes for a bone.

Hubert was at his country-seat in Ponchatuk when he read of his unhappy notoriety, but Voght still lingered in the house of his aunt Lexington, afraid to show himself as far as the threshold of its hall-doorway until those hateful purplish blotches had quite faded from beneath his eyes. Angela's days were now made heavier and more miserable to her than ever before. She detested lying about the affair to people as she detested, in the abstract, all lying of whatever sort—as she loved truth for its own clean, simple, noble sake. Her mother had long ago died of what certain friends had called a broken heart, and if this were a fact then nothing had broken the poor lady's heart except the wilful mendacity of her light-principled husband. Angela was all her mother's child; she loathed subterfuge and prevarication. But she was compelled to use both with the visitors who came curiously asking about her husband. Then there was Voght's incessant fury against the news-papers to meet and endure, day after day. There he saw himself repeatedly called a coward; but it was a fact that he had not a cowardly hair in his perverse, peculiar head,

˙and that he had gone back to his aunt's abode, that night, far more because conscience-smitten and morally disarrayed by Hubert's unexpected statements than because he had felt the slightest personal timidity toward his antagonist.

The plain truth was that Bleakly Voght, with all his vital faults, had for years hoarded in him the elements, the "makings" of an excellent man. All his worst traits were exaggerations of those evil tendencies which wrong training will so disastrously turn into vices. He stood before the world as a living example of what disaster may be wrought in human character by parental neglect and a careless handling of the powers of wealth. In the case of Jane Heath he had done a vile act; but if he had been a vile man the dread of social censure would not so have demoralized him as it then did; he would have rallied and become hotly bellicose toward Hubert instead of taking what seemed a flight to his observers gathered there on the stoop of the gambling-house. But now, while he sat and brooded on the indignity dealt him, vengeful throbs and shivers turned his dragging hours into unspeakable pain.

'My position as a man of the world, as a gentleman, as a person of honorable status,' he mused, 'is forever shattered. I have made an absurd mistake. I should have staid there on the piazza of the Club House; I should never have permitted that charge about Jane Heath to drive me away. What, after all, is a charge like that in the present condition of society, to a gentleman? I was a fool to be afraid that it would harm me in the opinion of society. . . . The real truth about the matter is my nonsensical conscience. That wrecked me after Throckmorton struck me as he did. My stupid trouble is that I've never been man enough to look at these peccadilloes in the proper way.'

He vowed to himself, more than once, while he staid a prisoner within his apartments at his aunt's residence, that he would never for an instant lose his temper with Angela. Yet he lost it constantly, and thus conducted himself in an explosive manner again and again. This temper of his was a question of long-scorned self-drill. It was a soldier that had deserted the army more than once, and had been pardoned each time. Now, when it came back again, he had no properly stringent pardon to give it; it evaded even his clemency; it had got the audacious idea that he would never have pith enough in him to order for it a summary hanging.

At Ponchatuk, that season, in his great, lonely homestead, Hubert tried repeatedly to write. Each time he failed. He had had in his head, for a long time past, the idea of writing a poem in pungent, fluent blank-verse that would merely be a metrical expression of the enormous nineteenth century taste for fiction. In the days that he had called his creative days—before he had known whether Angela Voght's eyes were or were not the rich blue-gray he had since found them, he had told himself that the poetic languor, the "twilight of the poets," apparently inseparable from this era, meant only a curious misunderstanding of its literary demands. 'They want novels, this queer public of ours,' he had more than once mused, 'and if some very able man should care to please them by a volume of hardier poetic worth, of wittier, stronger, less frivolous calibre than Owen Meredith's "Lucille," I think that he might so commingle worldly experience with the pure, sweet powers of poetry that he could please them past all reach of cavil. Should *I* ever be able to perform such a task? *Tant s'en faut!* But some day I may try. If I ever do I will call my work *Glenalvan*. . . . I don't know why, but I like the name *Glenalvan* as that of my hero. He shall be a sort of *Childe Harold* who journeys to this country, not to Switzerland or Italy. He shall come here as an Englishman filled with splendid beliefs and expectations about America. He shall teem both with beliefs and expectations—and he shall be frightfully disappointed. There shall be no dainty or dilettante pessimism about him; he shall simply be disappointed. He shall see the politicians at Washington and shall veil his eyes. After a little while he shall unveil them, my *Glenalvan*, and sing. He shall sing with acerbity, yet with piercing harmony; that will make my poem; he shall be so fascinating in his cynicism yet so accurate in his criticism that the entire Republic will notice him. They will do more; they will buy him. *Glenalvan* shall subvert all the practical literary *dicta* of his epoch. He shall sell thousands and thousands of copies before his multitudinous readers have yet realized the aggressive and palsying fact that he is—poetry.'

So Hubert, in earlier and more enthusiastic periods, had addressed his own youthful and ardor-teeming spirit. Now, at Locustwood, with ten times more of the technical power to create a *Glenalvan* than when he had dreamed of the poem years ago, he strove to forget a burning and poignant sorrow in writing of pangs that had once seemed to him easily conceivable.

At first he fancied that he could do nothing. Suddenly he made a discovery. He was not dipping his pen into ordinary ink; he was dipping it into his own heart's blood. The lines, many of them exquisitely musical, surprised him as they grew beneath his hand. He mixed with the life of *Glenalvan* his own anguish regarding Angela, and yet he had concealed it so that even the most merciless eye could not prove detective enough to discover this odd semi-portraiture. No one could actually recognize either his lost mistress or himself, and yet he had tried to photograph the sorrow and the blameworthiness of both, and to show just how forlornly either had lost faith in a love that should have defied misinterpretation. Strangely enough, his former incapacity to write had now wholly fled. He had come here to Ponchatuk and had lived quietly, seeing a few of the abominated newspapers and feeling the jibes of them, as every decent civilian does feel. And yet he had been able to write—to finish, in the latter part of August—his poem of *Glenalvan.*

He gave the book to his publishers. It was really "a book"; it had the bulk of a novel when he took it in his hands and scanned its bright, neat, modish binding. How had he been able to write it? Could it have been possible that he had lived here at this reposeful Locustwood, seeing as in a dream the smart traps of the swells and the belles flit past him on the opposite road, and yet composed such stanzas as these? All his passion for Angela was in them. It was not only that the hero had melodiously declared himself, in the earlier and intermediate pages, disappointed with America; in the concluding ones he had poured forth his supreme disappointment at life, destiny, all things. He requested his publishers to bring it out anonymously, and enjoined upon them the strictest secrecy as regarded his authorship.

. All this time he had been haunted by the desire to seek Bleakly Voght and offer him certain apologies. The more he had thought upon that wild, fierce impulse which had caused him to strike Angela's husband, the more he had execrated and condemned it. In the fervor of composing *Glenalvan* he had fully confessed to this clear spiritual trend. 'If I ever see the man again,' he had said to himself repeatedly, 'I will ask his pardon. My blow was a wound to my own dignity; I must have slight confidence in my own respect for truth if I cannot calmly endure being called a liar. I have reflected too much on the great meanings of life to let myself be swayed by any of its petty formulas.'

Meanwhile his love for Angela did not abate. *Glenalvan* appeared, was read by a certain few, was praised by certain journals, and finally, toward the latter part of September, was conceded to be a book which had, in spite of its power, *tombé à plat.* And yet that phrase should not truly be applied to it. It had shot too high; what really fine poem does not? It had fallen flat only in a popular sense; it had thrice the wit and force of that over-estimated literary snarl, "English Bards and Scotch Reviewers," besides possessing a story, a drama, a fine continuity. And yet it had failed. Hubert felt its failure no more than if it had been the visitation of an accidental horse-fly. He knew it had not failed with a certain limited number. Letters had already reached him (few, yet each of worth and note to him) telling him that he, and he alone, was the author of *Glenalvan.*

Suddenly one day it happened that a New York journal of great weight and authority appeared with a series of complimentary statements between four and five columns long, which declared that *Glenalvan* was not only a powerful but an era-marking poem. Its vigor, this journal affirmed, was past dispute; its originality was dazzling; its anonymous author not merely equalled Dr. Holmes in rich, swift, sharp humor, but transcended him in the nobler gifts of poetic authenticity. *Glenalvan* shot into success from that moment. Hubert, while the yellow leaves of the locust trees were falling in the woodland near his peaceful home, read of the great success his poem had suddenly made. He thought only of Angela while he traced the flow of these fervid eulogies toward the new poetic idol. 'Who is this master?' one man of letters had began to question of another, and Hubert wondered if Angela had recognized the half-hidden identity of his half-revealed passion. "There is nobody except Mr. Swinburne," affirmed one wise reviewer, "who has enough mastery of rhythm to have written *Glenalvan*. And yet Mr. Swinburne, with his fatal recent decadence, with his monotony of 'winds' and 'flowers' and 'lights' and 'dreams' and 'clouds,' could never have done anything half so vivid, so robust, so actual as this song of contemporary life, experience, and passion." Toward latter October Hubert was on the point of going to Russia again. He had wondered whether the quaintness of Moscow might not prove enlivening to fancy if not to feeling. The *réclame* of *Glenalvan* amused him, but it did not by any means satisfy him. He was an artist, and he realized that many of its verses were quite bad enough to have been signed by that brilliant yet insolently lazy poet, Browning. Being the artist that he was, and clearly admiring all there is to admire in this pietist, genius, and *poseur* combined, Hubert keenly regretted certain reviews that accredited the authorship of *Glenalvan* to him who wrote " Sordello " and " Feristah's Fancies." Perhaps the perusal of these reviews may have accelerated his impulse toward a departure from American shores.

Suddenly, one day, just after he had taken passage on the *Mesopotamia*, the fastest transatlantic steamer then afloat, Hubert learned that Mr. and Mrs. Bleakly Voght were his near neighbors at Ponchatuk. At first it seemed incredible. *They!* And then he remembered. Two or three miles to the north of him for years had stretched the big estate of Durand Lexington, which this gentleman had left his nephew, Bleakly Voght, at least fifteen years ago. A creek ran near the house, through a salt meadow, and all the lawns were one dark monasticism of pines. You could see Fire Island, a dim, pale streak, across the Great South Bay, from the upper windows. And this place, Pineland, belonged to Angela's husband! Of course it did! Dolt that he had been, not to recollect how the sweet, shaded, dreamy road called " Lexington's neck " led to it, beginning not far away from his own abode. And Angela was there!

He postponed his visit to Russia that autumn. After all, he told himself, the only time for one to go to Russia was the spring. One day, as he chanced to be standing at his own library window, he discovered a little break in the black line of pines that gleamed ridgy and dense against the Southern horizon. A short while afterward he had directed a small telescope upon this very spot, though his view was taken in the most surreptitious manner, from the window of a locked chamber up-stairs. A portion of lawn and the segment of what might have been a big, brown, commodious country-house were the nearest approach of even a visual sort that he could make to Angela. Presently he threw down the telescope in disgust, and began to arraign himself for having sought even a transitory glimpse of his former sweetheart.

'Confound it!' he mused, 'I'm not a fellow in one of Belot's novels. It's none of my business whether she ever walks out on that pine-needle carpet or not. I wish the old telescope had never found its way into this old house.'

But he used it the next day, notwithstanding, and the next, and the next. All his efforts, however, were equally fruitless and tantalizing. Adjust the instrument as he would, he could only penetrate so far and no further into the sylvan quietude that engirt the mansion. He compared himself, with sorrowful humor, to the man in "The Diamond Lens."

'Still, in my case,' he said self-correctingly to his own thoughts, 'there has been the drop of water without the sprite who dwelt there. She is a memory—a divine one—and bides in the realm of reverie alone. Perhaps I am fated never to see the reality again. And perhaps (most aggravating of fancies!) her feet may often walk the russet spaces of that lawn while I watch as now, yet never pass within my field of vision. I may be staring at some neglected old wing of the house that no one has lived in for twenty years.'

He laughed grimly to himself at this last reflection, and went and put the telescope away. That afternoon he took a ride on a beautiful thorough-bred mare that he owned, named Dara, gentle as a fawn and fleet as a hare. Dara was the perfection of a saddle-horse, and Hubert had often reproached himself for using her as little as he did. Still, it pleased him to own anything thus lovely and valuable in horse-flesh and not vaunt the possession of his treasure. He so detested braggadocio in others that he carried his quiet reserve in matters of personal proprietorship to what some people held the verge of affectation. And yet he had

seen so much raw, coarse pretension among the good-hearted
as well as the bad-hearted snobs of the world that he could
not resist, now and then, a deep and placid enjoyment of its
opposite.

The afternoon was full of those keen, tingling, wintry
hints that blend with a mellow sun and a variegated vege-
tation to make our American autumn a season of unique
charm. Hubert took the "Lexington neck" road, though
several years had elapsed since he had thought of taking it
before. As a boy he had loved it for its quaint difference
from any other tract of land in the neighborhood. There
were huge hemlock trees at intervals along its edge, and
their twilight boughs made the clayey soil of the road a
bewitching dusk even at midday, while now and then mimic
pampas of ferns would seem as if they only waited the rising
moon to have Titania and all her elves trip thither for a
fairy festival. Hobgoblin-looking toad-stools would spread
their mottled discs at the roots of half-decayed tree-stumps,
though the earth on every side was so humid and semi-
swampy that life, whether arboreal or merely weedy, was
forever replacing and concealing the hurts and scars of
death. Some of the branch-entangling oaks were bearded
with feathery, drab-tinted moss ; here and there a cluster of
the choicest maidenhair fern would strike the eye that knew
and treasured its garnet gloss of stem and its ethereal foli-
age. As Hubert now rode along, with the hoofs of Dara
making muffled sounds on the damp yet firm level beneath them, he recalled a hundred memories, not so
much of boyhood as of early manhood, when that romantic
glow which is the strange and sometimes fatal birthright of
all poets had first sent wakening thrills through his heart.

With the poetic temperament a cult for vegetable nature
is always primary ; its curiosity concerning human nature
comes afterward ; it wins more pleasure from brooding over
a wilding, waxen-cupped flower that wastes her delicate glory
amid the dimness of some lonely forest-haunt than in study-

ing all the growths of passion or caprice that ever inspired a Balzac's artistry. And so it had been to Hubert, who had known days when a red-and-yellow sunset was all the Byzantium he desired; when a jungle of fortuitous asters, in the hollow of a cow-pasture, served him for the whole Roman campagna; when a sudden-seen pool, glassy and luminous at early evening, with a vague hay-rick in the background, was all the Venetian lagoon or majestic San Marco that he dreamed of asking.

'How we forget things!' he thought, as he rode along through the rich-scented glooms while the short October afternoon was waning. 'Here I have been for years calling Ponchatuk so ugly, and have never recollected that this curiously beautiful part of it was hardly a mile from my own door.'

He did not attempt to deceive himself on the subject of why he had taken "Lexington's neck" to-day, after so pro-longed a discountenance of its beauties. He had done so for the purpose of gratifying a sentiment, even if the pictur esque little pilgrimage should result in nothing except a sense of augmented nearness. By-and-by the tread of his mare smote dryer ground, and an open space filled with the pointed ovals of small cedar-trees dawned on his sight. He was dangerously near the home of the Voghts; at a short distance away rose a gate, and behind this was their domain. The road now became two; one passed under the gate, and one swept toward the sodden, soggy shore beyond, winding for a little way past the leisurely silver creek with its bunches of tarnished salt-grass, its platoons of faded and brittle reeds. Hubert here reined in his horse and looked round him. Off to the left the pines crowded about the house, and still quite hid it with their gaunt, bristly flocks. To the right one monstrous plane of meadow-land slipped away to meet a sky that was full of rolling clouds, big and colored like iron. But from the changing blue rifts in the heaven shafts of sun would slant brilliantly upon the huge bay that faced our horseman as he was now stationed, and sometimes make flying paths of splendor on the waters, or sometimes turn two or three sails in its reach as white as Annunciation lilies.

Suddenly Hubert saw a shape coming toward him in the dubious, flickering sort of light. It was the shape of a woman, and the tricksy winds that were abroad to-day had unloosened a wisp of her hair. She turned so as no longer to face the gale, having both hands lifted to the back of her head. As she did so her draperies gave a windward swing like the canvas of a tacking yacht, and from the loosened tress that she strove to rearrange there darted an airy and evanescent gleam of gold. But Hubert had already gained one quick glimpse of her delicate profile; and this, brief a view as it proved, had told him that she was Angela.

VIII.

He felt for one instant as if his blood were ice, the next
as if it were fire. Almost immediately she managed to con-
fine the rebellious lock; she was coming toward where he
stood, still as an equestrian statue of himself; she had evidently not recognized him. The fitful wind had abated a
little; her gown and her wraps fell once more in their
wonted graceful lines. The chill of the brisk air had put a
touch of pink warmth into her cheeks. Her blue-gray eyes
had sparks in them that seemed caught from the blue-gray
waves of the neighboring sea. The old enchantment of her
beauty had fleetly and strongly captured him in its thrall.
He sprang from his horse as she drew nearer; she carried
a bunch of downy golden-rod in one hand, and its keen touch
of color lit up the mellow browns of her costume in the way
that painters love. Hubert was no painter, though he had
the instincts and tastes of one. He perceived, after a few
more seconds, that she had discovered who he was. Holding his fine horse, meek as a house-dog, lightly by the bridle,
he raised his hat. She had come so close to him, by this
time, that he could see she had grown pale. As he bowed
to her she paused; there were now only a few yards between them. A most serious look had overspread her face,
and she shook her head, with an inexpressibly pained effect
of veto and disapproval.

"You should not have dismounted," she said, standing
before him with the bunch of golden blooms almost dropping
from her lax hold. "I am sorry that you did. I—I wish
you would ride away." Her eyes burned toward him with
a great eloquence of entreaty. "You know it is best,
Please do it."

He drew Dara's head toward him and stroked it softly, though he did not take his look from her lovely appealing face.

"I can't say that you are wrong," he answered, with hesitation. "And yet . . ."

"I am right—right," she hurried, leaning toward him with great eagerness in gaze and mien, though not advancing so much as a step. "Please go; please go at once. I—I did not want to come here at all. It was not my wish."

"You remembered, then, about Locustwood?"

"Remembered? Of course."

Hubert pointed toward the sombre and spacious groups of pines. "And I forgot about that place of his," he returned. "It was very strange. I ought to have recollected. Still, he went there so seldom in past summers; he was always abroad, or at Newport, or somewhere like that. From childhood I knew; but only a few days ago I had cause to be vividly reminded."

"You heard we had come here?" she asked faintly.

"Yes . . . I have lived very quietly since I myself came; I have been leading a thorough *vie casanière* among my locust-trees. Otherwise I might have met you driving, and not had to wait for my old gardener to tell me that 'the house over across the neck,' as he called it, had become tenanted by its owner and his . . wife."

She looked downward at the flowers that she held, and brushed their velvet crests for a moment with one hand. As she did so a book dropped to the ground. He made a slight forward motion, but she stooped and picked the volume up, replacing it beneath the folds of her cloak. And in her expedition he read not only embarrassment but a distinctly imploring significance. As it was, his hand had just quitted the bridle of his horse and no more. He now began stroking Dara's head again while she brokenly murmured :

"We have not driven out at all. My . . husband has been ill."

" Seriously ? "

" No. He has been in much pain, however. He thought
this fine air would cure him. Before, when he had such
attacks he came here. He is better, now; the air *has* worked
wonders with him."

" And your life has been almost as lonely, then, as mine,
has it not?" Hubert said, after a short yet pregnant
pause.

" Yes," she answered; " very lonely."

" You have not lost your old habit of reading, I see."

" No . . . I suppose I shall always keep that."

" And you've been reading the new book, *Glenalvan*, have
you not?"

" *Glenalvan?* " she repeated, with a kind of softly frightened ring in her voice. " Why, how did you know—? "
And she drew the book out, looking at it flurriedly for a
moment, while the pink came with a sweet, rich rush into
her face again.

" I recognized the cover," he said. " I've read it, too.
Do you care for it ? "

She drew backward from him, clasping the book and the
nosegay between both hands ; and now he saw that her eyes
had taken that liquid, shining look which could only mean
tears.

" Oh, did not you write it ? " she asked. " I have felt so
certain it was yours ! "

" Why have you felt certain ? " he replied. His voice
broke, but he was unaware of this; eagerness to hear what
answer she would give made him unmindful of it.

" Oh, a hundred reasons have caused me to be convinced
it was yours," she hurried, quite self-forgetfully.

" Pray tell me one."

" First of all, the *story*—the . . the way . . . . ."

" The way poor *Glenalvan* found himself fooled ? "

She started, and he had never seen her eyes wear the
passionately mournful look that filled them now.

"He was not the only one!" came her fluttered cry.
" *She* was fooled as well . . . Ah, you *did* write it!" He
saw the tears glittering on her lashes, by this time, as their
rain quickened. "And again and again I've thought, while
I read it, that perhaps, in a certain manner, you might have
written it for *me!*"

"For you?"

"Yes. To—to show me that you realized just how I,
too, had been made the sport of that woman's deceit. . . .
You *did* write the poem, did you not?"

"Yes," he replied.

"I knew it!" she broke forth, with spontaneous, even
unconscious triumph. "And the newspapers have been
saying it was done by this, that, and the other! All the
while I was so certain of its being by you! Why, it's full
of your personality, your *façon*, your—"

She paused. A change swept over her face. She shook
her head excitedly and pressed her lips together, while
a frown of self-reproach, of entreaty, of affright, creased
her brows.

"All this has been wrong!" she exclaimed, petulantly,
desperately. "I've been dreading it—I've somehow felt
that it might happen. It can bring neither of us the least
good; it can bring nothing but sorrowful reflections, remem-
brances. I—I shan't be happy for weeks; I—"

"Then you were happy before you met me?" he struck
in. "You'd grown contented with your fate?"

She made an impatient, despairful gesture with the hand
that held the flowers; it waved him back from her, though
he had not changed his place at his horse's side by the least
fraction of a step.

"Contented—yes," she retorted, with her tones now a
tumult of gasps. "There has been a certain kind of contentment. You know what I mean. You know how a
woman might strive to make the best of things when placed
as I am. You know so much about the human heart. All

your poetry shows that ; *Glenalvan* shows it even more than
the other writings. You're wise enough to forgive, and
you're wise enough to be merciful."

" I'm wise enough to be miserable," he said.

" No—no ; that will not do ! You've the whole world
before you."

" I've a world of disappointment behind me, Angela ! "

" Ah, don't call me by my name like that ! . . . I'm
going—yes, I'm going, now. Good-bye. Try never to see
me again. *Try*. really. In a little while we shall leave this
place. He is better, at present, and we shall soon leave.
He has almost decided on Europe ; we shall perhaps pass
the winter in Nice, or somewhere on the Riviera—he has
not decided about that." She shot past him, and only
stopped when she had gone several yards away from him in
the other direction. The wind had begun its gusty assaults
again ; it blew the hair back from her temples, and by dis-
closing their sweet sculptural pallor, gave her a new look of
suffering, anxiety, dismay. " Promise me," sped her next
precipitate words, " that you will avoid us—avoid *me*. It's
all profitless, mad,"—here a fragment of bitter laughter fell
from her,—" and absurd, drearily absurd, as well. Promise
me, will you not ? Just say ' I promise,' and I'll believe
you ! "

He silently ground his teeth under the stress of an agony
that every line of her shape, every tremor of her speech fed
and aggravated.

" I promise—yes."

" And you'll go away from here, too ? " she eagerly pursued : " You'll let no more accidents like this happen ?
You'll promise that also ? "

He laughed, flinging the bridle loose upon the neck of his
mare, and advancing toward her a very little. Dara never
stirred, but her dark, gentle, humid eyes followed him with a
dumb wonder in their crystal depths.

" I'll make no further effort to see you," he cried, with an impetuosity born wildly of his pain. "There—let that suffice . . . And you proved—tell me if I'm wrong—that what I said to you about his past course of life was true— that the woman, Jane Heath, *had* been. . . . ?" ˙

"No," she broke in, receding from him as he drew toward her; "no, I had not any reason to verify your statement. I believed it, but even if I had not done so, his free admission would have confirmed it to me."

"Ah!" exclaimed Hubert; "so then he confessed all his sins to you? You've shriven him, I suppose, and he's the most contrite of penitents!"

A second after uttering the desperate sarcasm he regretted it. Her lips quivered; he felt almost as if he had struck her. "Pardon me!" shot his next words. "Oh, my God! if you only knew my anguish—if—"

"Hush!" she commanded, and raised one hand with a gesture whose import he almost instantly afterward discovered. The road leading toward Pineland was shut off, as recorded, by a gate, only a slight distance away. Hubert now perceived that a man had just opened this gate and was coming forward to where he and Angela both stood.

His first thought was that the man might be Voght. But no; in another moment he perceived that he had been wholly wrong. Meanwhile he had gone toward his horse again. But he did not mount. He had no idea of seeming to be a fugitive from scrutiny. On the contrary, he led Dara by her bridle toward the spot where Angela still stood, evidently distressed at the presence of the new-comer.

"Who is it?" he asked softly. "You are not alarmed? You have no fear of being spied upon?"

"No," she answered. "It is only Mr. Voght's servant. I think he has come to find me. I ˌ . . ."

She hesitated. The man was almost within speaking distance, now. To get rid of her tears this time was even less easy for Angela than it had been there in the moonlight at Elberon. Doubtless the man saw them as he now approached her. He had not just the face of a servant ; or if so, of a very capable one. He could not have been more than thirty years, at the oldest.

He addressed Angela in polite and impassive tones. He had what we Americans call the English accent. "Excuse me, Mrs. Voght," he said with his low and deferential voice. Then he ceased and gave a courteous glance at Hubert, as of thus tacitly asking the latter's permission to continue, no less than that of his mistress.

Wretchedly perturbed though Hubert was, he could not but value at its due worth the entire, tranquil, yet unexplainable tact of the man's behavior. Nothing could have been more respectful, and yet nothing could have been more intelligent. Indeed, if it had any fault, this was its very perfection. You might have said to yourself, witnessing it, "The man knows too much for a servant;" just as some adept in the art of acting might see a trivial part of one or two lines performed so admirably as to declare, with suspicion amid his praise, "No supernumerary ever did *that.*"

Almost at once (having allayed her agitation as best she could) Angela said : "Well, Bradbourne, what is it ? "

"Mr. Voght was restless about your stopping away so long, ma'am, and sent me to find you, if I could, and ask if you'd return to the house."

This was more in the style of the real servant, and yet somehow a doubt might have remained as to whether Bradbourne were not cultivated rather beyond his outward seeming. Hubert would hardly have given him a second thought had he not appeared at so malapropos a time. Afterward events made his image ineffaceable from memory. It was that of a slender, supply-knit man, with a short, close-clipped auburn beard and reddish-gleaming eyes. He was so far from being commonplace that almost everybody noticed him and found an antagonism between what might be called the emotional index of his face and the drilled formality of his air as a menial.

"Very well. You may say that I will join Mr. Voght presently," Angela returned. . . "Stay, Bradbourne," she continued, as if some new idea had flashed upon her, "I will go back with you now—at once." Her demeanor was full of a decision, a firmness, that seemed the product of effort, and yet was none the less cogent because factitious. Hubert had no sooner heard her use these different tones than he sprang upon his horse. While he gathered toward him the reins on Dara's neck, he heard the same voice as it now spoke to him, and with a collectedness, a self-possession that there was no misinterpreting.

"Good day. I hope you'll have a pleasant ride back. I'm sure you will, though, in this nice, breezy weather."

Hubert raised his hat. . . Without any other than this mute reply he let his mare take him fleetly toward the shaded road that led homeward. The brief October day was already waning. Before he had regained Locustwood through those elfish reaches of forest, he would hear the first shrill wrangles of crickets and katydids preluding the first scintillant small autumn stars.

Angela went back to where her husband, lonely and uneasy, awaited her. As she entered his room, on an upper floor of the great, rambling house, he rose from his chair, holding a half-crumpled magazine in one hand and a half-smoked cigar in the other.

"You staid a terrible time," he said querulously. "What on earth kept you?"

"It was such pleasant weather," she answered, beginning to undo her wraps, "I walked further than I expected."

"Pleasant weather!" he exclaimed, with a shiver, tossing his cigar into the big wood-fire that crackled not far away. "I think it's grown cold as Greenland."

"You're not so well?" she asked patiently, and with an intonation that some hospital-nurse might have used in one of her professional rounds among the sick in her ward.

" No. Those pains have come on again."

" You've smoked," she said, more critical than accusative. " You know that was wrong."

" I thought it helped this infernal neuralgia, the other day. But I see I was wrong; it's made me worse this time. Confound the weed—I wish I hadn't lighted it. It's got me so nervous I could jump out of the window. . . I shall want you to rub my head again ; that eases me more than anything else."

" Very well," acquiesced Angela.

The huge fire that he had caused to be built in the old-fashioned fire-place had heated the room so that it made her own temples throb while she passed her fingers in swift, steady motion to and fro on various parts of his aching head. She had now and then tried to be jocose about this task, which had grown an every-day one with her of late ; she had called it his " magnetic shampoo," and once had told him that she believed she must set up a kind of professorship, and call herself a cerebro-manicure.

All this had struck him as droll, and he had laughed most heartily at it while the tender nepenthe that for some occult reason her fingers knew how to bestow would soothe him past all telling. After she learned that she could amuse him amid his sufferings, pity made her seek new methods of doing so. But in a little while she discovered that the search involved no tax upon ingenuity. He was willing enough to laugh at all her jokes. Now and then he would be peevish, as we have just seen, but the cause of such outbursts was nearly always her own absence—her failure to be at her post, which was either close to his bedside or his chair.

The illness which had seized him shortly after they left Long Branch had wrought in him changes of the most acute kind. His sufferings at first had been beyond description ; there were times when the torture in his brain had been so exquisite that he had prayed the puzzled and distressed

physicians (who shrank from anæsthetics in too great quan-
tity) to mercifully end his life.   Then had come gradual relief,
and then the sense of Angela's quiet, steadfast devotion.

She had almost hated him before his illness began.   But
there is some mysterious law of our relations with our fel-
low-beings that forbids us to hate those whom we help.
Loathe our foe as we may, nothing can so quickly dissipate
such loathing as to do him a service.   There were times
when Angela bent above her husband's bed, after having
soothed him into slumber by the music of her own voice, a
dearer music to him than even any golden crash that might
come from the orchestras of Paradise—there were times
like these when it seemed to her as if she almost loved him.
He had needed love so piteously in the sharpness of his
affliction!   And then the discipline of pain had developed
in him more than one amazingly fine quality.   His occasional fortitude and endurance did more than merely astonish
his wife ; they roused her loyal admiration.

When a man like Voght has been half-spoiled by the
folly of his early instructors it is a remarkable fact that
traits often remain buried, so to speak, beneath the surface
of his nature which none but unusual or even extraordinary
events are able to bring forth.   Such men have been ruined
for the actual routine of their ordinary lives ; languor and
indifference have cast a blurring haze across those lines of
sacred duty which should be as clear in the atmosphere of
their own spirits as the morning-star is clear amid encom-
passing dusk.   But a sudden calamitous turn befalls the
current of their fortunes, and everything changes.   They
have now a new life to live—a life in which they can be as
much and as frankly their real selves as the influence of
perverse training has prevented them from being their real
selves in some other train of experiences heretofore.   And
so with Bleakly Voght.   Angela no longer secretly shuddered, now, when he took both her hands fondlingly in both
of his and looked up into her face with all the terrible

ravages of haggardness and emaciation so manifest on his own. His unhappy temper was like an extinct volcano; it smoked a little, now and then, but that was all. She had ceased to fear him (she had seen him so helpless from excessive prostration that a fly might not have feared him!), and there was such relief in this complete absence of physical alarm. Now that he was better and they spent the days of his convalescence here in the country together, she began to realize just why it was that he had been thought attractive by women in the past. Their mutual relations were now wholly changed. If she did not give him any evidence of personal love, she stood always toward him in a ministrant, alleviative, beneficent light; she gave him an incessant friendliness, which to one in his invalided state may be made quite closely to resemble love.

But in spite of all the change described, Angela had begun to dread the time when convalescence would be replaced by health. Not that she believed the tyrant in him would ever seek to harass her again, but rather that she feared lest his new demands upon her wifely tenderness might shake to its foundations the entire present structure of their intercourse. As long as he needed her aid, her stimulating prophecy, her arm to lean upon, her hand to do him a hundred little services, their mutual affairs might progress comfortably, acceptably, for both; but let restored bodily vigor render him assertive where he was now dependent, executive where he was now complaisant, and the resulting *-bouleversement* might bring discomforts past all calculation.

She had no doubt that the clamor which followed his encounter with Hubert had caused the horrible nervous malady now besieging him. There had been a period when delirium would succeed his worst attacks of agony, and then "Throckmorton" was a name frequently on his lips. The iron of an unspeakable humiliation had entered his soul. He had been knocked down in a public place and had retreated very soon after the chastisement. This much the world knew, and this much it insisted upon interpreting after its own arbitrary fashion. But his wife had observed with relief, of late, that the whole erosive memory preyed less than previously on his mind. One point gave her a frequent keen uneasiness, however, and that was the intensity of his jealousy regarding Hubert. If the latter had forgotten Pineland, he, Voght, had been very far from forgetting Locustwood. He had come hither for the delightful air, and it had already accomplished wonders with him. He had given secret instructions to his valet, Bradbourne (a servant who had but recently entered his employ and whose capacity he greatly esteemed), to find out for him whether Mr. Throckmorton had come to dwell at his country-place this summer; and Bradbourne, no less prompt than efficient, had soon brought his master word that Mr. Throckmorton *was* at his country-place.

From this hour Angela felt that she was watched, though without knowing why such vigilance was exerted. Her husband made no direct allusion to her former lover, but it was evident that he regarded a meeting between Hubert and his wife as among the odious possibilities of the situation. It had grown no new thing for Angela to have Bradbourne despatched in search of her. The reason given for this intrusive *espionage* always had an outwardly flattering form; Mr. Voght was lonely or nervous without her; Mr Voght missed her very much. But after a while Angela began to suspect that solicitude of another sort was at the root of Mr. Voght's persistent surveillance.

As she walked back to the house with Bradbourne this afternoon, she was once or twice on the verge of cautioning him against any mention of having found her in the society of a gentleman. Still, good taste forbade her from carrying out this impulse. It was enough of a sting to feel that Bradbourne had already guessed at the real explanation of her husband's behavior. No! she would not invite his pity, and wound her own dignity by so doing. Best to take the chances of his saying nothing. He had thus far struck her as a servant of the nicest prudence and discretion, without the remotest hint in him of guile or falsity. He had not a face that had ever prepossessed her. It was honest enough, but under all its decorum and gravity she had fancied that there slept an energy which might be of evil source. Still, such judgments as these were so apt, she told herself, to be quite *en l'air*. Living in this dreary old house and seeing so few people had doubtless made her moody. Bradbourne had come to her husband with the best of recommendations as an English body-servant.

"How far did you walk?" Voght now asked, while a sigh or two of gratification left him as proof that his neuralgia was being appreciably soothed.

"Oh, out into the salt-meadows, almost to Nicolson's Point," said Angela.

"And you met Bradbourne?"

"Yes."

"I suppose you were returning when you met him?"

"Yes."

Just then Bradbourne, with his gently official air, passed into the room through the half-open door that led from the outside hall. He at once began to fold up Angela's cloak, which she had thrown carelessly upon one of the chairs. Then he went over to the blazing fireplace and began to re-arrange the lurid logs.

' He will think it strange if I do not mention having met anybody,' mused Angela, as she covertly watched his stooping figure. ' But no,' her reflections quickly proceeded ; ' he may have told himself that there has already been time for me to have spoken on that subject.'

A silence followed. Angela continued her light, swift, delicate hand-motions. Voght's head fell backward on the cushioned easy-chair in which he sat. His distress was yielding to a pleasant sense of repose. *She* was near him, and her very presence wrought a placating effect upon his morbidly diseased nerves.

"Bradbourne," he suddenly called out, in a voice that held a certain amount of actual joviality compared with the peevish tones that both his hearers had so often heard him use, " Bradbourne, what are you thinking about, over there, so sombre and so solemn ; eh ? I sometimes believe, Bradbourne, that you do a lot of deep thinking which nobody knows about."

The man, in his stooped position by the fire, turned and looked at Voght. His face did not lose a shade of its customary calm as he answered :

" I was thinking, just now, Mr. Voght, of a very fine horse I saw a little while ago."

" A horse ? " queried Voght, " whose ? "

Angela felt a sudden chill sweep through her veins.

" I don't know whose it was, sir," replied Bradbourne. "A gentleman had it. I mean the gentleman Mrs. Voght was talking to when I met her. But I suppose she has told you, sir."

This was said as innocently as it was said respectfully. But from that moment Angela distrusted Bradbourne.

Voght gave her one look, and then settled himself a little further back in his arm-chair. She continued her rubbing process, though once or twice it seemed to her as if the power of moving her fingers coördinately might at any instant desert her.

She knew very well that her husband was waiting for Bradbourne to quit the room. Then the storm would burst.

Presently the valet did quit the room. He failed, however, to shut the door, leaving it just as it had been when he entered. Suddenly, Voght rose from his chair and went with steps of speed toward the door. He closed it, and then turned, facing his wife.

His face, grown so cadaverous since his illness, was livid. His eyes glittered with a savagery of accusation. Twice or thrice he essayed to speak, but only a husky sound came from his lips.

IX

STRANGELY enough, Angela did not now feel any of that physical fear with which he had once been able to inspire her. She stood before him, surprised at her own coolness. She met his enraged gaze with one quite unflinching. Was not this because of the illness through which she had for weeks nursed him, and in which her own strong young womanhood had been so contrasted with his variant stages of prostration and weakness?

"So.. you.. you make appointments," he at length managed to say, "that you do not tell me of?"

Angela bit her lip, and then shook her head swiftly once or twice, with a proud, sad air. "No," she answered, "I made no appointment with him."

"With *him?* with whom?" sped Voght.

"With Hubert Throckmorton. It was he who had the horse Bradbourne admired. I was talking with him when Bradbourne came up."

"You admit it?"

"Admit it! I should scorn to deny it!"

"But.. you—you did not tell me. You—you waited for me to learn it by an accident like that!—by the chance talk of one of my servants!"

"I did *not* tell you," answered Angela; "quite right. Why should I distress you by the account?—for I knew that it *would* distress you. Since the meeting was wholly accidental—"

"So you say!" he broke in, with a most acridly taunting tone. "So you say!"

"Ah!" she cried," is it to be *like that* again, between you

128

and me! I thought you had learned both to trust and to
honor me as your wife! I thought you had grown to freely
grant me my right to your courtesy and consideration! I believed those wild fits of temper (which have had much to do
with your wretched illness) were forever past. . . But have
I merely fancied all this? While I have watched at your
bedside through many a long day and night, I've fallen into
the habit of thinking that there was to be no more insult, no
more persecution. But have I been wrong? Will it all turn
out a foolish dream with me, and must I wake to find that
you're as tyrannical, unjust, childishly exacting as ever!"

Before she had ended her last sentence Angela saw that
these words had produced a decided effect upon him. He
hurried toward her, now, with both hands outstretched, and
his face twitching strangely.

"Angela!" he cried, "it isn't a dream; it's reality. All
that hateful time *is* past. . . You say your meeting with *him*
was accidental. Very well; I'll take your word!" He had
caught both her hands, and as that last exclamation left him
a harsh, queer laugh rang out, accompanying it. But at
the same moment Angela looked into his face and saw that
his eyes were full of tears. 'Most curious of beings!'
flashed through her mind; 'who could ever really explain
him?'

"I'll take your word; do you hear?" he went excitedly
on. "You need not tell me anything of what passed between
you. Perhaps it would even be *better* that you should not
tell me. . . Ah, you say truly, my darling; you're right, my
Angela, my rose, my pearl, my star! you *did* watch at my
bedside many a long day and night. And Angela. . . Oh,
ought I to say it?—is the time ripe for me to say it?—
Angela, I . . I've begun to imagine there's something
more than mere duty in all your goodness. Perhaps I'm
wrong . . ." He stared at her very intently for a little
while, and then, with a certain abruptness, he dropped
her hands walking toward his chair again. His steps were

9

a little unsteady, and his head, on which the gray hair grew so weirdly bushy, drooped in a most despondent way. "Don't tell me if I am wrong," he pursued; and his voice sounded as husky and hollow as that of some very old man. "I'd rather not be told if you still don't care at all— if you still can't care."

"I can care," said Angela, following him, a great compassion (which by no means every woman would either have felt or shown) rising and stirring in her soul. "I can care, Bleakly, and I do!"

He turned, and with a short, glad cry seized her in his arms. "My love! my wife!" broke from him. He showered kisses upon her; the strain of his arms hurt her. But while she was on the verge of uttering some sort of involuntary plaint, the grasp relaxed and his form swayed slightly backward. . . In another minute she had forgotten his passionate embrace and was assisting him, dizzy and full of a kind of nervous ague, to his chair a few yards off. . . All the rest of that day he was extremely ill, with touches of slight delirium that made Angela fearful of a relapse into mental conditions that she had already found fraught with anxious trial. But by the following morning a marked change for the better took place in him. During the next day he seemed to gain strength, peace, and gradual freedom from suffering, though his face still retained its terribly haggard look. Again and again she caught him gazing at her with a new elated intensity. He would avert his eyes as they met her own, and Angela's conscience would reproach her. What mere will-o'-the-wisp had she offered him for the steadfast lamp of hope itself? And yet, there was the other way of regarding it all—the merciful way. Allowing that she had let him believe a falsehood, had she really committed an evil act? She could never love him as a wife should love a husband; but perhaps hereafter, if he were good to her and dealt no more in those repulsive moods that had once made all their married future loom a hideous discouragement, she might feel for him (who could tell?) a sentiment somewhere between friendship and sisterhood. The whole emotional prospect, as it were, now looked very elusive, very precarious; it was not to be prophesied about; it had its delicate and stealthy developments yet ambushed in mystical shadow.

'I am willing,' Angela told herself, 'to make the best of a thwarted and spoiled life. The agony through which I have seen him pass has turned me more human toward him, as it has made him far more endurable. If the change will only last! There lies my sole chance of spiritual contentment in the coming years.'

Meanwhile the image of Hubert, as he stood at the side of his beautiful horse, with the far-sweeping meadows and the round, bluish, gusty clouds behind him, haunted her hour after hour. She recalled every word that had been spoken by him, though some of her own sentences she could not find again in memory's chamber of echoes. Ah, she knew well enough why! Her heart had leaped so wildly against her side as she addressed him, that sometimes the sound of her voice had seemed weirdly alien, with a thin, remote ring, as though a spirit were speaking there in the wind, in the mutable light, and not herself. She thanked Heaven that she had not let him even touch her hand—that she had had strength enough to pray he would never willingly see her again. Yes, she had thus begged of him—she recollected that such a vein of appeal had run through her eager protests, though here and there the substance of these latter was vague enough as reminiscence. . . And *Glenalvan!* he had really written it; he had acknowledged as much! Furtively she plunged from time to time amid its pages, and re-read them with a new sense of verification, confirmation. After all, she had not been mistaken! She caught herself kissing certain lines, and then, with a guilty tumult of self-reproaches, hid the book out of sight and vowed that she

would not re-open it for a twelvemonth.   But this vow was
unstable; it was writ in the water of her own secret tears.

The ensuing week saw Voght a greatly improved man.
For the first time since his arrival at Ponchatuk he took a
walk about the grounds of the estate.   The weather continued magnificent, with fewer clouds than formerly in the
crystalline sky, and an atmosphere that made the robust
pines crowding the lawns look as though their boskage had
been cut by a wizard chisel from some sort of greenish
ebony.   The invalid held his wife's arm during their first
stroll together, now and then leaning on it a little feebly,
while Bradbourne followed at just the proper deferential
distance.   But the second and third strolls were quite *à
deux*, Bradbourne being no longer needed.   Instead of
leaning on Angela's arm, Voght would sometimes draw her
arm within his.   It repeatedly occurred to Angela, at these
intervals, that she was the recipient of some very amiable
and gallant love-making.   But it was not by any means the
payment of an onerous or exacting court; it was merely a
pretty and delicate tribute, with the decisive hint in it of
past illness and present convalescence.   It made her mind
revert to the stories that she had heard before her marriage of
how unexpectedly fascinating this man could be with women
when he chose, and of how women the most difficult to
conquer had bowed before his adroit and subtle victories,
notwithstanding salient personal differences between himself
and the accepted type of heart-breaker.

A dread began to shape itself in her heart.   There seemed
every apparent reason for concluding that he would soon
be very much better—that, in fact, he would get completely
well.   As they moved about the lawns, which were half
bronzed with tawny pine-needles and bestrown, here and
there, with dry, ragged, swarthy cones, he spoke in tender
exhilaration concerning their coming winter in the Riviera
and the pleasures that awaited them on that wonderfully
salubrious tract of Mediterranean coast.   But blended with

such declared anticipations were professions of fondness that now and then almost took away poor Angela's breath. All this had been born of a few pitying words uttered by her under the keen stress of compassion! She felt as if she had been masquerading in the rôle of a millionaire and must soon reveal what emptiness of poverty dwelt within her purse. Might not the resistless disclosure of her incapacity to return such warmth as this when it had changed from mere warmth into ardent heat, restore those old horrible relations which had so grewsomely clad the initial months of their marriage?

As Voght's fine inherent strength of nerve and limb returned to him, he remembered that this was the shooting-season at Ponchatuk and that woodcock abounded for the sportsman among neighboring meadows. It soon delighted him to learn that Bradbourne knew about the handling of guns and the slaying of game birds. He held one or two rather earnest conversations with his servant on this subject, to all of which, as it chanced, Angela was a rather indifferent listener. Finally an expedition was planned, one especially brilliant autumn day, and it was then that these words, about an hour or so before the two started, were spoken quite gayly and carelessly by Voght to his man:

"You say you've only found two guns in the whole house, Bradbourne? Well, it's lucky there are even so many as that here. Several years ago I recollect taking three or four out of my stock when I went to make a long trip in the Adirondacks. One got hurt and I threw it away; one, if I'm not mistaken, I presented to a guide, one I lost on the train, and one I'm under the impression that somebody stole from me at my town house. Since then I've never shot at all—except a little, once or twice, while in England."

"These are very good guns, sir," said Bradbourne. He held one in each hand as he stood at Voght's side. He had cleaned them both thoroughly during the previous day.

Voght reached out for the larger of the two pieces. "Ah,"

he said, handling it with an adept's air; "I recollect this fellow very well. I bought him last of all my lot. A splendid gun for woodcock or quail, Bradbourne . . . By the way, Bradbourne . . ."

"Yes, sir."

"You've everything ready if I decided to start in an hour or two. I mean, dogs and all?"

"Everything, sir."

A little later Voght said to his wife. "I think I'm strong enough for it, don't you?"

"Yes," she answered slowly, as though perhaps not just sure what answer she ought to give. "You'll drive to the shooting-grounds, I think you said?"

"Oh, yes. We'll drive *to-day*, on account of my not being in trim. It's rather an unsportsmanlike thing to do, but I suppose it would be madness for me to take a tramp of seven or eight miles across the fields before I'm quite sure of my own strength."

"You're very right," replied Angela. "It would be an act of the most marked imprudence."

Hubert had ridden homeward that day with set lips and blank eyes. Dara took him almost whither she pleased; if she had brought him into some really dangerous swamp he would perhaps have discovered the deviation just in time to save himself and no more.

Through succeeding days he made at least twenty different resolves about quitting Ponchatuk. Perhaps if he had had some definite preference of one place over another he might have departed forthwith. But all places held out the same inadequate lure to him. Besides, his home was here, after all, and the most sumptuous hotel-accommodations could not equal its simple comforts. It was true that she had asked him to go—had implored him to go, in fact. Well, he would grant her prayer; he meant to grant it. And yet what if he should linger here a little longer and watch the season die, with its heavens like aerial turquoise and its woods gorgeous as the tapestries of Turkestan? She had merely meant that they should avoid meeting one another in the future; what was their nearness to one another, provided no further actual encounter took place? And if he had erred once he would never repeat his folly. It had been with him like bringing a burn near the fire again; only fresh ache and sting had resulted.

Different from many men of the so-called æsthetic temperament, he was by no means a lazy moralist. It had often been said of him that he possessed no religious belief, which may or may not have been true, and which, if entirely true, would not have emphasized any reason for his not being a devout believer in more substantial things. Happily, the days are almost past when people of the higher and better intelligence regard religion and morality as transferable terms. Hubert would have been quite sure to tell you (if he cared about discussing the subject with any living confidant) that it needed no stronger force than his own sense of ethical fitness to keep him from either torturing Angela Voght by his presence, or weakening and harming his own spiritual nature by stolen interviews full of storm and dolor. He was a man who looked for no supernatural explanation of the laws that bind society together. He saw in them the plain and direct energies of that justice which is either subjective or objective, and which defends me against my fellows, as it restrains me from my fellows. Some men, knowing that they possessed the power over Angela which Hubert could not doubt that he still possessed, would have found easy arguments to justify them in the unscrupulous employment of that power. Hubert simply clenched his teeth, and told himself that to employ it at all, to do anything except stamp it underfoot, would be to commit one of those criminally rash misdeeds which are so many thorns in the flesh of human advancement. Voght's wife was his own, and so was Angela's wifely honor hers. It would be vicious theft in

him not to leave both unmolested. He might urge the plea
of peculiar sundering circumstances ; but we are all subject
to misfortune, and there is hardly any case in which it may
not be made an excuse for sin. No, his course lay clear
and straight before him. He meant, with all the force of
will that was in him, to take it, and to hold by it.

One morning he received a letter from O'Hara, who had
just had time to read *Glenalvan*, and who was quivering no
less with enthusiasm than with conviction. " I recognized
you at least twice on every page," wrote the Irishman.
" Oh, my friend, there can be no mistake. There is only one
Throckmorton in this particular epoch of ours, and sooner
or later the world will come to realize it. Why, my dear
boy, it isn't your 'manner' that betrays you ; it's your
charming freedom from one. Your verse is the soul of
lucidity, just as it is of sincerity. You're above all trick ;
your individuality is wider and deeper than any dialect could
make it. You rest your claim upon beauty, pure and simple.
But good heavens! how you throw the spell of beauty
about everything you touch ! Who will ever claim that agnosticism is not a noble theme for poetry after reading that
conversation in Book II. between *Glenalvan* and the Catholic priest ? Who will deny that science isn't capable of the
most splendid emotional treatment after that apostrophe ·to
it in *Glenalvan's* copious but sublime soliloquy ? And I
have never dreamed that the so-called Religion of Humanity
could be clad in as much burning eloquence. But that is
not all ; it amazes me to mark how you have contrived to
mingle, in your political reproaches against America, so
much imagination with so much pitiless logic. To think of
making the Muse talk about Protection and Free Trade !
It did not seem possible that she could do anything with
such subjects except stammer gracelessly. But you make
her glitter with wit at one moment and melt with sentiment
the next. . . Ah, wondersmith ! how have you wrought this
enchanting poem ? No marvel that they are babbling about

it over in England, where it needs almost a new Shakespeare to thrill the languor of their Saturday reviewers. . . . ."

This letter of O'Hara's caused Hubert to remember that he had mentioned something about the autumn shooting at Ponchatuk when they were together at Long Branch. He soon afterward wrote : "Come to me for a day or two if you can, and I'll try to tell you what I think of your having saddled me with *Glenalvan*. The shooting, as far as I can learn, is very bad this year ; but if we can't shoot we can always talk, and I've some Madeira here that they thought fine before I was born."

O'Hara accepted the invitation with promptness. He arrived one evening just at twilight; it was cold enough for Hubert to have had fires lit in all the lower rooms ; and outside, just behind the gold-leaved locusts, a new moon, shaped like a cup of glistening silver, hung over a sunset that was like a great pool of spilt wine.

" *C'est une fête de vous voir,*" said O'Hara, with his Celtic French, and wringing his friend's hand as they met in the wide old lower hall of the homestead. "My dear boy, if I missed the train you told me to take, I do hope you've not missed your dinner in consequence. . . . "

"Dinner hasn't been served yet," said Hubert, in his quiet way, as they were entering the fire-lit library. "Since the evenings have grown so long, I rarely dine till eight o'clock."

O'Hara stood undecidedly for a moment, glancing now at the dark, tasteful, book-lined room and now at his handsome, high-bred host. He ran one big white hand ruminatively through his coarse, red, curly locks, and that little live spark that was forever floating about in his hazel eyes brightened into the keenest of twinkles.

"Bless me ! " he said, "how fortune showers her blessings on some men ! "

It was impossible to avoid seeing what he meant. "Blessings ! " repeated Hubert. Just as he spoke the word

he approached one of the broad windows to pull down its
shade.   Off there against the fading sunset sky those pines
that stood about Angela's home lifted their black massed
boughs.   'Blessings,' he said again, but this time to himself.

"You've the blessing of genius, my dear fellow," cried
O'Hara, "even if you have nothing else."   And then, as
though this subject were one magically inspiriting, he
branched off into a eulogy of *Glenalvan* by no means less
florid than that which was contained in his letter.

Hubert never recalled having seen him more charming
than during dinner and for two or three hours afterward.
He abounded with wit and geniality ; he told three or four
convulsingly funny stories which also had the rare merits of
being both decent and brief ; he spoke on the literary outlook, as it is called, with blended acumen and scholarship.
He was *bon camarade*, gentlemanly, captivating.   Hubert,
who had rather dreaded having anybody at Locustwood,
even after his invitation had gone forth, now felt most
happily disappointed in the result of his little anti-ascetic
experiment.

O'Hara's blithe spirits were in a manner born of self-grat-
ulation.   It had not needed what he held the almost unique
qualities of *Glenalvan* to strengthen his belief in Hubert's
exceptional worth.   O'Hara, as we know, had started his
career with an ideal.   That ideal seemed impossible of
attainment, now ; he had done things for a certain number
of years that made him wonder how he could ever have got
out of their miry rut and landed himself in the comparative
cleanliness of his present life.   But this life still failed to
suit him.   There were features of his journalistic career that
wakened within him a dull, ceaseless remorse.   There were
lies which he lived if he did not actually tell and which at
times made sick the something in his spirit no mundane association could render callous.   Of course heredity was at the
root of these repentant pangs, and education had helped

heredity, as it invariably must. He had been born and reared not merely a gentleman, as the ordinary phrase runs, but he had been born and reared so that every impulse and tendency had prompted him, at one time of his life, to cultivate an unchangeable fineness. He had wanted to be fine just as Hubert was fine—Hubert, who seemed to him the one shining type of *parfait gentilhomme* at which the index of experience could safely and accurately point. Whenever Hubert paid him the least civility he felt proud and keenly gratified. The thought of having been asked to Locustwood had exhilarated and cheered him. His expansive Irish nature yearned toward his host with a loyal and grateful tenderness. It was during the progress of dinner (a repast which he praised with deserved epicurean compliments, and of which he partook with an appetite verifying such encomium) that he merrily yet seriously said :

"Ah, I see you've taken my advice about writing *for* the public and not beyond it. And yet the devil of the matter is, my dear boy, that you've written beyond and *yet* for it, by that miraculous method which genius alone understands."

Hubert laughed while he bit an olive. "So you cling to that 'fad' regarding my authorship of *Glenalvan ?*" he said.

"Oh, yes, you needn't either deny or affirm. I know you better than you think I do."

"It occurs to me," said Hubert, "that there should be a special kind of moral law to cover the case of an author who has made up his mind to preserve the anonymity of a certain work. If he says 'I did not write it,' his honor should remain just as untarnished as if he had told the exact truth. I don't see that he has any other way of getting along except by turning wrong into right with the most topsy-turvy depravity ; do you ?"

O'Hara's eyes twinkled. "Is this the prelude of an open confession ?" he asked.

"Oh, no. I'm afraid that if I were to tell you I really wrote *Glenalvan* your critical modesty would be shattered forever; you'd become a greater autocrat than Dr. Johnson. Besides, you admire faith and deplore the scientific spirit of the age; you've told me that you do. Now let me see you preserve your faith, live in it and draw from it the sweet peace that passeth understanding."

"The peace that passeth understanding is the kind that comes to a Browningite," returned O'Hara; "but with *Glenalvan* it's a different affair . . . Well, if you won't let the cat out of the bag, all I can say is that I know she's there; I've heard her mew."

After dinner, when they were both seated near the fire in the library, O'Hara again referred to the poem which had so captivated him, though this time with no marks of curiosity regarding its authorship.

"It amazed me, Throckmorton," he said, making a smoke-cloud from one of Hubert's good cigars, "that you should (pardon me—I mean that the unknown *writer* should) have succeeded so brilliantly with the management of those modern questions. You know, we talked on that subject while together at Long Branch, and I then declared that what the great public wanted in poetry was precisely opposite to what you—to what the author of *Glenalvan*—has given it."

"Yes," nodded Hubert oracularly; and then, after a little silence, his friend continued, at first with grave sarcasm:

"I regret, for several reasons, not knowing the author of that very notable work. I should like to ask him if he truly believes with the hero of the history that science—*scientia,* knowledge—is hereafter to answer every question relating to the destiny of man."

"It would be highly probable, I should imagine," said Hubert, "that *Glenalvan* and his creator were of one and the same opinon."

"But the philosophy of agnosticism makes all knowledge pause before the unknowable. 'In its ultimate essence,' says Herbert Spencer, 'nothing can be known.'"

"True enough," replied Hubert. "But what now *seems* to us the unknowable, the unconditioned, the absolute, may really be within the future reach of science. There was a time when to prove molecular motion would have looked almost as wild as it now looks to try and get *on the other side* of matter. Some day science may tell us that what we have been taking for final causes are nothing of the kind— that . . . "

"Science," here broke in O'Hara, "is forever behaving just that way. She is forever pushing on, yet never reaching an end."

Hubert made a slightly impatent gesture. "My dear fellow," he returned, "what sophomore has not learned that? But why shall we presume to say that sooner or later the vision which *Glenalvan* intellectually sees may not be substantiated here on earth? Science will then have told man all; man, the ultimate yet infecund product of a race which it has taken quintillions of years to develop through numberless grades of evolution, walks the earth as the mythic angels of Milton walked their mythic heaven. His mighty destiny has at last been accomplished; he is lord of this planet—perhaps of the entire solar system as well. Civilization, which is he, has reached its highest condition of heterogeneity, which means perfection. He has mastered everything; he has conquered physical disease, and utterly annihilated another form of disease once known as sin. He will live on, perhaps, in a condition of statical faultlessness, for many thousands of years, until the first traces of disintegration manifest themselves both in himself and in the earth which he peoples. Such disintegration will doubtless be brought about by the cooling off of the sun, and as that process must be enormously gradual, so will the downward lapse of the race be gradual as well."

"It's tremendously poetical," said O'Hara, leaning back in his chair and staring for a moment at the ceiling; "yet I can't help but think it would be finer if you let the race reach one still higher plane of grandeur instead of going so miserably to seed."

" You mean ? " questioned Hubert.

" I mean, of course—God."

Both smoked in silence for a little while. At length Hubert said : " Perhaps, in a way, it *might* be finer. That is, pictorially. But how if it were not true ? "

" Ah," cried O'Hara, " I've always been a poor enough religionist ; but why may it *not* be as true as the other prophecy ? "

" Why ? " repeated Hubert, a little sharply for him. And then his manner grew much quieter, and he slightly shrugged his shoulders. " My friend," he said, " in order to find *that* out you'll have to meet the author of *Glenalvan* personally."

" Oho ! " exclaimed O'Hara, " that's altogether too Mach iavellian for a poet. There was one thing about this poem which I insist upon maintaining you wrote : from beginning to end I did not find in it a single line that was the least ambiguous."

" Nor should there be in any poem," declared Hubert, with a touch of half-betraying fervor. " There is something to my thought equally sad and trivial in seeing an age like the present one waste precious time over metrical enigmas. This is an age whose best philosophers have set us a hand-some example of perspicuity. It is an age with a very wholesome contempt for metaphysics. Germany allows a few such cobwebs to hang ; they ought to be nearly harm-less there, as most of the mischievous spiders once inhabit-ing them have died a good while ago. England's brooms, on the other hand, have swept all *hers* away ; the philo-sophic thought of no other country in the world is to-day so exempt from metaphysical delusion as that of England. But of her modern poetry this by no means is true. It has often seemed to me as if she thought any speculative frag-ment of dogma were good enough, nowadays, for poetic treatment. Of course I include America, when I say England; there should be some international adjective to express the colonial character in which American letters must, for centuries yet, stand toward English."

"Let us invent a word," said O'Hara, laughing. "Hereafter when anyone refers to the literature of the two great English-speaking peoples, let him call it 'Anglimerican.'"

"Charming," decided Hubert. "It may be indifferent philology but it is irreproachable euphony."

"But by the way, my dear boy," proceeded O'Hara, "you surely don't claim that poetry and metaphysics should be forever divorced from one another."

Hubert looked into the lurid fire, while a slow smile began to steal about his lips. "Ah," he said, "future generations will have little patience, I think, with those who beat the air. If you will examine closely the work of any poet who tends toward mysticism you will find that he tends toward superstition also. But sooner or later I feel confident that every vestige of superstition will be banished from life. If from life, why not from literature, which is a form of life or else nothing? No, my friend; there will no more be obscure poets 'when the years have died away' than there will be obscure historians, obscure moralists."

"By Jove," said O'Hara, jumping up, with both hands thrust into his pockets, "I'm prepared to take issue with you there—blessed if I'm not! Now I hold that imagination (which no doubt is another word for superstition in your new scientific dictionary) will never be banished from any sort of literature! And moreover—"

"I could have no such designs upon imagination," Hubert here broke in; "let me assure you, on the contrary, that I have the deepest regard for it, except that phase of it which might be defined as superstition . . . However" (and now he rose with his easy air of hostship) "perhaps if you mean to fight it out with me you would like a little of the sinew of war."

He rang, and when two or three decanters had been

brought, with their satellite glasses, O'Hara began both to
talk and to drink. Hubert made himself some sort of dilu-
tion and took sparing incidental sips of it ; he had already
had a glass of madeira at dinner, and his was the temperament that inherently shrinks from all save the most moderate
stimulant. His companion, on the other hand, had not
only taken several glasses of the madeira, but had drunk
rather copiously of other choice wines besides. That former weakness for strong drink in O'Hara had been suffi-
ciently conquered to make his future career promise far
more hopeful things than had once seemed possible. But
occasionally the old bad greed would get the best of him
still, and its terms of brief mastery for the most part made
themselves felt when life seemed to treat .him, as now, with
a special softness and indulgence. He had always thought
it a privilege to know Hubert ; he felt a proud thrill, this
evening, in the realization that for the first time in his life
Hubert had asked him to be something ·more than a mere
guest of the hour. He was delighted by the sense of personal association with one whom he so heartily and devoutly
respected. He differed from his entertainer, now, in their
present rather vehement discussion·; but the pleasure of
drawing Hubert out, of watching his mind flash or glow
under stress of varying attack, was more agreeable to him
than his alert and often vigorous antagonisms denoted.
O'Hara was himself a man in whom 'liberal theories offered
a charm to which an unconquered orthodoxy had not yet
permitted his entire surrender. He loved to hear Hubert's
dauntless and cool-headed responses, delivered against his
own more conservative postulates. He had not " followed
the time " in his reading half as much as Hubert had done.
He had always wanted the leisure to do it ; he was trained in
methods of scholarship, and most efficiently so. But the
immense modern intellectual movement had escaped him
in the demand and worry of continuous journalistic work.
The more that Hubert calmly and logically defeated him

now, the more amazed he became that his contestant should actually be the poet whom he knew him. This was indeed a new kind of poet who made cold science underlie all his points of controversy. But science did not seem cold, somehow, as Hubert dealt with it; the chill hardness of mere fact vanished, and the warmth, the expansiveness of truth appeared instead. He began to feel convinced that superstition and imagination were *not* one—that much of the romanticism in past literature had been a vast mistake—that the province of all art was to express human experience and not fascinatingly to misrepresent it—that many literary reputations had been built up, in preceding years, upon falsehoods no less untrustworthy than engaging.

But he argued still; "e'en though vanquished," nearly every clever man does; and O'Hara was now in the position of an exceedingly clever man who will not admit himself worsted while he has a single big argumentative gun left with a big crashing-power in its throat. Meanwhile he drank copiously and carelessly. It seemed to him that he talked with a greater brilliancy while he drank; it seemed to Hubert that he talked with considerably less. The hours slipped on, from ten to midnight, from midnight till a good deal past. . . Hubert began to find himself rather severely bored. O'Hara had said a great many complimentary things to him; he had sugared a number of stout denials and contradictions with profuse personal admiration. . . . After a little while longer Hubert told himself, in annoyance and regret, that his guest, on this the first evening of his visit, was getting somewhat repellingly drunk.

It was quite true. . . O'Hara's head at last fell back on the tufted support of his arm-chair, and thick, husky snores ensued a little later. Hubert, more grieved than irritated, rose and strove to awake him. But it was quite impossible. He looked at the decanter toward which his friend's hand had so often strayed during their long *séance* together, and started when he saw the liquid evidence of his present torpor.

'Well, well,' he reflected, 'it's too bad. I'll leave him here. He knows his room; he'll wake up some time before morning, no doubt. . . His old folly; I fancied he'd quite outlived it.'

Next morning O'Hara met his host at by no means a late hour. He was perfectly himself again; his superb physical health had been one of his worst temptations toward excess, as it so often is with men of the same large and sure vitality. His liver, his nerves, never troubled him with a "to-morrow." But his conscience troubled him now, and he poured forth a strain of remorse as voluminous as it was sincere.

Never had his deserted "ideal" looked more sombrely remote from him. After he had fiercely damned himself to the lowest infernal depths and yet proved by eating a plowman's breakfast that mental disturbance did not interfere with bodily welfare, Hubert feared lest melancholy might so cloud him as to render his company both tedious and uncharacteristic. This was an error of judgment, however, and proved how little the lord of Locustwood knew his visitor. O'Hara's despair had in it an element of humor which made Hubert think of something he had somewhere read about the rules for writing good comedy, and in which the axiom had been laid down that a vital seriousness should crouch at the root of all exquisite fun.

O'Hara's despair was certainly serious, and Hubert furtively reproached himself, now and then, for presuming to hold it as droll.

" I came to you—*you*, my nonpareil of moral strength and high personal cultivation," he effusively mourned, " and . . and *did what I did !* Oh, it's detestable; it's . . But it's just like me ! It comes from sinking myself years ago ! I began well . . .yes, dear boy, I began with as hot a hatred for coarseness as you have now ! I've longed from the first to be . . to be just as fine and high as you are this minute! I've . . ."

" My dear O'Hara," said Hubert, interrupting him for at least the tenth time in an outburst similar to that just recorded, " I'm not fine and I'm not high. I'm quite as human as you are. Pray don't exalt me ; and pray forget last night. I agree with you that to bathe one's brain in vinous fumes must always be a wild imprudence. *Je me suis encanaillé* is a good motto for the man who finds himself doing it. . But I don't preach ; I don't know any better parson than experience for a man of your age or mine."

O'Hara, who had already seized his hand, now wrung it. "There's that about you," he exclaimed, "which ought to make the whole world cherish you ! It's not so much your mind as it is your nature. You find forgiveness so easy ! "

Hubert laughed softly at his hyperbole. " Perhaps I've had much more than your peccadillo to forgive in my lifetime," he said.

O'Hara's mind instantly flew to the Long Branch scandal; he remembered how the engagement to Angela before her marriage had been heartlessly bruited abroad as only newspaper cruelty could bruit a matter of such commandant privacy. But before he could reply, Hubert, with a light gesture, as if wishing to dismiss the whole uncongenial subject, continued :

" You wanted some Ponchatuk shooting. They say, as I wrote you, that it's miserable this year. . . But we'll try it this morning, if you agree."

The shooting proved miserable indeed. Their two dogs were good " setters," and the meadows they roamed had their past glories of exceptional *trouvailles* for sportsmen. But hardly a bird rose, and the few that did rise proved to be hopelessly far away. Either was an excellent shot. They took no servant with them. The meadows were so near Locustwood that to return for lunch was at their easy option. After a little while they became separated, and Hubert, with

one of the dogs meekly following, found himself at the out-
skirt of a wood which he knew well, having wandered it
often in boyhood.

The sun shone so bright outside its verge that as he
passed now amid the shade of the close boughs a momentary
dazed feeling fell upon him. But soon he saw quite clearly
again. The stems of oak and birch grew plain to him,
with the little knots of weed and of wild-flower growths
at their roots. He walked onward for a few paces. Suddenly a dog of the " pointer " breed sprang growling toward
his own. He seized the latter by the collar, but in a trice
saw that there was no danger of canine combat ; the differing
sexes of the two dogs made less harsh relations immediate.
He unloosed his " setter," while the " pointer," mollified
and playful, began a kind of gambolling minuet. As he
went a few paces onward he remembered that there was a
small open space in the wood not far off, where a huge
pine-tree had fallen, the rugged remnant of primeval
years. .

Boughs of saplings pressed their tinted leafage before him
as he sought this spot. He parted them with waving movements of the right hand, holding his gun in the left. On
he went, with an idea that the owner of the unexpected
dog might at any moment confront him.

He was not mistaken. A few seconds afterward he met
a tall man, with a peculiarly haggard face, standing by the
great fallen trunk of the pine which had been known to him
from boyhood. On the prone stretch of half-decayed wood
lay spread a white napkin, with tokens of a light repast,
either recent or in progress.

The man advanced a few steps toward him as Hubert
approached. It is perhaps true that their mutual recognition occurred at the same instant. But Hubert, for some
reason (possibly one born from a sense of intrusion) was the
first to recoil.

The man whom he had found in the little glade where
lay the fallen pine-trunk, was Bleakly Voght.

X.

Hubert had started back, on seeing Voght, and with a most visible agitation. Swiftly, however, he regained what looked to be perfect outward composure. But he did not speak. It seemed for him as impossible to speak as to retire. The latter course would, he fleetly realized, be ridiculous. But if he spoke, how equally ridiculous would be any words that he might say to this man, whom, on last meeting him at a gambling-house in Long Branch, he had smitten upon the face!

Bloodless, indeed, and like a worn-out invalid's, that face looked now! Voght unconsciously drew his brows together as he continued to stare at the intruder. And then words left him, spoken quite low and most probably born of combined rage and hatred.

"So . . it's you? You've thrust yourself in upon me here?"

Hubert felt his embarrassment vanish on the instant. He slightly raised his hat, and answered:

"Pardon me. I did not thrust myself in upon you, as you are pleased to put it. I chanced to be shooting on my own grounds,"—he distinctly accentuated those last three words,—"and I passed into this wood by the merest accident."

"Your own grounds!" burst from Voght, as he looked to right and left of him in the way that a man might look who finds himself environed by hostile soldiery. "I—you're mistaken, sir; these grounds belong to Mr. Gansevoort Lawrence."

Hubert smiled. "Mr. Lawrence's property begins," he

said, "about a quarter of a mile further eastward. However, it is a matter of no consequence. You are wholly at
liberty to remain in this wood, or to ramble about my fields if
you so wish."

Hubert was about to lift his hat again and quietly move
away. But merely to look on his calm, gentlemanly visage
had re-opened Voght's old wound. He hurried forward
several steps; his lips and his eyes had both grown sneering
in the extreme, and his voice, the next minute, was a sneer
also, as he said :

"When I last had the pleasure of meeting you, sir, you
were not so civil as I find you to-day."

" I had less reason for civility then, I think," said Hubert.
He scanned the grass at his feet, for a moment, dark-green
and cool under the shade of the frosted trees. Then he
raised his eyes again, and added softly, but with much firmness : "Do not you ? "

Voght gave a short, dry, harsh laugh. " I'm not in the
health I then was. If I were, you might find quite as much
cause for calling me rude as you then had . ." His pale
lips writhed apart in a smile that seemed pregnant with
malice, and he lifted one tight-shut hand.

Hubert stood before him for several seconds with com-
pressed lips and a gaze that bespoke deep if swift reflection. Suddenly he gave his head a slight toss, and went so
near to Voght that he could with ease have touched him.

"Will you let me tell you," he said, "that I greatly regret
what I did that evening ? Your insult to me was plain; I
could not misunderstand it; and I need not remind you that
the general usage of the world holds one placed as I was to
be without blame. But the world's opinion regarding such
matters cannot alter my own feelings. I believe that I was
wrong to strike you—that I should have controlled the angry
impulse you roused in me. I therefore ask your pardon, and
ask it sincerely, repentantly."

He put out his hand, and held it for a slight time

thus extended. He soon saw, however, that Voght was looking down at it with an undisguised disdain.

Hubert shrugged his shoulders. "As you will," he said. And now he spoke with darkening face, with the flash of threat in his eyes. "Wrong as I declare myself to be in having struck you," he said, "I insist that your conduct was aggressive, that night, and my own purely defensive."

Voght had entirely disbelieved the genuineness of this proffered truce. He had promptly become convinced that Hubert desired to make up with him for some subtle reason wholly apart from any high and noble liberalism. '*It is she,*' had darted through his mind, and this abrupt conviction set his jaw at a more ugly angle, filled his small gray eyes with balefuller sparks. This old lover had met Angela not long ago—he had ridden on horseback, prowlingly to the very limit of Pineland. His present high-flown generosity breathed of some shrewdly politic move. Perhaps he wanted to become an *ami intime* in the Voght household—he, Angela's former lover, whom she had possibly never yet ceased to care for!

The human brain can freight minute lapses of time with hours of self-torment. This is what now occurred with Voght. The entire detestable drama of Alva Averill's deceit swept before him with electric speed. He reviewed everything—the forced separation between the lovers, caused by infamous guile—the matrimonial acquiescence of a maiden half-crazed by shame and disgust—the probable horror of him who had permitted an evil woman to make him her dupe—all this, and as much more as duly completed such a malign sequence of facts, passed in repulsive panorama before his inward vision.

"Your own conduct, sir!" he now cried, with a bitterness that had in it enough piercing reproach to have served a far better cause than his own insensately jealous one. "Pray, what has that been? I am ill, as I have told you—feeble in body, and therefore not fit to meet your new insult as I would meet it if I were possessed of my former strength—"

"Insult!" here exclaimed Hubert, with a doubt of the man's real sanity crossing him, and hence taking both from his face and voice all irate signs.

"Yes—insult! Do you suppose I don't see through your damned plan?—But we'll say no more of it, sir! You try to place yourself most adroitly in the right as regards that little affair at the Long Branch Club-House. I grant that I gave you the lie there, and I'll . . yes, I'll even grant that what you said about a certain bad bit of scandal was true. But how do you presume to excuse yourself for having gone with that story to my wife hardly an hour before then? What sort of an action do you call such miserable meanness? You had lost her for yourself, yet you could not let her remain at peace with me; you must find a chance to tell her what could only mean discomfort, if not the deepest wretchedness."

"Ah," said Hubert, with a sorrowful scorn, "this is mere madman's talk! I sought no chance to tell your wife anything. A frightful act of treachery had divided us; it was only through a blunder of our host that we were brought together again beneath the same roof. If, in the few private words I held with your wife, I yielded to the impulse of telling her by just what infernal trickery we had both been snared, my motive was not to create any new unhappiness. The woman before me, I found, was unhappy enough already. Still, it was but justice that she should know I was not guilty of the crime which had formed her reason for breaking all ties between us. What man, placed as I was, could or would have acted differently?"

"Crime!" scoffed Voght. "What right have you to call it so? What right had you to let her so regard it?" He spoke, now, indeed like a madman; he showed himself the searcher for any pretext, no matter how flimsy, wherewith to fling hostile sentences at Hubert. "As if you could know—

you, a stranger to all the events in my life—how much at fault I was, or how little?"

Hubert felt his face flushing, now; there was something that savored of so despicable an attempt at bullying in this new train of pompous sophistry.

"Good God, man!" he retorted, "do you suppose I was fool enough not to make inquiries about the act I had been accused of, after Alva Averill's dying confession was made to me!"

"Ah? You began inquiries?" demanded Voght, with a sort of leering belligerence. "You played spy, in other words?"

"Yes!" Hubert cried, now stung to an unconquerable anger. "And I found out every fact regarding Jane Heath. You behaved to her like the damned rascal that you are." He wheeled about and passed to the edge of the little glade, where a faint pathway ran among some golden birches and scarlet-tinged maples that made in comminglement a tumult of splendid tinges. Here he paused, and turning again, saw that Voght's face had grown still more blanched and furious.

"If the poor girl had had a single near male relation in this country," he went on, "you might have paid dearly for your scampish treatment of her. As it was, her father had recently died, and except some kindred as far off as Australia there was not one of her own blood to defend her. That was lucky for you, Voght. The world deserves to know just what a devil you made of yourself. You dare to accuse *me* of meanness. If I had your record I should feel like ending it with this gun I carry. By heaven, there are times when I feel as if I could kill you myself—not so much because you stand between me and the woman I cared for immeasurably and care for still, but because of that scoundrelism so doubly base when seen in a man born and trained as you've been!"

He had no sooner hurled out these assertions, in a ring-

ing and excited voice, than he regretted them. The desire
to rid his sight of Voght—and forevermore, if fate would
concede him such a boon!—was strongly uppermost in his
heart as he shifted his gun with a rapid motion from one
arm to another, and turned a second time, quickly losing
himself in the dense trees. But the next instant a shrill
report cleft the stillness, and he knew that the •weapon in
his hold had discharged the contents of a barrel. The
" kick " of the gun would have made him sure of this, even
if its smoking muzzle had not promptly confirmed the fact.
A hateful singing noise, too, sounded in one ear, and almost
dazed him. But his brain was clear enough to hit speedily
on the cause of the explosion, which was no doubt a branch
that had caught in the trigger of the gun as he changed its
position. Immediately, moreover, he realized that the dis-
charge had been toward the open spot in which he had left
Voght. As he hurriedly parted the trees again, in eager
wish to learn if any mischief could have resulted, a long,
wild, unearthly shout smote on his ears.

That sound set every nerve tingling. He sprang past the
obscuring leafage, and saw what blurred his gaze, for a
short space, with its untold horror.

Voght had fallen upon the grass. There was a bleeding
wound near one of his temples. His eyes were still
unclosed, but they had already begun to wear a glassy
vacancy.

"Oh, my God!" broke from Hubert, as he knelt down
beside the prostrate man. "Voght—you're terribly hurt—
how can I help you? . . Was it my gun? Ah, it must have
been! . Here, let me bind up your head with this." He
had begun to tear a cambric handkerchief in twain, when
the noise of steps made him pause and look round.

It was Bradbourne, who had come dashing through the
brilliant autumnal boughs almost within a yard or two of the
point at which Hubert had quitted them.

He carried his gun, but flung it aside and fell on his

knees quite close to where Hubert also knelt. He seemed swiftly to have comprehended that there had been a dire accident; this was revealed in his pale face and gasping tones, as he addressed Hubert.

"Where was he hurt? . . Oh, I see . . . How was it caused?"

"My gun," said Hubert, with a stifled groan. "Some bushes in yonder must have caught the trigger . . . Here— you're nearest his head. Just bind this strip of handker- chief round it as tight as you can; then I'll give you another. The chief thing to think of now is stopping the blood. Afterward we'll—"

Bradbourne was about to obey when Voght's hand lifted itself and made a most strange motion toward Hubert. Over the ghastly, blood-stained face there had come a look of fierce detestation. But very soon the eyes of the wounded man closed, and his head sank quite inert on the grass.

'Is he dead?' thought Hubert. In a few minutes he and Bradbourne together had bound up Voght's head. But just as they had completed (and very ineffectually) their forlorn task, O'Hara appeared in the glade. He was soon followed by the coachman who had driven Voght and his servant over from Pineland, and who had been waiting with his vehicle not far away. Two other men accompanied the coachman; they were workmen, and had been cutting corn- stalks in a neighboring field. All three had heard the shot sound within the wood, and all three had heard Voght's hor- rible cry.

With O'Hara it had not been quite the same. The wind had, in a measure, blown the cry away from him, though he had very plainly heard the shot which preceded it. He was considerably farther from the glade than the men had been, but he had instantly gone in search of Hubert, half curious, half worried; and his long, alert limb had, in consequence, brought him at a fleet pace to the spot where Voght was lying.

There were now six men gathered about the unfortunate man. For some time Hubert had felt doubtful as to whether Voght still breathed or no ; and now, with a sudden shivering movement, the latter not only unclosed his eyes but showed their look to be endued with intelligence vivid as it was perhaps flickering. Once again, just as he had done a little while ago, he uplifted one hand and made with it motions toward Hubert. But at present the gestures were more expressive of a decided meaning, and this meaning unmistakably denoted extreme, loathing repulsion. A frown of great malignancy accompanied them, and seemed to darken with each tremulous back-drawing of the upraised fingers. All hint of film had now passed from the small gray eyes, as if the scathing fire that brimmed them had burnt it away. Twice or thrice he struggled to speak and failed. Then, at last, the choked and husky voice found articulate power :

" *He, there . . that man, Throckmorton, shot me . . . It was purposely done . . .* " For a second or so it seemed as if those would be his final words, as if no immensity of effort could drag forth another from the colorless and fluttering lips. But at length he did speak again, and to Hubert his convulsed face wore a satanic malignancy as he panted forth :

" *He meant to kill me . . . 'twas no accident . . . he meant to kill me, and . . he . . did !*"

" Ah ! no ! no !" cried Hubert, with a note of agonized denial in his voice.

But by this time Voght's head had sunk backward, his accusing hand had fallen forceless, and the next instant that change which none of us can see on the face of a fellow-creature without knowing it past all chance of error, had overspread his features.

He had died, then and there, with the charge against Hubert as his murderer the last utterance on his lips.

XI

STUPEFIED, Hubert remained standing. The bright-dyed woods were reeling all about him. A monstrous oppression, as of guilt, weighed on his brain; he strove to shake it off, yet with a failure that he innately knew to be mere nervous dismay. He glanced downward and saw that some of the group were preparing to bear away Voght. Suddenly a hand fell upon his arm. He shuddered, drew back, and then burst into a wild yet soft laugh that had almost the intonation of mania.

It was O'Hara who had approached him. "What *does* this mean?" came the latter's eager question. Then Hubert saw that the speaker was avidly searching his face. "You—you heard what *he* said?" O'Hara hurried on, pointing toward the group that had gathered round Voght. "You *heard*, didn't you?"

"Yes," answered Hubert, trying to moisten his lips, that felt as if they had become like some sort of flexible chalk; "yes, I heard."

The next minute O'Hara's hand had caught his own, and was pressing it with a vigor that would, at any other time, have caused him pain.

"It isn't true!" burst from his friend, now. "It *isn't*. I don't ask you whether it is or not, Hubert Throckmorton! I simply say, and I mean, and I know, as I know that the sun shines, as I know that I'm alive and breathe, that *it isn't true!* there, now—do you understand me? *He* was mistaken—he fancied it was you. Or, if it was, you did it by accident—you *must* have done it by accident!"

Hubert grasped at those two words. They seemed to

strike a rational ray through his confused brain and give
him a kind of inlet for sane thought.

" By accident," he repeated. " Yes, O'Hara, it *was* that.
He may have believed otherwise—I suppose he did."

" You suppose he did ! " echoed the Irishman, in a fleet,
troubled whisper. He made a sign in the direction of the
men who were now lifting Voght from the turf. " Be care-
ful. How could he suppose such a thing? were you not
near one another ? "

Hubert pointed toward the thick trees whence he had so
lately emerged. " I—I was in there," he faltered.

"Then he did not see you ? How is that possible ? "

" See me ? He had seen me a short time before."

" Ah ! you had met, then ? "

" Yes."

" And exchanged words together ? "

" Yes."

" They were . . . angry words ? "

" They were very angry, on both sides."

A short, vehement sigh left O'Hara. " The devil they
were ! " he muttered, under his breath. " Ah, if those four
other men had only not heard him speak as he did ! . . .
Well, after leaving him you—you went in yonder ? "

" Yes."

" You were going away from him ? "

" Yes."

" Just to end the quarrel, and for no other reason ? "

" What other reason could I have had ? " Hubert asked.
" I began by asking the man to pardon me for that blow I
struck him at Long Branch. He refused to take my hand,
and soon became sarcastic, insolent, abusive . . . But
though I retorted hotly enough, I did not choose to remain
and wrangle like that, so said my say and left him . . . I
had got but a few yards into the wood when I shifted my
gun " (here he made a descriptive gesture) " and as I did so
one of its barrels went off. Immediately after that a great

cry sounded from Voght. I hastened toward him and found that the charge had wounded him as you saw."

'And soon afterward,' sped the pained thoughts of O'Hara, 'Voght died, accusing you, before five witnesses, of having deliberately killed him. A rather bad showing, it must be owned!'

But aloud he murmured, close at Hubert's ear, with a voice full of the deepest meaning :

"Speak scarcely a word in the presence of these men. Let me do all the talking that is needed. You must understand why this bit of counsel is given you."

"Very well," said Hubert, after a little pause ; " I will do as you say."

A slight while before that he had seen, or fancied that he had seen, one of the workmen give him a furtive and rather scowling look. Whether reality or imagination, the effect of this impression had been poignant as a knife-stab.

Angela was seated in her room at Pineland, answering an invitation which her husband and herself had lately received to go and spend a week at Newport. Somehow, while describing Voght's wretched ailments to the lady who had made kind proffer of hospitalities, Angela fell into a train of rather morbid thoughts regarding her own destiny. Surely it was slave-like enough! She was going to do her best with it, but each year would bring her, she knew, a more desolating fatigue, a more heart-breaking oppression. For some time she had sat there in the big, still room, with pen poised over her sheet of half-filled note-paper. The house was so large that a good deal of noise might be made in certain parts of it without becoming audible in others. The window near which Angela sat opened upon the rear portion of the pine-shaded lawns. Hence it so occurred that she neither saw the vehicle which bore her dead husband home nor overheard any of the alarmed bustle which his ghastly return created among the servants. And O'Hara, who had

made himself an apt and able superintendent of all that
must now inevitably and solemnly occur, had arranged to
have the whole grisly tidings kept from Mrs. Voght until the
dead man was laid peacefully within one of the down-stairs
chambers.

Hubert had found himself forced to endure a most harrowing little episode after the body had been placed in the wagon which had brought it alive to the shooting-grounds. He
had then turned to O'Hara, saying :

" I will go back to Locustwood, now. It is best that I
should ; you understand why, of course. Come over to me,
will you, as soon as possible ? "

The coachman, whose name was Hugh Magee, and who
had been for years in the employment of Voght, started a
little as he imbibed the sense of these low-uttered yet distinct words. He was an intelligent man, with character
and some rather bovine obstinacy as well in his clean-shorn,
florid face. Several times Voght had discharged him for
" answering back " when reprimanded, though later clemency
had always re-installed him in his former position as master
of the stables. Whether an affection for his employer existed or not on the part of Magee, some sort of relative mutual adaptability did certainly exist between the two men, in
their differing social grades. The death of Voght had been
a horrible shock to the coachman, and those words delivered
actually with the sufferer's dying breath had formed an
ample factor of his present emotion.

" Excuse me, sir," he now said, looking straight at Hubert, whom he knew well by sight and of whose former quarrel with Voght he had long ago learned every particular,
" but considerin' how things has turned out I'm afraid it
won't be right for you to go off that way alone."

Hubert's brow darkened. That a servant should dictate
to him was indeed a novel sensation. And yet his natural
wide-minded tolerance and charity would have perhaps
caused him to answer Magee with a good deal of sensible

calmness, had not a harsh, fierce oath now suddenly sounded from one of the workmen.

" Not a divil a bit does he get loose," the same fellow proceeded, eying Hubert in a most ugly way, " so long as I've a pair o' legs to catch up wid 'im. If he's kilt a man in cold blood, he mus' wait till the law o' the land takes its coorse, so he must ! "

The other workman, endowed with a less assertive spirit, contented himself by an emphatic grunt, coupled with a hitch of his dingy blue overalls.

Hubert's eyes were blazing by this time. " Let me see one of you men dare to prevent me from returning home ! " he said. " I am ready to answer for everything I have done when called upon. I have killed no man in cold blood—"

" Then the gentleman that's layin' here," broke in the last speaker, " towld a lie win death itself had a holt on 'im. An' I guess *that* ain't much likely ! "

With a grin that disclosed scarlet gums and yellow teeth, the man looked about him as if for confirmation of his grewsome logic and approval of his defiant attitude. That grin seemed to Hubert of a more hobgoblin hideousness than any which he had ever seen on mortal face. Just then, O'Hara threw an arm about his shoulders and drew him slightly aside.

" My dear fellow," O'Hara began, in excessively earnest whisper, " you'd best make no objection and just come along with us. This fellow in a certain way is really right. You know, after what Voght said when he was dy— But never mind about that now. Take my advice and come along with us."

Hubert began to feel that chill which will creep about the bravest heart when surety that one has put himself under ban of the law becomes definite.

" But you are going to—to *his* house," was the answer soon received by O'Hara.

11

"Yes," the latter said. "Of course we must go there with the body."

Hubert shuddered. "*I* go *there*!" he faltered.

O'Hara gave a great start and involuntarily drew a little away from him. Hubert reached out one hand in a helpless, piteous manner.

"You—you doubt me," he said, in a half-choked voice. "O'Hara—you *do*! I see it in your . . ."

"No, no," came the swift interruption, as Hubert felt his hand again warmly clasped. "I'll be frank—just for an instant I *did* doubt you. But it's past; I'll never have that feeling again, old fellow. And I remember, now, precisely why you *should* feel a reluctance about going there. I've heard, of course, that his wife—that you and she once . . ."

"Were engaged to marry one another," said Hubert.

"Yes. But it need not be so intensely painful to you. That is, I will smooth matters for you as much as I possibly can. There must be an inquest, you know—and this afternoon, I suppose. Do not speak another word. Go with myself and these men, quietly. You and I will walk by the wagon, arm-in-arm. Leave all the talking to me; pay no heed to anyone except myself."

'How strange!' O'Hara thought, a little later. 'What swift intimacies calamity deals in! Much as I cared for Hubert Throckmorton, I have always felt that an impassable little mound of ceremony rose between us. It has been something, too, not so much made by caste as by that secure moral superiority of his, evasive yet undeniable, and which you hear in the very creak of his boots or see in the very poise of his walking-stick. But now a mere flash of time has done what years of ordinary acquaintance couldn't have done. He's in trouble, needs me, and presto! we're equal. God bless him! By just standing up for him through thick and thin and proving what a friend I can be when such a man as he wants one, I may get a certain queer sort of self-absolution . . . why not? I've done a lot of things in my

day that I'm more than half ashamed of. Now for something to be a good deal more than half proud of—sticking
fast to a man like that when he's down and almost up to his
arm-pits in mire. . . And d—— it all, he'll be lucky if the
mire doesn't close over his head ! '

Voght's body had been brought into the house and laid in
one of the lower drawing-rooms before Angela was even permitted to suspect that anything extraordinary had happened.
Then a pale, scared maid-servant knocked at her door, and
in a little while she was being told everything that had
occurred, gradually and with a most exquisite tact, by a tall
man who had a reddish moustache, hazel eyes, and a wonderfully sympathetic voice and look. This, of course, was
O'Hara, and their memorable conference took place in a
small sitting-room which communicated with the library.
O'Hara proved himself possessed of astonishing skill as a
bearer of dread intelligence. He had guessed instinctively
that the news of her husband's death would deal Angela no
sharp pang of grief, however seriously it might shock her
nerves ; for, having had some experience in the personality
of Bleakly Voght, it seemed incredible to him that so
sweetly human-looking a creature as the lady whom he
addressed should have loved so thoroughly ill-favored a
spouse. Before the talk had progressed very far he was
ready, with his impetuous Irish way of drawing conclusions
about people, to wager that there must have been some powerful emotional reason to have caused a separation between
his admired Hubert and a *fiancée* of such enchanting personal attractiveness. Minutes like these that now passed
between himself and Angela will reveal truths which months
of ordinary intercourse fail to betray. As the exact details
of the shooting began to imprint themselves on Mrs. Voght's
mind, he could not but observe the peculiar quality of that
agitation which she strove almost pathetically to hide. At

last it was all clear to her, and she stood pale and tremulous before his wistful, searching, expectant gaze.

"I am glad you bear it so well," he said, at last breaking the little pause that had ensued upon his sentences of purely expository recital.

"Bear it so well?" her pale lips repeated. She pressed the backs of the fingers of either hand against either momentarily closed eye. "It—it isn't at all real to me yet. I feel as if I were dreaming it—and in some hateful nightmare." She looked at him suddenly, with a wild plaintiveness. "And you believe they will accuse Hu— Mr. Throckmorton of having *intended* to kill my husband?"

"My dear lady," said O'Hara, as he lifted both hands with a gesture at once deploring and deprecating, "I am reluctant enough to believe so; and yet it now seems unavoidable!"

"Those words that you all heard him say," she ran on, feverishly—"the words that made it appear as if Mr. Throckmorton were guilty! Those will have a terrible weight, I suppose." Her voice broke, and she tried to hide an inward shiver as she added, with a glance of most fervid appeal at her listener: "Tell me—do you think they would have weight enough *to—to?* . . —But you know, you know!"

"Yes," said O'Hara, solemnly, after a slight silence; "But I don't think *that* . . . Your husband," he continued, wishing to change the subject, or at least the dismal view of it just selected, "is in one of the drawing-rooms—as I may have mentioned to you before. Is it your wish to see him?"

"See him?" she panted, rising. "Oh, yes; I must—I mean, it will be right for me to do so, and at once; will it not?"

She said this so excitedly, helplessly, and irresponsibly that O'Hara felt a fresh pang of pity for her pierce his heart. It was evident to him that though she desired to do what would seem "right," she nevertheless felt herself shrinking

in spirit, just then, from the idea of looking upon her husband's dead face.

"If you are at all unstrung now, Mrs. Voght," he therefore gently said to her, at this point, " I should advise you
not to go and see him yet. You can wait until later—
a little while before the inquest—if you prefer."

"The inquest?" she repeated. "Oh . . there is to be
one then?"

"There must be. They have gone, now, for the coroner."

" And they will hold the inquest here?"

" Yes; I suppose there is no other place. This house is
so far from any of the hotels; it's off here so alone by
itself."

She kept her eyes fixed on the floor, while he stood at
her side, watching her and wondering whether or no he
would turn out a correct prophet as to the question that
she would presently ask him.

It proved to be just the one he had expected. "If
the inquest is held here," she asked him, as she raised her
eyes to his once more, liquid and burning with anxious fires,
"will not Mr. Throckmorton be obliged to come?"

" Here?"

" Yes."

" Here?" O'Hara softly iterated; and then with a faint
smile, he added: "That will not be necessary; he *is* here,
now."

" Here now!" She gave a violent start, and the color
surged up to her temples, afterward leaving her whole face
perhaps paler than before.

O'Hara pointed to a heavy mahogany door, closed between this room and the library. " He is in there," said
Hubert's friend. " He is . . waiting, you know. Will you
not go in and see him for a little while? You and he have
already met, I think." O'Hara tried to make his mode of
speaking that last sentence as neutral a one as possible.

She had turned a good deal away from him, but he could

see across one of her shoulders that she had got the fingers of both hands tensely tangled together and that she was gnawing her underlip so that every second or two a white gleam showed from her teeth. Quite a long silence followed between them, and then she abruptly broke it by facing him full again and asking:

" Does he expect me ? "

" I can't be sure of that," returned O'Hara, with sombre diplomacy. " Shall I go and tell him that you will . . a . . look in upon him ? "

" No," she said, shortly and quite vetoingly. She at once seemed to meditate again, standing with her head bent, and her form as full of pliant curves as though she had been a lily in a breeze.

Until now O'Hara had taken for granted that her skepticism regarding Hubert's guilt was just as cogent as his own. But now, for the first time, a doubt of her disbelief crossed him. " Pardon me," he presently said ; " but after the account I have given you of all that has happened and of just how decided has been Mr. Throckmorton's assertion that the shooting was wholly accidental, I can't help wishing to know whether you yourself hold the man whom your husband accused as really guilty of crime."

" Guilty of crime ! " This first brief reply, all in one key of indignant amazement, shot forth like an arrow. The others followed more slowly, but they were forceful enough to leave O'Hara very firm in his opinion as to how criminal Angela Voght esteemed the recent unhappy act of Hubert.

" He no more deliberately meant to kill my husband," she pursued, " than I deliberately mean to kill you at this moment. I am as certain of it as I am of my name, my birth, my coming death—anything of which one *can* be certain. What my husband said just before dying may have been a mistake, a delusion, or it may have been . . . "

' A jealous, malicious lie,' O'Hara mentally supplied, as Angela paused, and with the intonation of one who has

ventured among imprudences. ' Ah,' he added, still to himself, ' this woman is aware what manner of man she married
—she has gauged all his capabilities and potentialities of
mischief ! '

Soon after this he perceived that Angela gave every sign
of being beset by new painful reflections. He watched her
as she began to pace with what was no doubt unconscious
restlessness a small tract of carpet immediately adjacent to
that big mahogany door behind which he felt sure that
Hubert yet remained. But at length she came to a stand-
still, and as she did so she addressed O'Hara.

"I think I will go in and see Mr. Throckmorton. I—I
don't know of any reason why I shouldn't go ; do you ? "

" There is every reason why you should go," replied
O'Hara urgently.

She glanced from object to object throughout the room,
with turns of the head that had the quickness and grace of a
bird's ; it seemed as though she had made her resolve and
now would receive some stringent reprimand from somewhere
—the furniture, it might be, or the bodiless air itself.

" Do you think he will expect me ? " she asked, and he
now saw that she had moved very close to the door and had
even reached out one hand toward the knob, letting it fall
a minute later. " *Don't* you think that he will consider it
dreadfully ill-timed of me ? "

" Decidedly I do not," answered O'Hara. " Of course
this is a frightful blow to him. It may turn out that every
friend he has will refuse to believe his story—that is, except
you and myself. I think that if you go to him now you may
give him fresh courage and strength for those piercing
ordeals through which he will be compelled to pass."

" Then I will surely go," she said ; and there swept a
gladness over her face that for some vague reason reminded
him of starlight. " Yes," she continued, with a slight catch-
ing of the breath, " I will go at once." And she put her

hand quietly on the knob and passed into the library with-out another word, closing the door behind her.

O'Hara, as he observed her, asked himself why she had apparently not even thought of knocking. Was it because she dreaded the effect which the very sound of Hubert's voice might produce upon her? The Irishman had known some women intimately in the past. Something made him almost certain that this was why the widow of the dead man now glided almost stealthily into the next room as she did.

XII.

THE library at Pineland was a really lovely old room, and altogether the most tasteful that the house contained. The kinsman who left Voght this estate had spent years in collecting rare books, and had placed them in a chamber that looked as if its heavy oaken wood-work, its polished floor, and its monstrous fireplace surmounted by a superb mantel of carved black marble, were all quite unfamiliar with even the existence of our western continent, not to mention that small segment of it known as Ponchatuk, Long Island. Voght had always detested this room; he used to affirm that it gave him the horrors, it was so gloomy. He liked bright walls, with gay patterns in them, like those of his own ill-tied cravats. Gloomy the library certainly was, but Angela loved it all the more, during certain moods, on this very account. She had often read pages of *Glenalvan* over and over again while seated there; and more than once she had heard the tones of a certain unforgettable voice float among its silences.

To see Hubert standing there, now, with one of the black marble mantel-columns behind his golden head, and a shaft of sunshine intensifying both the pallor of his face and the delicacy of its high-bred profile, was for Angela more like reminiscence than actual and novel experience. She went toward him with the still step of a ghost and with eyes that peered at him in that eagerly straining look we sometimes give to those whom we immeasurably pity.

He returned her gaze in such a troubled and dubious way that when she had reached the great, cheerless, empty fireplace near which he was standing, she broke into a note or

two of listless, dreary laughter. Then as if this grim kind
of masquerading in the rôle of mirth-maker had supplied her
with some sort of initiatory verbal formula, she began by
saying :

"I . . I came in so softly, did I not, that I'm afraid you
must be wondering if I'm not my own shadow."

And then, trying to smile with her wan lips, and knowing
that she wofully failed, she let both arms fall at her sides
and stood before him, stirred by unutterable compassion.

Hubert had scarcely moved. She saw how intently he
was looking at her. She waited for him to speak, and
meanwhile a qualm of shame hurt her for having sought to
hide her own piteous disarray at an hour like this behind the
least meagre similitude of a jest. ' I ought to have hurried
right up to him,' now sped through her mind, ' and assured
him that he had always one devout, unalterable believer in
his perfect innocence . . . But might not even such an approach as that have wounded him ? Has it not been best
for me to wait until he asks me whether I doubt him or no ?
Then I can tell him how confident I am ! . . . *then* . . .
then ! '

"I hoped you would come," he presently said, with something underneath his characteristic calmness that was like
the sense of push and throb a smooth yet swollen lapse of
sea will sometimes rouse in us. "I was not sure, however . . . Well, you have come, and there's that about you,
somehow, which leads me to hope in . . in another direction." He left the dark height of stone that had thus far
made so relieving a background for his head and frame ; he
drew nearer to her and put forth one hand—his right hand.
And then he said, in a voice of great appeal, of great sorrow :

"You must have been told it all by this time. O'Hara
promised me that he would see you at once and make everything clear . . . So, now, you don't believe, do you, that I
could meaningly, wilfully have done anything so infamous as
that ? "

She sprang close to his side. Her eyes burned into his unhappy soul as she answered him:

" *Believe* it ! If you swore to me now that it was not an accident I should . . . yes, I should say you had gone mad and *fancied* yourself guilty ! *You !* oh, *Hubert !* . . ." And then she stopped short, frowning troublously and moving her fair, delicate head from right to left, as though she were looking for some ethereal ally, shaped out of the blended dusk and sunshine of the peaceful room, to come and verify before him her sincere and unswerving faith.

Hubert stared down at one of her hands as if he wanted to touch it; but he did not do so. He soon spoke, however. " Pardon me if I have misunderstood you," he said. " Once, you know, I had reason to recognize your . . your lack of trust in me."

The stab went home, with her. " True," she said, just loud enough for him to hear. Then she added, while her voice rose again : " *That* sort of distrust is so different ! "

" Well, I thank you," said Hubert, " for the faith you show now." He smiled, and with what struck her as a supreme melancholy. " Half a loaf is better than no bread, I suppose. I feel proud because of your trust—I feel immensely proud because of it ! "

" Now," said she, looking at him steadily, while she pointed toward a chair and sank, herself, into one but a yard or two away from it, " will you tell it me all over again ? I heard it all from your friend ; he kept his word. But I want to hear it all from you. Will you grant my wish ? "

" Of course I will," he answered.

He took the chair that she had indicated, and for quite a long time his low tones made one continuous murmur amid the soundless room. He narrated everything, from the moment of his meeting with Voght until the death of the latter under conditions that were so hideously unforeseen. After he had ended, Angela sat silent, with a brooding look on her face, for what was perhaps not half so long

a time as it seemed to her companion.   And then, slowly,
with the stress of a deep significance, she said :

"I understand just why he spoke as he did.   Ah, I know
him so well by this time !—I have such excellent cause ! "

" You think, then, that he was not convinced I had inten-
tionally shot him ? "

" Convinced !   No.   He realized that he was dying, but
he also realized that he could revenge himself on you—that
there was time left to do it in.   And he did it ! "

"He hated me like that ! " exclaimed Hubert, with a
shudder.

" He hated you very much ; you had cut into his pride as
possibly no one ever dreamed—except myself alone—when
you struck him there at Long Branch.   And then there was
the other reason . . ."

" The other reason ? "

" Yes ; you surely know what I mean."

" Ah . . you mean that he was afraid you still cared for
me ? "

" Well . . yes."

Hubert spoke with great softness here.   " And it was
true, was it not ? " he asked.

" Ah," she cried, " why refer to that now ?   It is no time—
no place."

" Good heavens ! " he broke forth, " I dare say you
intend that only as a prelude to something with a far colder
chill in it !   One day you will say to me : ' It will never be
the time—it will never be the place.'   Ah," he went on
passionately, " how can we mortals ever be such fools as to
maintain that we're not the merest whims and freaks of a
mindless and sightless chance ?   Our best happiness is a
blind accident, like our worst misery !   Here are you . . . "
he rose from his chair and spread out both arms with a gesture of fiercely rebellious pain . . . " Oh, my God, Angela,
here are you, *freed* again—with the bars that caged you from
me broken by death—and yet this liberty of yours that I've

caught myself longing for so often, brings to me, at the very hour you win it, a captivity bitter and horrible ! "

" Captivity ! " she repeated ; and here she also rose, and went toward him. " How ' a captivity ' ? Are you thinking of . . of what may happen ? "

" No," he replied ; " I am thinking of what has happened."

" Then . . then you are not anxious about the . . the immediate future ? " she hesitated.

" Anxious ? . . I should not be much surprised if they said I'd murdered Bleakly Voght. Perhaps, though, the charge may not be proved as the law wants charges of that sort to be proved . . ."

She clasped her hands together as he paused, and drew a little nearer to him. " Oh, pray Heaven it is not ! " she exclaimed.

" Perhaps," he proceeded, " they will even quite acquit me—after a time . . ."

" Yes—yes," she said, with eager impetuosity. "I'm so glad you have that idea ! Mr. O'Hara has it, too—or something like it. They won't take such evidence as . . as those few words from a half-unconscious man—will they ? No, I'm sure, myself, that they will not ! But it's so hard to make predictions thus early ; isn't it ? "

Her speech was tumultuously emotional ; her bosom seemed to show him the pulsations of the heart beneath it. The poet in him gave adoration to her beauty, seen in this unwontedly tragic light ; the lover in him longed for some admission more direct and real than any which had thus far fallen from her. It had grown certain to him, now, that the unimagined potency of recent events had exerted over her a great weakening force ; and this, he perceived, might effect, at his bidding, a self-humiliation of surrender, a nakedness of impulsive candor, such as all that he had formerly loved in her for being a symbol of the most modest and gracious womanliness would hereafter keenly repent.

Hubert proved himself, then, notwithstanding his agitation, his revolt against the despotism of fate, his wretched bewilderment at the new and strange ill amid which his life had suddenly swept, a man nerved and braced by such innate nobility as only natures of true intrinsic honor may claim.

He caught her joined hands in his own and held them thus for a brief little interval. "Angela," he said, "I have been foolish to speak as I did. We are all the slaves of destiny, and yet . . and yet it is always more or less clear to us that if we can't radically alter we can at least partially shape this destiny, by will, by courage, by self-control ! Let us be brave, you and I ! Oh, my love, my lost love, let us be brave !" He dropped her hands and receded from her, while she stood before him and felt their pressure yet glowing on her flesh almost as if some fiery contact had left it there. "Remember," he hurried on, "that his corpse lies in this very house now! Remember that I killed him ! yes, I killed him, as we must both concede, no matter what torture it deals us both ! Remember—"

But she broke in, there. "I remember everything !" she exclaimed. "And I remember how you must suffer—how much more than I, greatly as I do suffer! Ah, you say truly that we are destiny's slaves !" She came toward him again, and her eyes swam before his perturbed gaze like two beautiful oscillant stars. "Oh, Hubert, I don't believe I am doing the least wrong thing in telling you how I pity you—how I'd meet tortures to help you! While he lived I never swerved from my duty to that man. He's dead, you say ? Why, so must *we* die ; but when we do, let us hope we will not die with any such blasphemous falsehood on our lips as the one he spoke against you this day !"

"Angela !" he protested . . . and then there sounded a knock, clear and unmistakable, at the door which led from the library into the outer hall.

Hubert went to this door and opened it. He expected to

find that one or two of those who had gone for the coroner had returned to tell him of that official's arrival. But, instead, Bradbourne, the valet of Voght, alone presented himself; and Hubert knew that this man had remained in the house, to all appearances as a sort of guard left by the others upon his own future actions.

" Well ? " he inquired, as Bradbourne entered the library. " Are they back yet ? "

" No, sir," the man replied. He was stroking his short-cropped auburn beard in a nervous, perplexed way. He started when he saw Angela, who had withdrawn a little into the shadow as he advanced. " I—I didn't know Mrs. Voght was here, sir," he proceeded. " If you say so, I'll . . I'll not disturb you, sir." And he backed slightly toward the threshold that he had just crossed, with an awkwardness quite unlike his usual quiet security of movement.

Angela at once spoke. She had felt an antipathy toward this man ever since the hour on which he had apparently gone out of his way to acquaint her husband with the meeting between herself and Hubert. From that time she had always been suspicious that some duplicity underlay his capable, methodical conduct, and she was by no means certain that an acrid enmity against herself did not lurk at its root.

" What have you to say, Bradbourne ? " she inquired, a little imperatively. " Whatever it is, I do not think Mr. Throckmorton will object to my hearing it also." It seemed to her, while she spoke, as if the man had been listening outside before he knocked; she disliked him so that she could believe almost any bad thing about him. At the same time her sense of justice told her that this was a most unfair posture, since what had seemed in him so artful a piece of malice might have sprung from entire innocence.

He now looked full at her with his reddish-tinted eyes, and she promptly saw in them a new expression of grievous worriment. It occurred to her, indeed, that she had not thought

his collected, sedate countenance could ever concern itself
with so much evidently poignant feeling.

"The—the truth is, ma'am," he began, stammering at first
but soon gaining much of his usual composure, "I came to
ask Mr. Throckmorton a question or two about the inquest.
I mean " (and here he addressed himself wholly to Hubert)
" with regard to the testimony, sir."

" The testimony ? " queried Hubert.   " Whose testimony ?
Yours ? "

" Yes, sir."

There was a silence.   Angela's look was fixed steadily on
the new-comer's face.   It struck her, once or twice, that he
was disagreeably aware of this fact.   He had begun to feel
at his beard again, and the hand with which he did so (unless Angela's covert though rather keen scrutiny deceived
her) was a trifle tremulous.

"What questions have you to ask me in the matter of
your own forthcoming testimony ? " Hubert now made
inquiry.

Bradbourne gave a swift, uneasy glance in the direction
of Angela.   Then he took several steps toward Hubert, who
stood much nearer to him than did his mistress.   And here,
abruptly, he showed a perturbation that was in sharp contrast with his former restraint.

" I don't want to have anybody except you and me know,
sir, that I—I came along quite so soon as I did.   Whatever
words passed between you and Mr. Voght, sir, before . .
before *it* happened, I might just as well *not* have heard.   You
understand, sir?   You *do* understand—I'm sure you do.   *I
needn't have heard anything at all*—if you'll only make it
seem that way in your evidence ! "   He went still nearer to
Hubert, and his tones took a touch of entreaty.   "Say we
fix it like this, sir," he eagerly continued : " I didn't strike
through the wood and find you till you'd bound Mr. Voght's
head up ; you *bound it up yourself,* sir . . don't you see ? . .
it was all your doing.   I only got there a second or so before

the . . the other witnesses.   Is it clear what I mean, sir ? . . is it clear ? ''

He was undoubtedly very much in earnest, now. The sweat-drops glistened on his forehead, and he had become so pale that Angela grew amazed at the change this pallor wrought in him.

" It is clear," said Hubert, " that you wish me to suppress some of the truth at the coming inquest, and that you will abet me if I do so.   I take for granted that you can have only one motive for this proposition—a desire to be of service to me.   I cannot, indeed, conceive of your having any other.''

Bradbourne nodded several times in swift succession. " Yes," he acceded, " that and no other.   My motive, sir, is only to make things . . . a . . well, *easier for you, sir.*''

It had meanwhile sped through Angela's mind that Bradbourne had seemingly taken her own sympathy toward Hubert quite for granted.   This tended to confirm her theory that he had perhaps listened at the door, and it also augmented the general aversion she felt for him.   In the matter of blaming this man for having assumed that she had given credence to Hubert's version of the shooting, Angela judged with an absurd lack of self-perception ; since to any servant of medium intelligence, living as long in the Voght household as this one had done, it must weeks ago have become plain that tolerance was the warmest kind of wifely sentiment existing there.

" Easier for me ? " Hubert said, almost repeating Bradbourne's own words to him.   " It is *only* because of making things easier for me, then, that you are willing to commit perjury ? ''

" How, sir ? " shot the man, drawing himself up with a sudden scowl.

" It would be perjury and nothing else, my good fellow," said Hubert, with a sweet, frank smile.   " Remember, you will be on your oath.   It isn't my safety you must regard ;

12

it's the safety of your own word." And then Hubert, with
his manly, winning air, stretched out a hand to Bradbourne.
" I thank you," he began—

" Don't ! " exclaimed Angela, taking several steps forward. Both men turned and looked at her. Hubert dropped
his hand before the other could grasp it. She fixed her
eyes on Bradbourne's face, and with by no means an amiable light in them, as she proceeded :

" Why should you wish to shield this gentleman ? "

" Why ? " repeated the man, with a slight toss of the head
that had bravado in it. " If I tell what I heard there behind the branches it might go very hard with this gentleman. That's why, ma'am."

" What were *you* doing behind those branches ? " asked
Angela, with austerity. " You must have been eavesdrop-
ping, I should say, to have heard so much."

Bradbourne's face darkened again. " I'd sat down for a
few minutes on the stump of a tree," he said, " to eat my
lunch. Mr. Voght had given me three or four sandwiches
after I'd laid out *his* lunch."

" Then you must have heard our entire conversation together ? " Hubert said, half questioningly.

" I did, sir," was the reply.

" Very well," Hubert pursued, and he now let his hand
rest for an instant on the shoulder of Bradbourne ; " say your
say, my man, and don't have the least fear on my account."
He was silent for a little while, after that, and when he
again spoke his voice vibrated with a new depth of feeling,
though its gentle gravity remained the same. " I think I
would rather go to the scaffold because of true evidence
than be saved from it because of false."

" Ah ! " cried Angela, with a heart-pang in her tones. " If
you are innocent, as you most certainly are, you should rejoice all the more in being saved, by whatever means ! "

" If I am innocent, as I most certainly am," he responded,
with a tranquil solemnity that thrilled at least one of his

listeners, " then let the law look to it that my innocence is not degraded into guilt."

Perhaps Bradbourne would have spoken further (he still appeared fluttered, irresolute, worried) had not an interruption now occurred which was rather grimly irrepealable.

The coroner had been secured, and had come with several wagon-loads of curious, wide-eyed, excited village-folk. All Ponchatuk was by this time aflame with the disaster. It was a fearful ordeal for Hubert. O'Hara stood near him, and once or twice helped to nerve him with a few whispered sentences when self-continence was on the verge of being replaced by desperate personal revolt.

Bradbourne gave his evidence in a way that struck Hubert as having been forced from him against his will. It was damning in its character; having been an auditor of the quarrel in the glade between his master and Hubert, the man repeated every fierce verbal detail of this quarrel with a fidelity that rarely erred from the minutest point of accuracy.

'Poor Angela!' Hubert said to himself more than once during the loathed progress of the inquest. 'What publicity this will pour upon her! Thank Heaven she is not required to be present now. But if there is a trial (and it looks as if there must be one) can they not force her to appear?"

The evidence of the coachman, Hugh Magee, and of the two workmen who had gone with him to the glade after hearing the shot and Voght's wild subsequent cry, contained a single dread factor of accusation. All three had gathered from the dying man's gasped-forth charge one same fatally compromising import.

As for Hubert, he attempted no defence. He narrated all that had happened without a shadow of reservation or prevarication. Lying had always been a lost art with him. It was now his dreary and agonizing pride to tell the truth, and he told it with a candor whose merciless rigor pierced O'Hara by admiration and pity in equal degrees. O'Hara himself could do nothing but testify as the other five witnesses had done.

The verdict of the coroner's jury came rapid and unsparing. It declared that Bleakly Voght had met his death through wilful murder at the hands of Hubert Throckmorton.

The idea of bail, to any amount, was peremptorily refused.

The county jail was at L——, an ugly, lifeless town about twenty miles distant. Hubert went there that evening by rail, under close custody, O'Hara faithfully accompanying him. The prisoner did not see Angela before he left Pineland. O'Hara might have arranged a brief meeting, and indeed somewhat pressingly volunteered to do so. But Hubert refused. He slept at L—— that night, in a common cell of the prison. Or, rather, he did not sleep, but lay awake brooding over the dire catastrophe that had befallen him, and now and then telling himself, with a half-miserable sort of comfort, that Angela was perhaps as wakeful and as woful as he.

XIII.

THOSE days in L—— prison, before the trial took place, were fraught for him with a momentously novel experience. The New York newspapers might almost be said to have rioted in the *cause célèbre* which they were now called upon to exploit and commemorate. The Long Branch episode had been the merest trifle of incident by comparison. Hubert's past was remorselessly raked up; lines of his poetry were quoted by the column; Angela's engagement to him was narrated in a hundred different versions, and her marriage with Bleakly Voght was made to-day the impulse of a coquettish pique, to-morrow the mercenary manœuvre of a hard-souled worldling.

After a while Hubert ceased to read the papers at all, and refused to have them brought him. Except for O'Hara he passed most of his days in solitude. That is, he preferred such a life when he had fully made up his mind that O'Hara had turned out to be the only real friend he had ever possessed.

Hours of the most keenly despondent thought had oppressed him while reflecting upon the conduct of persons whom he had once believed to be his friends. Without a single exception, everybody who sought him was the bearer of disappointment. Some who professed to hold him guiltless did so with the shabbiest parodies upon loyalty. Not a few of those in whose adherence he had instinctively trusted, never came near him at all. The quality of the evidence at the inquest, and that of the journalistic disclosures concerning his former relations with Voght, had cast over his entire acquaintanceship a spell of the most lukewarm tendency.

His own kindred were of all the least encouraging, for the simple reason that behind their assertions of fidelity he read nothing except a timorous forecast of his possible criminal fate.   O'Hara would sometimes bring him news of Angela, who was dwelling in New York amid the utmost privacy, not so much crushed by the *scandale publique* of the ruffianly press as by dread of what the coming trial might accomplish. Hubert would not bid her to write him, though he yearned for her letters.   There were times when he yearned to write *her* voluminous letters, breathing of his anguish and loneliness.   But he refrained from doing so.   'Whatever happens now,' he desolately told his own heart, ' she and I can never become one.   The world would say that she had married her husband's murderer.   It would follow us wherever we went.   *I* should not care a straw except on her account ; *that* would make me care intensely—so much, indeed, that though she begged and pleaded of me to marry her I would never consent ! '

Thoughts no more cheerful than these were forever taunting and harassing Hubert here in his onerous solitude.   It is wonderful that his health did not break down ; perhaps if he had eaten the unwholesome prison-fare and not had meals that were specially cooked for him, it would indeed have succumbed.   His fellow-prisoners were a vicious and often filthy class of beings—more odious in certain ways than even those who fill the larger metropolitan jails.   And yet Hubert sometimes felt that their contact was a moral tonic to him.   The horrors of social inequality were brought closer to his vision than ever before.   He realized, as he had never done till now, what pitiless tyranny of antenatal preference had made one man the child of an unlettered or perhaps drunken clod, and the other to be born with every monetary and educational aid forcefully on the alert.   He heard the histories that some of these half-imbruted creatures had to recount, and he perceived with a startling clearness how great is that fallacy which claims opportunity in life to be the handmaid of ability; for not seldom during these gloomy and growled-forth recitals he had traced from its juvenile beginning a will to rise in the world and prosper, coupled with a dearth of every helpful agency. Lastly, too, he found his sympathies broadening and deepening toward temptation, so often an energy that simply seizes the individual as a tiger might seize an antelope in its teeth and bears him to a spiritual death if not a bodily one!

Hubert's wealth made it easy for him to secure the most skilled lawyers in the country. These soon gave him as their opinion that conviction would hardly be possible in his case. It might come, but as all the evidence was now rather plainly *en rue* beforehand, its coming did not seem by any means probable. After a few days of intercourse Hubert thoroughly confirmed his lawyers in the belief that he was innocent. He made no effort to bring about this result; the quiet naturalness of his story, the subtle and delicate fragrance of honor, refinement, cultivation, good taste, which his personality unconsciously diffused, wrought their due and potent effect. The men who had at first let Hubert's dollars tempt them into trying if they could not make the black of guilt look for a certain time to twelve fellow-mortals as though it were a sinless white, presently found that no such tricksy species of legerdemain was needed. Hubert had shot Bleakly Voght by a lamentable accident, and nothing else. They were prepared to defend the prisoner against what they now felt confident was a hideously false charge made in a spirit of moribund malice. Like the majority of those lawyers with whom the dealing in truth is a question not wholly dominated by the size of the fee, they exulted at the idea of having secured a case in which they must not only do some pretty hard fighting, but do it as the most stanch believers that they were fighting for a really noble cause. For even a high-priced lawyer can appreciate the nobility of a cause. As he might betray to you, if you caught him in some confessionally mellow moment, across the walnuts and

the wine, it is not a matter of clients you shrink from taking, but one of clients you can't afford to shrink from taking.

O'Hara was from the first their devout ally, and may
almost be said to have acted, on more than a single occasion,
literally as the proxy of Hubert. Terms of comparative
intimacy had been established between himself and Angela.
Every possible turn of developments at the coming trial
they discussed together again and again. One evening in
early December, while he and she were holding an interview
amid the tasteful tapestries and bright embellishments of
Angela's New York drawing-room, the latter most meaningly
and deliberately said:

"There is one portion of the case, is there not, Mr.
O'Hara, which the lawyers feel somewhat afraid of?"

"Yes," acquiesced O'Hara.

"And that is," continued Angela, "the portion where five
men will all testify to my husband's . . having . . accused . . ." Her voice loitered and sank. He presently broke in, with a brisk, relieving manner.

"Yes," he said again. "That is the portion. Or rather
half of it."

"How?" she queried repeated. "Is there more, then?"

"There is the quarrel. I mean, you know, what Brad-
bourne overhead. His evidence will be most compromising.
It will have the effect of verifying those last words of Mr.
Voght's. You comprehend this, of course?"

Angela stared down at her own black robes for a moment
—the habiliment that seemed to her so exquisite a mockery,
and yet, in another sense, was so well adapted to her
present despondency.

"Yes, I do comprehend perfectly," she said. "How I
wish," she added, "that he had only suppressed his evidence
at the inquest, as he proposed, offered, almost begged to
do!"

"I remember," said O'Hara, stroking his chin ruminatively. "You told me something of that before. The man's behavior at the inquest was odd. He seemed so agitated, once or twice, that I really thought he was going to faint."

But on the following day intelligence of a still more "odd" character reached O'Hara regarding this same man, Bradbourne. The Irishman went down to L—— and passed a night there, as he had so often done since Hubert's misfortune. The more he contemplated the bitterness of tragedy in which that high-strung, honorable, almost totally unselfish life had been steeped, the more he felt real thrills of indignation against what one might term the brutality of circumstance. A futile enough wrath to waste thought and time upon, it must be owned; and yet this very revolt has now and then proved the threshold of a subsequent philosophy from which foolhardy anger against the unavoidable has been as absent as foolhardy faith in the insoluble. Some of the hours which he had spent with Hubert in his prison-cell had made the profoundest of impressions upon O'Hara. If he had not known how forcibly his friend suffered, Hubert's excessive patience might have wakened an opposite belief in him. This very agnosticism which had long ago seemed to threaten the fine ideals of O'Hara (though for any injury of those ideals he had solely his own perversity to blame) was apparently doing, in the case of Hubert, all that religion had ever achieved with martyrs of past periods. Hubert was a martyr of fate; and yet the stoicism with which he met his unmerited scourges drew its quiet strength from no surety wrought by the airy axioms of pulpiteers. A stern hostility of events encompassed him; his hope against their worst assault was centred in his trust of that equity which long sweeps of evolution had bred among his fellow-men. Over all spread the Unknowable; here might lurk providential mercy; on this point he neither denied nor affirmed; he simply granted that some sort of aid might be working in his behalf.

And yet he was so calm, so uncomplaining! O'Hara

envied him his brave, cool resignation. He had once believed that no such serenity could result from the non-religious point of view. Hubert's repose was a revelation to him. Whence had he derived it, since the accepted codes of orthodoxy were all one valueless fable to him? . . . By degrees O'Hara, through the very admiration which he had always felt for what was clean and high and secure in his contemporary, began to accede that a lofty moral condition may base itself neither upon expectation of reward after death nor a dread of posthumous punishment. For the first time in his life he recognized not alone how essentially Christian an agnostic may be, but how wisely consistent with that so-called audacity of his rationalism.

" If Bleakly Voght really meant to bring me to the scaffold by that dying accusation of his," Hubert had once said, " I forgive him for the baneful impulse no less easily than I would forgive a wild beast for having sought to maim me. His attempt was evil; so was my resentful speech to him. Both are explainable through mentally material reasons. I believe that all harm inflicted by man against his neighbor is the product of insanity. Diogenes might better have said that he sought a sane man than merely one worthy of the generic name. Some day, I also believe, there will be no wrong in the world, and hence no rage that shall seek to repress or avenge it. How shall we probe the mind or the soul? Who has yet either explained to us the wherefore of the human devil or the human saint? Science may do so, some day; when it does we shall have the same trustworthy amulet against spiritual evil that vaccination has given us against physical evil. We are, all of us, the heirs of innumerable ancestors. I dare not allow that I ever lift my hand without allowing that there has been hereditary, ancestral cause for even so simple an act millions of years ago. Forgive one another? Ah, my friend, it is only when we fail to forgive ourselves that we cannot find it possible to forgive our fellows." . . .

Many words like these fell from Hubert's lips, while he was girt by the shadow and duress of his unmerited calamity. O'Hara, who had almost reverenced him for being exceptionally upright and admirable amid the levities of ordinary living, now felt within his soul a respectful homage larger and richer than he had dreamed of even furtively paying before. But on this especial occasion of meeting, neither the philosopher nor the poet in Hubert had much to communicate. During the previous day he had received a visit from Bradbourne, and it had both dismayed and perplexed him.

"The man was admitted into my cell," he told O'Hara, "and the instant that I looked at him I saw a great change in his appearance."

"He seemed ill ?" asked O'Hara.

"He must have lost at least thirty pounds. He was never a particularly robust fellow, you recall? But now he is emaciated almost to a shadow of what he was."

"And he said ? . . ."

"For some time I could not even make out what he desired to say. I took for granted that he had come to me with the desire to say something definite, appreciable. But for the life of me I couldn't get him, at first, to do anything except besiege me with a kind of feverish, wandering compassion."

"Compassion ?" sharply asked O'Hara.

"Yes. He lamented that I was here. I struck him as so sadly unsuited to my surroundings. It was an outrage. My forthcoming trial was also an outrage. They ought to have understood that a high-bred gentleman like me couldn't, no, *couldn't* have committed an actual murder. . . And all this was spoken so disjointedly, so erratically, so often with the suggestion in it of a dazed if not a demented brain, that I began to regret the absence of the turnkey and to cast my eyes about the niggard space of this abode, thinking just what stout thing I might turn into

defensive account if incoherence should suddenly take the
form of ferocity. But my caution proved needless. After
a while Bradbourne became a good deal more lucid. He
still remained a little wild and unsound in demeanor, but the
improvement had nevertheless been marked. Gradually I
began to learn that he wanted my consent and that of my
lawyers in a successfully mysterious escape from the country."

"Ah!" exclaimed O'Hara, as if he held this news to be of
piercing importance. "And he thought you might abet him,
so as to avoid his testimony! How little he knew you!"

"It was certainly a miscalculation," said Hubert, in his
placid way. "But then there was no excuse for it, this time,
as he had made a similar one before the inquest at Pineland."

"You showed annoyance?"   .

"How could I? The man's whole appearance was so
pitiable. With his gaunt figure, wasted face, and hollow
whisper, he gave me an absurd idea of a conspirator in some
opera. After a short time I found myself forgetting to take
him seriously. . . Australia seemed to be the one country
of refuge that he particularly craved. He knew it, having
lived there before—during nearly all his boyhood and a part
of his early manhood, in fact. He spoke of you as being my
chief possible aid in getting him safely away before the trial.
The whole proceeding, he affirmed, could be managed
between the lawyers and myself. He had money enough to
defray all the expenses of the trip ; he did not ask me for a
dollar—not he ! There were two people whom he would
like to take with him ; one was a woman, and the other a
child. Would I not think the plan over ? Let me recollect
that what they would compel him to say at the trial might
have a damaging effect upon me only second to Bleakly
Voght's awful declaration. It was true—oh, yes, he admitted
it was quite true—that he had been forced to speak harm-
fully about me at the inquest. But if he were not to be found

when the trial came off, all that the prosecution might say about him would not influence a jury half so much as what he might say in his own voice. And suppose lots of people *did* claim that he had been spirited off as a dangerous witness against the prisoner. Are not people forever babbling like this about everything and everybody? The great point always is whether or not they can prove their imputations . . . And so on, my dear O'Hara, until weariness grew no name for his imploring monologue."

"You finally silenced him, of course, by a flat refusal."

"I silenced him, at first, somewhat painfully. After I had spoken the word 'no' for what sounded to my own ears about the hundredth time, he literally fell on his knees before me, with the tears streaming down his face."

O'Hara shook his head most puzzledly, like a man who has begun to ponder something with zeal. "Strange," he murmured . . . "strange."

"But his swoon was still stranger," Hubert continued; "for in a few minutes I found myself kneeling beside him here on the floor of my cell and looking into a face that very closely resembled a dead man's. He had fainted completely away. . By a lucky chance the turnkey appeared soon afterward, and together we succeeded in resuscitating him. As soon as he was able to walk I caused him to be conducted from the cell. He had me, with his impetuous appeals, at a sort of physical disadvantage, cooped up here as I was. Besides, there had already been more than enough for me of these half-savage supplications, to which no inducement could make me listen. 'Get him away,' I whispered to the turnkey, 'or I shall be ill myself'. . . There was no danger that he would recommence his attacks before a third person, though he turned to me with a look of fervent pleading on his altered face just as he was being pushed across my threshold. Subsequently I learned that he had left the prison in a tractable state of mind, though

not until he had begged without avail permission to see me
privately once more."

O'Hara acted for a long time like a man who would
rather remain silent than speak. "This behavior on the
part of such a person," he at length broke forth, "is
deucedly perplexing. He cannot be acting solely through
motives of regard for *you*. He had never even exchanged a word with you until the day of Voght's death.
Merciful reluctance to testify so adversely against a fellow-
being? That is at least improbable. His evidence, after
all, is but the truth, and he's intelligent enough to see
clearly that he can only show himself an honest man, in such
an emergency, by declaring just what happened. . . No,
there is some mystery . . some mystery. . . " And O'Hara
tapped his bowed forehead as he now scanned the floor of
Hubert's cell.

The latter gave a little weary sigh. "Well, if there be a
mystery," he said, "I can't see how any special benefit to
myself may result from it."

"You can't see," returned O'Hara, "nor can I. But
that is no reason why the solution of the mystery may not
prove of the utmost worth and weight."

Hubert slowly shook his head. "I don't understand you,
O'Hara," he murmured.

O'Hara gave a laugh that had in it only the vaguest echo
of his once gleeful hilarity. "I'm afraid I don't understand
myself," he said.

"It couldn't turn out, I suppose," suggested Hubert,
with melancholy sarcasm, "that Bradbourne really killed
Bleakly Voght instead of myself?"

"Are you serious?" exclaimed O'Hara, starting and
looking at Hubert with great intentness.

"Serious?" echoed Hubert. "Good heavens, man, how
could I be?"

"True," admitted O'Hara, a little sadly, and as though he
recollected something. "It couldn't possibly be; could it?

There was but one shot fired. Yes, if there had been another we would have heard it—we people, I mean, outside of the wood. Besides, you had been standing in the presence of Voght only a few seconds before. Oh, no ; there simply *could* not have been any criminal act perpetrated on the part of Bradbourne, against his master. He . . . "

But here Hubert broke in, with his manly, thoughtful, collected tones. "You are indeed right, my friend," he said. "This Bradbourne *cannot* be guilty of any murderous act against Voght. To have done that he must have had an absolutely noiseless weapon, and have darted forth with it. . . . But you see, we at once get into the realm of 'penny dreadful' fiction. Air-guns, and pistols that go off without the slightest report, are not much in vogue nowadays, even if it were ever true of them that they made no noise at all. . . . I think the explanation of this man's behavior may be found in a disordered state of his nerves alone. I would not, if I were you, postpone any other work preparatory to the trial for the purpose of investigating his eccentric course more closely. Remember, pray, there is not much time ahead. Within two weeks from to-day, you know, the trial takes place."

"Two weeks from to-day," O'Hara repeated. The sentence held for him a deadly chill in it, as though he had felt the touch of an icy hand upon his flesh. Then, with rallying spirits, he added: "Well, be it as you say about Bradbourne, my dear fellow ; but I think the lawyers have made every needful preparation, as it is. And they're immensely confident of success, too—but then no less so than I am."

Hubert smiled. "Success ?" he asked. "You mean, by that, 'acquittal,' do you not ? "

"Why, surely, yes. What else could 'acquittal' mean ? "

Hubert slowly shook his head while his eyes fell. "It might mean," he said, "a cleansed name, and not the stained one that I must bear through the rest of my life, even if they leave me my life after they have done with me ! "

XIV.

NOTWITHSTANDING the advice of Hubert, future reflection induced O'Hara to begin a series of close investigations regarding Bradbourne's whereabouts and mode of living. The young man, as a noteworthy witness in the forthcoming trial, was already under vigilant watch. O'Hara had merely to make inquiries with respect to his address. He then set certain detectives at work, and in a few days he had learned facts which filled him with strange amazement.

Bradbourne was not Bradbourne at all. His name was Heath, and he was living with his sister, Jane Heath, a fragile, faded-looking girl, in a decent Second Avenue flat on the outskirts of Harlem. This name, "Heath," let in a world of new light to him; for Hubert had concealed no item of information concerning all that he knew of Voght's past misdeed. The detectives worked more boldly after they had gained an infallible clew. They discovered that this Jane Heath, although living under what she had given as a maiden name, was the mother of a child who did not at present share the home of her brother and herself. And a few days later further disclosures were made. Disguise had now been cast aside, and the so-called Bradbourne was threatened with immediate arrest, provided he did not reveal the whole truth about himself and the unfortunate young woman with whom he dwelt.

"His sister is the woman who was the victim of Voght's wickedness," O'Hara hurried one day into Hubert's cell for the purpose of telling him. "There's no doubt of it—not a vestige! I wrote you that his real name had turned out to be not Bradbourne but Heath, and now comes the

192

news that he is unquestionably Jane Heath's brother. The story of his Australian life is perfectly true. He was separated from his sister, Jane, at an early age. She was left here with a relation, and he was taken thither by the father of both. The elder Heath was seized with a desire to win rapid riches among the gold-fields. He failed to do anything of the sort, like so many others; and when his son, Julius, had reached the age of about nine years, he died. Julius had always recollected America, and now longed greatly to revisit it and to see his sister once again. But for a long time circumstances forbade such a step. He passed two or three years of the most pinching poverty, and at last succeeded in getting a fairly lucrative position at Melbourne. Meanwhile he had written the most affectionate letters to his sister, whom he idolized, and passionately desired to see again. Jane answered these letters punctually and with affection for a long time. At length the relation with whom she had lived (an aunt somewhat advanced in years) rather suddenly breathed her last. Jane wrote quite hopefully to her brother that she would go into service at least until the happy time when he could rejoin her here in New York; and then . . . she wrote no more during a period of about two years. One day, however, Julius Heath received a letter from her in his Melbourne home. It told him a story of miserable shame, and made the blood in his veins boil for vengeance upon Bleakly Voght. He had by this time accumulated a fairly large sum of money; he had lived with the most rigid economy on first securing the situation which proved such a godsend, and afterward some lucky turn of affairs had most radically improved his prospects. In a little while longer he had delighted to tell himself, the hour of his home-coming would arrive. Then there would be a great surprise indeed for Jane! She would pardon him for having played the miser thus long that she might rejoice and be comfortable hereafter. The continued silence of his sister had been an agony to Julius, and her horrifying letter arrived when he was on the verge of setting sail for these shores. He now swore a fiercely determined oath that he would spend every farthing of the money he possessed in seeking to force Bleakly Voght to marry his sister. . . But when he at length did reach America, it was to find Bleakly Voght the husband of another woman. . . And here his story becomes most improbable," O'Hara said, with that change of manner which accompanies the desertion of narration for criticism. " He admits that he entered the employment of Bleakly Voght knowing quite well who that person was, and that his entire method of operation was underhand in the extreme. If Voght had not been oddly careless about recommendations, I suppose that Heath could never have got himself engaged as Julius Bradbourne. It's most probable that Voght was prepossessed with his nice manner, and omitted, in his own severe illness, to verify whatever documents were presented to him."

" Strange," said Hubert, at this point, "that *Mrs.* Voght should have made no personal inquiries."

" I saw her this morning," O'Hara proceeded, " and I touched on that very subject. Mrs. Voght says that ' Bradbourne' came at a peculiarly trying hour. Her husband's last valet had been discharged for a flagrant refusal to obey some order given him on the previous day. She is certain that the new man showed her a note of recommendation which bore the name and address of a person living in a highly proper part of the town, and that she thoroughly intended to seek this person out for the purpose of having the reference authenticated. But almost immediately after ' Bradbourne' had been told that he could at least temporarily begin his duties, Voght was seized with a worse attack of his complaint than any from which he had yet suffered. For almost a fortnight, Mrs. Voght further told me, her own attendance upon the invalid was continuous. Meanwhile the newly-engaged servant had so pleased and satisfied her husband by his deftness and efficiency that she had grown too grateful for having him at all to think of corroborating his credentials. " Indeed," she added, " the plan of going to Long Island for change of air had suddenly been formed, and my chief thought was to move the whole *ménage* thither as quickly as could be done, since at any hour a new seizure might have made the departure of my husband impossible." ' These were Mrs. Voght's words to me yesterday. Now, whether Bradbourne's recommendations were forged or not, it is hard to tell. Doubtless all of them were genuine enough. A little money, used judicously in a great city like New York, can buy the vouchers of seemingly respectable people. If he wanted to get into the Voght household he must have wanted to do it very much indeed, and hence, being possessed of funds, he did not scruple to pave his way."

Hubert had been listening to all this with the most fixed attention. " Pave his way?" now came the interrogating answer. " Pave his way, O'Hara, for what purpose? If he had intended to wreak any revenge on Voght for having wronged his sister, he would certainly have taken advantage of those weeks which elapsed after he had secured a footing near the invalid. And yet he did not do so; we know that he did not do so." Here Hubert rose and began to pace the floor of his cell, while O'Hara felt pangs of pity at the way in which confinement and mental distress had thinningly told upon his robust figure. " I think his conduct implies insanity," Hubert went on, as he again drew near his friend during this nervous little walk; "but I don't see how it really can imply anything more definite in the way of explanation. If Bradbourne had made up his mind to kill Voght he would have carried out that intention; he wouldn't have waited . ." And now O'Hara saw a smile of bitterest humor touch the speaker's lips . . "No, he wouldn't have waited for me to have performed the bloody business ! "

" How can you ! " cried O'Hara, springing up and grasping his friend's hand. "Ah, this hateful prison and these intolerable days of suspense are spoiling all your splendid manhood—or beginning some such vile work, surely ! . . . Thank God, Hubert, the ordeal will soon be ended. In a little while, now, this cursed waiting, this abominable inaction, will have passed. Your trial will begin, and whichever way it turns, its very agencies of change will prove a relief."

"Right, O'Hara," murmured Hubert, as he answered the pressure of his friend's hand. " Anything will be better and more endurable than this monotony, this torpor, this stagnation ! "

He drooped his eyes as he spoke, still grasping the hand of the man who had so richly and profoundly surprised him by an undreamed-of loyalty and fidelity. But the eyes of O'Hara, as they gazed on the bowed head before him, were brimming, at this moment, with compassionate tears.

The trial began on the appointed day. Throngs of people came down from New York to be present at it, and drowsy, ugly little L—— had never before been so actively roused into a sense that it was not a place which civilized persons saw only from the windows of cars. The trial lasted eight days. Among the witnesses for the defence (as it is best here to record) was Angela. She chose to appear and testify that the violent irascibility of her husband's temper might have made him accuse Hubert of being his murderer even at the last mortal moment itself. Many of her friends and acquaintances had held up their hands in horror at her willingness to aid the prisoner by what they chose to term such terribly self-compromising means. But Angela had shown an inflexible purpose. No one opposed the step more than Hubert, and this she knew. As for the opinion of the world, she had but a single reason for not laughing at it, and this was that her heart felt too heavy to let her laugh at anything.

"What I can do I shall do," she persisted. "Let propriety shudder all it pleases. Let decency declare that I am trampling on it. If I can influence judge or jury the very least imaginable I shall be rewarded for all the discomfiture this ordeal costs me."

It cost her more, poor Angela, than she had anticipated. Her deliberate choice had been made to perform a sacrifice which the law did not necessarily demand or even request of her, and such an attitude was regarded by the prosecution as a kind of haughty challenge flung at their own strength. They forced her to feel this, and with poignancy. But she never once regretted her measure. Some of the cross-examiner's questions had made her dizzy and set her cheeks tingling; the worst of these, however, were "ruled out," and she was therefore allowed to escape from answering them. Meanwhile a horrible dread stole through her lest by having appeared at all she might be doing harm and not good to Hubert. This thought agitated her so wildly for a short interval that she was once or twice on the verge of rushing down from the stand and asserting a new-formed disinclination to testify at all. Were they going to drag out the whole hateful story of Alva Averill's treachery?—of what motives had caused her own marriage with Bleakly Voght?—of whether, after such marriage, her affections had remained with her former sweetheart? Would they make her lay bare all the weakness and faultiness of the past in order that they might pour upon it their vitriolic sarcasms? But no; her counsel beat them back; they were strong men, those lawyers of Hubert's, and to fight against them was to recognize it. A few cheering whispers to Angela wrought with her sinking heart like as many draughts of wine. She very distinctly rallied, and from that time forward held her own. It shocked some sensitive auditors wofully to hear her cast disrepute upon her dead husband—her "murdered" husband, they put it—in order that she might shield from just conviction a man who was known once to have loved her passionately and doubtless did so still. Defenders and traducers took hot sides for and against the brave young creature, who stood pale and resolute before the unpitying stares of the packed court-room, bent only upon telling the truth and telling it in such a way that it would help to save *him.* What friends praised as her fine womanly fortitude, was called by foes her coarseness, her effrontery, her brass. The Voghts, the Lexingtons, and a few other relations of her husband cut her dead from that hour. Some of them were in the court-room while she spoke the precise facts regarding Bleakly Voght's wayward and domineering nature. They knew that these were facts, and that the public revelation of them might materially assist the working of justice, and yet they ground their teeth with vexation, and said to one another : " She has got hold of his money and is living on it, and yet she dares to talk against him like this !" " Oh, what ought one to expect from the daughter of such a father ? Poor Bleakly should have been warned by the girl's tainted blood !"

But Angela did not care for the Lexingtons and their patrician allies. She would have torn out her tongue rather than have wronged Bleakly Voght's memory by the faintest untruth, the dimmest reflection of a calumny. She believed, however, that he had charged Hubert with his assassination, while he felt himself to be dying, from impulses which were a certain result of his old jealous hostility. She believed this down to the inmost depths of her spirit, and thus believing, she judged herself irrefutably right in giving publicity to her faith.

The witnesses for the prosecution had rendered her position all the more difficult and unpopular. Hugh Magee and the two workmen had stated honestly enough what they had seen and heard, but Bradbourne (or Heath, as he should now be called) had exhibited so much perturbation, prevarication, and palpable insecurity of statement that here and there he produced the impression of struggling to shield the prisoner

whom his unvarnished story would have otherwise plainly
injured.   The account of what he had overheard Hubert
say to Voght was wrung forth from his hueless and quivering lips.   He looked like a man beset with a perilous
illness, and once or twice he placed an emaciated hand
against the region of his heart, as though to still pulsations
there that were almost costing him his consciousness.   But
the full sum of what he had to disclose was finally forced
from him, in so far as concerned anything which might
jeopardize Hubert's favorable chances.   He gave an ex-
haustive account of the disputatious parley between the
prisoner and his master, and created the profoundest sensation
by this most implicating narrative.   At last he retired, totter-
ing, *énervé*, while everybody felt as if one of the beams had
been firmly planted which was to help make a scaffold for
Hubert.

Still, the adverse evidence began and continued purely
circumstantial.   Hubert's own plea was that the death of
Voght had been caused by an accidental explosion of his own
gun, and although Heath's testimony had pointed toward perjury on the part of the slayer, it nevertheless had substantiated no such proof.   Many a man has been hanged on a
good deal less actual certainty of guilt; but Hubert's lawyers were astuteness itself: they allowed no point to slip
their lynx-like visions.   The shooting had occurred, and so
had that harsh previous conference; but Heath, though he
may have heard one, had not seen the other.   Then the admission on this man's part that he was the brother of a
woman whom Bleakly Voght had wronged and that he had
engaged himself in the service of the latter for purposes of
possible yet unachieved vengeance, threw an *arrière pensée*
of cheapening influence over nearly everything that he had
said.   Or, at least, the dexterous counsel of Hubert spared
no pains to produce this result.   What, they queried with
scorching irony, was the credibility of a witness who admitted himself to have perpetrated so insane a freak?   Or did

he merely write down his own cowardly pusillanimity, and
concede that he had entered the Voghts' home for the purpose of killing its proprietor, but later had found courage fail
him?   Could any intelligent jury be asked to believe this
tale of a hot quarrel between the prisoner and Voght, when
told by so curious a blending of the jackanapes and the pol-
troon?   One moment the witness granted that he crossed
Bleakly Voght's threshold with the intention of dealing death
to that gentleman; the next he affirmed that "from day to
day he lingered on, undecided regarding his actions at
almost any hour."   And to the statements of so vacillating
yet vicious a being was to be entrusted the very life of a man
with so flawless a personal record as that which Hubert
Throckmorton had long conspicuously possessed! .

This turn of the argument secretly troubled Hubert very
much.   Heath had spoken the complete truth concerning
his turbulent interview with Voght : why seek to prove the
truth a falsehood?   It was an odious course of procedure,
Hubert passionately meditated, and as he sat listening he
became almost over-mastered by an impulse to leap up and
hurl denial at his own advocate.   And yet what mad folly
would attend a step like that?   No; he had given himself into the hands of these men because they were nimble
manipulators of the law, not because they devoutly served
the spirit of it.   If no straight path could be found toward
the legal assertion of his innocence, he must resign himself
to the discovery of a crooked one, provided this reached for
him the acquittal that was his right.

Many "exceptions" had been taken by the defence.   In
case a verdict of "guilty" were pronounced, his counsel
were hopeful, toward the close of the fourth day, that a new
trial could be secured.   As before recorded, the trial occupied a space of eight days.   The jury were "out" four,
and several hours previous to the bringing in of the verdict
a report had got wind that they would soon make known
their inability to agree.   O'Hara, who had seemed to himself

like a wretched blasphemer while delivering those compul-
sory statements which aided the arraigners of his friend, dis-
played toward Hubert, during that almost insupportable in-
terim of suspense, a devotion as spontaneous as it was charming . . . And at last the end came. It had been a trial
rather more replete with drama than most affairs of the same
criminal sort. In some ways it had been as technically dull
as far more ordinary trials; in others, it had almost equalled
that lurid intensity of development which the trials loved of
conventional novel-writers are sure to exhibit. Its termination was a surprise to everyone, a delight to some few, a
source of shocked regret to a good many others, and to a very
large majority indeed the opportunity for scornful comments
upon those miserably perverse methods by which our re-
publican justice is too often administered.

Hubert's astonishingly clever lawyers had saved him.
There had been one missing link in the evidence against
him, and on the existence of this they had harped with so
consummate a skill of iteration that the judge, while making
his charge to the jury, had re-clad it in terms of decisive offi
cial injunction.

The verdict, delivered amid the bluish wintry dusk of a
cheerless afternoon, was "Not guilty." O'Hara's hand was
the first to grasp Hubert's in vehement congratulation.

"Thank God, my boy!" he said, with tears in his voice.

"Thank God—for what?" asked Hubert, with a quiet,
searching look.

"For what? why, that you're free," broke forth O'Hara.

Hubert slowly nodded once or twice. "Yes, free," he
murmured. "But how? Free with a stained name. Free
to be despised and shunned by my fellow-men for the
rest of my lifetime! . . . Ah, do you think I do not understand just *how* free I am?"

"No, no!" denied O'Hara. "There may be some people
who will—"

"Don't talk that way," interrupted Hubert, laying a hand

on his friend's arm. "The entire world of my acquaintance believes, at this hour, that I have just missed the gallows by a hair's breadth, that I have been adroitly steered to acquittal by the shrewdness of my counsel, that I am and shall remain the unpunished murderer of Bleakly Voght."

These words were very composedly uttered. . . . O'Hara simply wrung the hand of him who had spoken them. He had no honest response ready, and any other, at such a time, would be the most piteous of mockeries. For all that Hubert had said he felt to be most dismally true !

XV.

THAT same evening Hubert returned to New York. As the dusky starlit levels of Long Island slipped past his view, he made a mental vow that he would never set foot there again. While the train was plunging through malodorous and slatternly Hunter's Point, just before it came to a final pause, he caught himself laughing audibly.

O'Hara, who occupied the seat in front of his own in the almost empty car, turned sharply at this extraordinary sound.

"I suppose you're thunderstruck, are you not, old fellow?" Hubert said.

"Well, yes, I am, rather," O'Hara replied. "But it's a hundredfold better to laugh than to cry, if you'll forgive my platitude."

"I was laughing," Hubert said, "at the positive refreshment that these horrible Hunter's Point smells from oil-tanks and bone-factories were able to afford me."

"Refreshment!"

"Yes. If anyone had told me such a thing were possible a few months ago! And I had got so to dislike New York before a certain . . misfortune occurred. Now I've an actual throbbing desire to walk its pavements once more! There's the thought of release—of getting abroad into the world again and merely moving one's limbs at liberty—that is mixed up, no doubt, with local feelings like these. The last time I breathed New York air, you know, there had never been a shadow across my personal freedom. Oh, that hideous kind of absence has all made such a difference! I shall go back with sensations that I ought to apologize to Fifth Avenue for ever having denied it was beautiful."

As the ferry-boat landed them at Thirty-Fourth Street they
heard boys crying extras, and in a little while had succeeded
in making out that the apparent gibberish yelled from several lusty little throats at once, was— "The acquittal of
Throckmorton." Hubert stepped into a carriage, shuddering. But just as O'Hara was about to follow him he said in
a low voice, "Get one of those things, will you?" And
O'Hara complied.

Hubert did not glance at the paper until he reached home.
There were lights in the drawing-room windows of his spacious old dwelling; he saw this through a sudden mist of
tears. They had received his telegram; one or two of the
servants who had been with the family in his father's and
mother's time must be met and spoken to. He controlled
himself by a severe effort while springing from the carriage
and ascending the low, familiar stoop.

"Through every stage of life my feet have trod the stone
of these very steps," he murmured to O'Hara. "How little
I ever dreamed that I should ascend them *like this!* I have
come 'back home,' you know, from many various parts of the
world, and with, ah, so many varying emotions! Once my
poor father was lying dangerously ill, and I had taken the
steamer with wild haste at Southampton, ten days before, on
hearing the unhappy news. I remember how my heart fluttered in my breast as I went up these steps then, fearing to
meet the truth which must be met in a minute or two . . .
My God, *if it were like that now!* . . I should be standing
here praying that I might find him dead!" . . . .

A little later, as they entered the hall, Hubert said to his
companion, motioning toward the drawing-rooms: "Go in
there, and I will join you presently."

O'Hara obeyed; he had seen a pale gray-haired woman
and an elderly man standing in the rather obscure background of the hall, and soon he heard something that
seemed very much like the sound of a feminine sob or two.
But after the briefest of absences Hubert made his appear-

ance. He tried to smile as his gaze met O'Hara's, but the attempt bore a sadder result than if he had failed to make it.

"Poor old Ellen!" he said. "No wonder she's over-come. She used to be my nurse . . . Then there's Richard, too; he was our butler thirty years ago." Suddenly he seemed forcing his manner into a factitious brightness. ' I ought to be gay to-night, oughtn't I?" he exclaimed. "What do you say to a stroll, O'Hara—a long stroll somewhere among the quiet down-town streets, where we're sure not to meet a soul that will know us? (I mean after dinner, of course; it's almost ready to be served now.) We might find some clean, out-of-the-way place and have a glass of beer there, quite *à la Bohème*. . . It's so strange; I've a longing to do something that will prove to me I'm a free man again, and yet I shiver to think of going where people may by the least possible chance recognize me . . . Oh, that paper you bought. Have you it? I'll just glance at it before we go upstairs."

O'Hara had already done a little more than glance at the sheet. It was lying on a table near which he stood. He put his hand on it, saying:

"If I were you, old fellow, I wouldn't look at it. Anyway, not now."

But Hubert did not heed the warning. He took the paper up and began reading it. The account of the trial and the announcement of his acquittal were not what O'Hara had been thinking of. These were inserted in a flaring, sensa-tional, but not specially offensive way. On the editorial page, however, was a column in big type, headed "Our Aristocratic Murderer." This Hubert soon saw, and this he let himself read. It was one of those pieces of newspaper frenzy which contain about as much moral force as a rattle-snake's bite. Its innuendoes were founded on noxious falsehood; its accusations were all cowardly stabs in the back. But it hurt Hubert, nothwithstanding its paltriness, for it made him realize that it stood for a certain phase of public opinion; and to reflect that there were any of his countrymen whatever now looking on him as a red-handed assassin who had bought himself free from the righteous grasp of justice, was galling beyond all speech. There was one long, vituperative paragraph, toward the close of the article, which drew forth a deep sigh from between Hubert's clenched teeth; and one sentence here, mephitic and rancid beyond the others, had been put into this hatefully memorable shape : "*No honest man should hereafter associate with the criminal who has thus insolently flaunted his money in the face of our law; and every honest man whom he meets ought to try and help teach him that in thus having skulked away from the just recompense for his crime he has only stamped himself more deeply with the brand of an unpunished infamy.*"

All this was a vulgar, flaunting tirade enough, and yet it affected Hubert at the special forlorn hour of his homecoming, with an unspeakable pang.

He flung down the paper. His colorless face was working; his hands were lifted as though to smite some viewless foe. All his accustomed quiet had vanished; he sank into a chair beside the table and bowed his head; when he lifted it again O'Hara saw that his mouth had taken a downward curve whose meaning could only be the darkest kind of dejection.

"Why should I go on living, now?" he softly yet miserably cried. "I have nothing to live *for*—nothing!"

O'Hara, infinitely pained, stretched forth a hand, grasping his arm. "You have *her*," he said.

Hubert sprang to his feet. "Her? Whom? Angela? Drag her down to my level? make them think harder things of her than what she did to save me has already made them think? Ah, no, no! how little you know me, after all!"

'That was an impolitic move,' spoke the voice of O'Hara's exquisite loyalty. A moment later he said aloud, going up to Hubert, putting a hand on either of his shoulders and

staring with fervor straight into his desperate, gloomful eyes :
" Look here, old chap ; that trash shouldn't trouble you ;
you're too big for it. Judge K—— is an enemy of that
paper. It always was filthy in its manner of showing its
dislikes, and it's got as many as a porcupine has quills.
The judge that sat on your case offended it a year or two
ago by stumping the State contrary to its rotten partisan
opinions. Can't you see that *you're* not so much black-
guarded as the official who gave the charge to your jury?
Come, now, be a man. This won't do at all. You've lots of
friends and supporters left . . you'll see to-morrow if you
haven't." . . .

To-morrow did not corroborate O'Hara's rosy prophecy,
nor the next day, nor the next. A few congratulatory letters
reached Hubert, but decidedly a few. Before long he
learned that the most prominent metropolitan club of which
he was a member had seriously debated the question of
demanding his resignation. But no such demand reached
him. There was a friendly element working in his favor, or
at least one that expressed the refusal to accredit him with
cold-bloodedly murderous motives. A certain faction declared that if he had really shot Voght with intent to kill he
had done so from a terrible previous exasperation. Another
faction shook its head cogitatively, dubiously over the evidence of Heath, *alias* Bradbourne. Still another (smaller,
decidedly smaller) credited his claim with regard to an accidental manslaughter. This one leading club was large
enough to contain many men of many varying views.
Hence, after a little while, Hubert's legal exoneration was
socially admitted, and the final mordant humiliation was
spared him of being officially treated as a man not worthy
the companionship of gentlemen.

But in a practical sense he soon perceived that his ostra-
cism had become a partial if not a complete fact. He never
entered the doors of any of his clubs ; he lived a life almost
thorough in its isolation and solitude, except for the visits of

O'Hara, which were frequent, and excessively welcome. Sometimes in the day he would walk abroad, avoiding, for the most part, streets in which he would meet former acquaintances. Yet such occasional encounters were unavoidable, and when they took place a cold bow or a distinct cut would sometimes be the consequence. He grew to hate New York as he had never hated it before; always previously his distaste for it had been of the dilettante kind; he had said to himself that it was a bad sort of place to live in, that it failed to give a fellow the least chance for dreaming nice dreams, that to an idler like himself who spent most of his time *avec les bras croisés* it was fatally unsatisfactory. But now it had become for him a metropolis teeming with loathsome associations. Some of his kinsmen and kinswomen had paid duteous calls upon him, and after each one of them had done so he thanked God that he or she was but remotely allied to him by blood and that the chill hypocrisy of such sympathy as theirs need not be encountered more than once.

"I hate to lose you, and yet you should go abroad," O'Hara repeatedly said to him. And one day he added: "In my last issue of our paper, you know, I almost constructed an editorial on the advisability of it."

Hubert's eyes filled with tears, then, as he grasped his friend's hand. "My dear old boy," he said, "I can't but remember how you studiously avoided mentioning that Long Branch quarrel in your paper, and how, afterward, while the trial was pending and while it was in operation you never allowed a single line to be printed there. You had a devilish hard time with your co-editors, too; you needn't deny that you did; a chance word, unintentionally dropped every now and then, told me so. . . But now, when half the town—I may almost say half the country—is hot against me, you make your journal brim with my attempted vindication.... . Well, you ask me why I don't go abroad and quit the whole abominated environment. Shall I tell you why? There are two reasons. One is what my prison-life has led me to look for and help in this woe-begone town."

O'Hara nodded : " I know ; you spend hours every day in the dens and slums. You've tried once or twice to keep it from me, but I've found you out; so now, I suppose, you're going to make a clean breast of it . . eh, my boy?"

Hubert answered his friend's nod. They were' sitting together in his dining-room over their after-dinner coffee and cigars. "That *is* my first reason, precisely as I have told you." His face flushed, his usually grave eye sparkled, as he went on : " O'Hara, what I find among the poor here is beyond all my powers of telling. The so-called charities of Christianity never dream of reaching those horrors that I see. . . I go everywhere ; I dive into the lowest quarters. I nearly always had detectives at first, to go with me, but now I very often go alone. There are holes so horrible that you would not believe their existence unless I brought you there. Think, my friend, of cellars where Chinamen sell opium to young girls—often girls not more than fifteen or sixteen years old—at a price too revolting for me to do more than hint its vileness. Think of dance-houses where quadrilles are formed on big board floors every night, with each male dancer a thief and each woman at his side the strumpet by whose harlotry he lives. Think of countless low sheds, with rickety doors, at the end of reeking alleys, where eight and ten people, male and female, lie on shelves reeking with vermin, between walls whose pendant cobwebs are a ghastly parody of Mrs. Manhattan's or Mrs. Amsterdam's yellow old family laces. Think of children born in holes like these by mothers who are drunk when they bear them; think of taverns where the only drink sold is a stale malt stuff, the leavings of drained beer-kegs. Think of all brutality, bestiality, infamy, desperation, grovelling and wallowing sinfulness, grown an incessant part of the daily and nightly events our sun and our stars gaze upon in this monstrous town. . . Well, I prowl about through all these base, lewd haunts, and

14

thank heaven I'm rich enough to drag some few wretches out of them that are willing to be cleansed and given a decent chance against the curse of heredity. I go deeper than most of the best charities go. Some of these are very good ; they are trying to work wonders. I don't know that I have half the beneficent aim *they* possess. I'm merely trying to show myself, all the time, that the experience I've passed through *might* have sunk me in the grossest pessimism, but has'nt ;—that, in other words, it's taught me how fortunate I am, after all. I don't claim that my motive is other than a really selfish one at heart. But you see it now for what it's worth."

"I see it," said O'Hara dryly, as Hubert paused. For a little while he remained silent . . . A remembrance had visited him of his old half-deserted ideal ; he thought of how closer association with Hubert, of how intimacy with this man's stoically-borne agony, had roused and kindled him to a finer and sincerer action ; of how he had fought with his co-laborers on the paper which he and they edited for a truer and loftier standard of journalism, and of how he had finally prevailed with them and won them to his cause, notwithstanding a certain decrease in immediate and temporary profits.

A little later he went on, puffing at his cigar with a commonplace pertinacity, as if it had gone out, which it had not done at all, and which the volumes of smoke that it exuded quite nebulously told :

"I see—of course I see, my dear Hubert. You've about forty thousand dollars a year, and you might keep a coach, a yacht, and goodness knows what else. You don't, however ; you go into frightful places like that, and God bless you for doing it . . . So here's your first reason for not wandering off into Europe, Asia, anywhere you might choose. A mightily commendable reason, I admit . . . But now for the second reason. Recollect you said there were two."

Hubert began absently to pass his forefinger round the

rim of his finger-bowl. "Oh, yes, there are two reasons . . I said so, and I meant it."

"And the other," said O'Hara softly, after a renewed pause, "the other is . . .?"

Hubert lifted his head and stared at his companion. "You know," he murmured.

O'Hara put both elbows on the white table-cloth, and ransacked the face of his host with those hazel eyes that Hubert had learned to read and to love so well.

"She never ceases thinking of you, my boy," he said. "She's there, up town, waiting for you to give her a sign. Why don't you? Why *won't* you?"

"A sign?" repeated Hubert, with his voice grown very low; "what sign?"

"Ah," said O'Hara, looking down and shaking his head; "you understand me; you must!"

"Yes, I do," he answered, with the hoarse note of pain in his modulated tones. "But it's of no use. Perhaps . . I only say perhaps, mind . . . she would even agree to marry me—"

"Agree!" shot in O'Hara. "Ask her, and find out for yourself. Just ask her—that's all!"

Hubert turned paler. Those words of O'Hara's pierced his heart; they told him what he had already been a good deal more than half sure of regarding Angela—that she had longed to see him, or at least hear from him, for weeks past.

That night, some time between midnight and morning, when the large house was still as death and the larger city which encompassed it was almost as still, he sat alone and wrote Angela a letter. He poured out his love and his sorrow to her equally. It was a letter meant to be final. She would ever remain the idol of his life—he would never marry. But they must try to forget one another. Not that either would succeed, but that both must try. A dire fatality had launched itself between their loves. Once—not so very long ago—it had looked as though death might bring light to them in place of darkness. Then death had come, and with it a darkness that must prove, for all they knew, one eternal night . . . It was a hopeless, unanswerable letter. And yet Angela answered it at once, on the following day. She sent her reply not by mail but by messenger. It was very short, and its chief sentence ran thus : " I concede all that you say, from your point of view, and yet I beg that you will let me give you mine, not as I might write it here on paper, but as I desire to express it in spoken words." She furthermore mentioned an hour when she would be at home on the following afternoon. If he refused to come to her she would know it by his silence. If he accepted, then let him write her a line to this effect.

Hubert sat gnawing his lips for quite a long time. At last he took a sheet of note-paper and wrote on it at great speed :

" I will be with you by five o'clock to-morrow afternoon."

Then, sealing and directing this brief response, he rang for a servant and bade that it be immediately sent. He was in dread lest he should recall it if it were not despatched with the greatest promptitude ; and about a half-hour or so later, as he had indeed anticipated, a mood of excessive regret overcame him that he should have agreed to meet Angela at all . . .

On the next day, however, he punctually kept his appointment. Angela was living with extreme quiet, just now, in a house which she had rented on East Fifteenth Street, directly facing Stuyvesant Square. The situation was one of considerable retirement ; " out of the world " a good many of Angela's acquaintances thought it. She herself had been won by the view of the spacious parallel parks from her upper windows, and the fine boulevard-like sweep of Second Avenue, broadly dividing them. There is a pathos in the fact of how New York has left to shabbiness and vulgarity her only two really noble thoroughfares, the Bowery and Second Avenue. Angela could see nothing save the prosperous and handsome part of the latter street, however, from her own semi-retired dwelling. She had made herself very comfortable as far as material surroundings went. Her home had been her chief mental recreation during the past winter; whenever she had a specially keen heartache she would go and talk with an upholsterer, a keeper of curios, a seller of etchings. The New York of 1880 or thereabouts was far from being the same meagre market for all artistic wares that twenty or even ten previous years had seen it. One could make a very charming home for one's self, she found, without going to hunt up precious rarities in Paris or London. Besides, Angela did not desire any particularly precious things. The income that Voght had left her was a large one—sixty thousand dollars a year if a dime. But she had as yet spent only a comparatively small portion of it, and for reasons that will presently be shown. Those who knew her either well or ill equally marvelled, as the months of her widowhood succeeded one another, that she kept no carriage. Indeed, her life amid the calm of Stuyvesant Square was hardly less sober and sedate than the dreary hues of her widow's robes. Her eye craved brightness, grace, and felicity of encompassment, and these she permitted it to enjoy. No one had ever supposed that she had loved her husband, and therefore no one could understand her reasons for a course of comparative economy, even while the period of conventional "mourning" was in progress. But Angela herself understood, and kept her own counsel unalterably. The most intimate woman friend whom she possessed could never gain from her a single satisfactory response on this point. It might be added with strict truth, by the way, that she had no really intimate friend, now that Alva Averill (with those terrific posthumous revelations of the latter's unworthiness!) had passed away. To Alva she had given an immense confidence, a romantic ardor of admiration. 'I seem to have shut myself in my shell,' she would sometimes muse, ' toward all other women, ever since that unspeakable deceit of Alva's became known to me. I am *sure* that I'm wrong in doing so; there are myriads of splendid women in the world, and no one realizes this more clearly than I do. Perhaps my reserve will wear off before I die. I hope it will, for I believe that the woman who loses all faith in her own sex runs the chance of becoming, sooner or later, almost suicidally odious to herself.'

But the reserve had not worn off, and there were forcible reasons for its having failed to do so. Her behavior in appearing, not long since, as a witness against the cause of her dead husband, had created much assertive discussion among many interested cliques. The *droit du plus fort* had proved, as she well knew, operative against her. A good many people sought her company and outwardly professed a certain sympathy with the posture that she had taken. She could not be sure, however, whether hypocrisy or sincerity was, in more than a single case, at work among just these same professed adherents. Meanwhile she did not specially care on the subject. She was incessantly hopeful, suspenseful, expectant as regarded a totally different matter. But hope, suspense, expectancy, all three remained unaltered. ' Some day he *will* make some sign,' she kept telling herself; ' O'Hara says that he will—that it must appear before very long—that he will never leave the country without coming to me.'

The winter had blown, rained, frozen, and snowed itself into early March. Second Avenue had been piled with white drifts more than once, and Stuyvesant Square had been for weeks a glassy, bluish monotony of ice, previous to that gusty, heavy-clouded afternoon when Hubert at last ascended the stoop of Angela's house.

He sat for quite a little time in her front drawing-room, before she entered. He had leisure to note in the apartment certain evidences of her personality which almost thrilled him like the whispered words of dead friends. It was indeed no drawing-room at all, but a sitting-room and library combined, with a big garnet plush curtain separating it from the remainder of the floor. Here, in low cases against the wall, were some of the books they had read together through past untrammelled, inestimable hours. Here was a glimpse of color that he knew she had always loved. Here was an engraved copy of some picture that she had professed attachment for . . . Oh, how her individualism breathed to him on every side, in slight, yet vivid ways! . . And presently he heard the rustling of a dress, and felt certain, in the hyperbole of his passionate sentiment, that it was, it must be, *her* dress. It might just as well, of course, have proved to be that of her maid, or of some other feminine being who was a total stranger to himself. But when its prophecy seemed confirmed by the entrance of Angela, he felt that love should have some new word which would aurally correspond to what clairvoyance had given a visual definition.

She placed her hand in his, for a moment. "You were very punctual," she said, with her blue-gray eyes meeting his own just long enough for him to see both fear and grief in them. Then she sank into a seat quite near the one which he had taken, while he resumed his own.

"I thought," he answered, with a little gleam of smile, "that if I came at all I might just as well be on time."

"If you came at all!" She stared down at her hands where they lay white and delicate as curled lily-leaves against the dead-black of her dress. He saw her under-lip quiver for a second; then he saw her tighten it against her hidden teeth, as though to be prepared for another such tremulous movement, should one arrive. After a slight pause, she added, again looking up at him: "And so you did not want to come—you debated about it in your own mind, and almost refused to come, even . . even after the letter I wrote you?"

He answered her with a sudden gloomy bluntness for which she was unprepared. "I was mad to come; I knew

it, felt it, when I sent you back that 'yes.'   It's tearing
an old wound open.   Not that the wound had ever healed,
or ever would heal."

She clasped both her hands tightly together, and held
them pressed thus.   A little spot of the chilly March sunshine swam in through a window near by, and rested like a
yellow jewel amid the auburn waves of her rich, dense hair.
'How lovely she is!' he thought.   'What might not such a
woman, if she were bad, make a man do for her?'

She began in a low and hesitating voice that soon grew
louder and firmer :

" I should be prepared to hear you speak just like that ;
I should be prepared because of your letter.   So much of
exactly that expression, that tendency, was there.   You say
it is best that we should not even exchange any further
words together at all.   You insist that you have forgiven me
for marrying as I did—"

" Yes," he interrupted ; " I have forgiven you.   I know
how you have suffered since.   That you *could* have done it,
I . . well, I hate to reflect on the point of your having *been
able* to do it.   But, as I say, your punishment came to you
and you've expiated your fault.   Mind, if you had cared for
him, I would not have called it a fault—if you had cared for
him enough, that is, to become his wife with the least . . the
least . ."

It was her turn to interrupt now, and she did so with a
ring of sharp censure in her tones.   " Oh, I see that you
have *not* forgiven me for marrying him.   You have *not*, and
you never will !   That is why you treat me as you do !   That
is why you declare that your coming here is a madness ! "

" No, no, Angela ! "

" Yes, yes," she protested.   " Men never pardon certain
things in women—never.   I've thought it all over so much
and so often."   Her accent had become as bitter as it was
mournful, now.   " You assert—you are so self-satisfied in
your assertion—that consideration for *me* is the only motive

you have, in . . acting as you are. But it's yourself that you're remembering all the time—it's that wound you've just told me about—that wound which will never heal! You don't mean any wound that comes from losing me ; you could heal it if you did, and . . and you know how. Oh, I dare say this may sound unwomanly, immodest, to you ; but I don't care. I want to face the truth and speak the truth. Your *self-love* has been wounded ; you won't acknowledge it, even *to* yourself, but that explains everything in your present course. I'm . . I'm . . impure, defiled, repellent to you, in a certain way—"

"Angela ! "

"Yes! If you'll sound the depths of your own feelings towards me, you'll find that I'm right—right. Now that I'm free, you discover that there are gossips and scandal-mongers in the world who might destroy my peace of mind, provided a . . a certain step were taken by me. As if I had not trampled on all that, months ago, when I chose to appear in court and say what I did! As if my action *then* were not proof enough how I minded the *pros* and *cons* of popular opinion! If I'd been afraid of what society's cackle and clatter could do to my peace of mind, do you suppose I would not have shown it then ? "

"You showed it then most heroically, Angela," he said. "But even that was a torment to me. I hated seeing you clad in such glaring publicity—and on my own account ! "

"Why not on your account ? I owed you some reparation. Was I not the cause of all that had passed ? "

"You mean," he asked, "the—the killing of Voght ? "

" I mean everything."

" Good heavens," he began, "you don't think, then, that I really—? But no ; it's impossible."

" No, no," she swiftly agreed ; " and you should not wrong me by even such a fleeting suspicion."

" Your pardon ! " he entreated. " How could I think you doubted whether I was a murderer or not ? you who. . . ."

"Ah, say it all right out!" she exclaimed, as he paused. The color bathed her face as though all the air of the room had suddenly grown rosy, and her eyes were like two winter stars. "I who am willing to be your wife—who have almost begged you, in so many words, to marry me!"

"Angela!" he said once more, but this time with an intonation of the most melancholy remonstrance.

"I will not molest you ever again," she went on, "if you will once assure me that I've not made a misjudgment. Only say to me 'I swear that it's true I never could quite forgive your marriage, and this is my actual motive for my present course toward you.' Only say those words, giving me your oath—yes, your solemn oath as a man of honor— that you mean them, and I will promise sacredly on my part never to write you, and never to try and see you from this hour. . . . I will even promise that if we should meet anywhere at any future time I will not show by the faintest sign . . "

He rose, then, waving one uplifted hand. "What are you saying? What is this absurd vow you wish me to take?" And he walked over to a table on which there was a low vase brimming with violets, and leaned his face toward them for a moment or two.

She rose also, but she did not follow him. She stood with the fingers of one hand slipping over the polished filigrees that surmounted the back of her chair, and her gaze directed downward upon its clustered ornamentations as though there was something symbolic there in the way of advisory help.

"You call it an absurd vow, then?" she queried. "There's . . there's nothing to keep us apart from one another except your dread of censorious things which the world may vent about me? On your word of honor there's nothing except just that?"

He turned and faced her. The light struck him so revealingly then that she saw his great pallor with an inward start, and one caused by sadness and joy strangely blended. But

the joy took swift predominance as she now heard him reply
to her, with a tone infinitely familar, infinitely welcome.

" On my word of honor there *is* nothing except just that."

His manner was so ardent that she waited for him to speak
still further, knowing he would do so; and very soon he continued, with all the love of a life in his tumultuous utterance.

" Oh, my Angela, my treasured, my idolized Angela!" he
exclaimed. " If you could only realize that I cannot and
will not endure to have you scorned!"

" But if I am not scorned by *you*," she dissented, bridling,
and almost fiercely.

" No, no," he murmured, and he recoiled as she advanced.
" Some day you would repent. I feel it—I am certain of it! "

" Then," she cried, " you are convinced that some day I
would cease to love you as I love you now! "

" Not that! "

" What else? . . . what else? "

" All such love as ours takes a change, a tarnish, sooner
or later."

" That is your old cynicism . . pessimism . . what is
it? You always had it. . . But you would remain *you*,
Hubert! *I* would never change. You might, but I never
would! I'm willing to take the chances of your changing! "

" Still . . still, you are his widow. That is, in material
ways."

" Material ways? How? "

" You understand."

" I do not . . . Ah! you mean that I am living on what
he left me? I would give everything up—yes, everything!
They say it's very large—the lawyers have told me—I've
only taken a little of it. Look about this room. You see?
I have only made it pretty; I've gone into no extrava-
gances; I've hated to *spend* much of what he left me. It's
mine, but I've always felt that some day you might say just
what you've said now."

" I? And what have I said? "

"That I'd be the possessor of his money ! . . . Hubert,
do you hear me ? I'll give it all up. I'll give it up because
I love you. If you don't want me to have a dollar of it I'll
hate to keep even one ! Do you hear me ?—even one ! I
don't care, I don't care, why *should* I care for riches, when
you will give me riches I prize a millionfold more ? Why
should I care, Hubert ? I love you and you love me !
You've said it ! It's the whole world to both of us ! You're
not forcing me into a sacrifice; you're simply choosing
whether I shall die or live—whether I shall go plodding on
for a few years longer with sorrow in every breath I breathe,
or whether—"

He caught her to his breast, then, and she clung to him
while he rained kisses on her lifted face . . . But suddenly he took both her hands by the wrists and forced her
away from him.

"No . . no . . no," his choked voice got breath to say.
"I won't—I will *not.* You have your life before you—I
have mine. You will give up everything and find a consolation in me. But what will that consolation prove hereafter ? They will make you a jest and a by-word ! They
will declare that you planned to have me murder your
husband and defended me in open court afterward. They
will heap their infamous charges on your spotless character
. . I am a branded man, a man with a stained and tainted
name, and you *shall* not join yourself to me . . . I love you,
I love you, I love you ! Man never loved woman more, I
think, through the whole sweep of that human history which
makes up the sum of all man's and woman's loving ! . . .
But you must not plead with me—you . . ."

"Hubert !" She had flung herself on her knees before
him, and stretched out her hands in lovely, surrendering
supplication. "Woman never loved *man* more !" she cried.
"Will you leave me ? Will you make my future an
anguish ? I don't speak of *your* future—I'm thinking only
of my *own.* I'm so selfish as that; I'm selfish as love

always is! See what I'm doing now! You remember how we talked together" (her voice came in quick, hard gasps, here) "of—of the novels they write to-day? You remember how you used to say that the—the—realism . . . what was it? . . never grasped the . . the whole actual truth about human suffering, human desire?" She broke into a wild, hard, quick laugh. She was still on her knees, and her beautiful bosom almost broke the leash of its bodice as she let her form sway backward while she watched him, standing over her, in his misery, his temptation, his great love, his invincible sense of right.

"Good-by," he said. He stooped and caught her delicate, flower-like head in his grasp. He kissed her brow, her cheeks, her lips . . . there he lingered, for that one long kiss was indeed a good-by, and to him an eternal one.

Then he fled out of the room. He had conquered himself. He would not make her his wife because he believed, with every impulse toward fair-doing of which his soul was capable, that in the rendering of such concession, either to himself or to her, he would be committing a fault no after regret could expiate.

XVI.

ANGELA passed a fearful night. But she rose, the next
day, with a certain resigned outlook toward the future that
surprised even herself. It was all settled. He had gone
for good; they would perhaps never meet again. She could
not blame him; he had acted, altogether, just as she might
have known that he would act. From the hour of that
terrible farewell with him his image in her thought took a
shining idealism which it had never worn before. He was
lost to her forever, and yet the splendid unselfishness of his
choice must always thrill and sway her moral being throughout the future. A great happiness had been forfeited, but
she would never recall Hubert, among the years to be,
without a glow of pride in his nobility that would prove as
triumphant as it was mournful.

"I doubt if we ever meet again," she told O'Hara, a few
days later. "I am going abroad to live."

"Really!" he exclaimed, astonished by the news. "To
live?"

"Yes," she replied. "All ties are now broken here."

"And there you hope to make new ones?"

"Only the ties of place. I have scarcely seen any of
Europe but a few of its larger cities, and those when I was
quite a little girl."

"It is too bad . . . too bad," O'Hara softly said, looking
down, and after quite a pause.

Angela gave one of those little flute-like laughs that seem
to carry a sigh in it. "What is too bad?" she asked.
"My going?"

" Yes—or rather that which makes you go." And then, with an irrelevancy which, after all, did not sound like one to Angela, he added : " Do you know, I still think so much of that Bradbourne—or Heath, as we should now call him ? "

" And I ! " she exclaimed. " For hours at a time I am haunted by him in the strangest way. It is simply, I suppose, that the unexplained mystery of his dealings with my husband has made upon me a deep, ineffaceable impression."

" The mystery ? " O'Hara inquired.

" Is it not one still ? "

" If you choose to call it so. And yet he entered into your husband's employ with the motive, no doubt, of some revengeful project."

" Some revengeful project which he never carried out ? " said Angela. " But if so, *why* did he never carry it out ? "

" Lack of opportunity . . of occasion . . of courage, if we are to credit his own statements."

" Opportunity and occasion he certainly had at a hundred different times. As for courage, he never seemed a man lacking in that . . . And then it is so strange : Hubert Throckmorton's quarrel with my husband, there in the wood, was partially relative to his sister; and he *heard* those words that Mr. Throckmorton spoke about Jane Heath."

" Yes, he heard them," conceded O'Hara.

" If *he* had shot Mr. Voght it would have been . . well, it would have been so much more natural, somehow. Don't you think so ? "

" I have often thought so. He was near enough to have aimed a deadly shot and fired it."

Angela was biting her lips and staring straight past O'Hara in a most absorbed fashion. " But he did not fire," she murmured, slowly shaking her head. " He did not ; he *could* not have done so; he would have been heard if he had."

O'Hara smiled and shrugged his shoulders. " There can

hardly be any two opinions on that point," came the response; "he would inevitably have been heard."

"You have had news of him lately?" Angela asked, discontinuing her mood of reverie and giving O'Hara her wonted
glance of direct frankness.

"About a week ago—yes. I made inquiries, or rather
caused them to be made. If you ask my reasons for doing
this I can't precisely tell you them. Possibly they are the
same as yours for being haunted by recollections of the
man."

"Well," said Angela. "And you learned . . .?"

"That he had been ill—confined to his rooms in that flat
where he lives with his sister."

"You have seen *her?*" Angela inquired, a little tim-
idly.

"No."

But it was not long before Angela was destined to see her,
and in the most unforseen of manners. One morning, between breakfast and luncheon, a servant came to Mrs.
Voght with the news that there was a rather strange-acting
young woman down-stairs, who refused to give her name but
begged to see the mistress of the house.

"'Strange-acting' isn't a word with at all a safe sound to it,
Margaret," smiled Angela. There had been a number of
very indigent people applying for help at the house in Stuyvesant Square, ever since Mrs. Bleakly Voght had taken it.
The fact of her new wealth had rather widely transpired
among her needy fellow-citizens, for such events are apt to
do so even in cities as large as New York. "I hope," she
now continued, "that this person didn't strike you as being
at all out of her head."

"Oh, no, ma'am," hurried Margaret self-correctively.
"Not *that*, ma'am, at all. I only mean that she had a way
as if her mind wasn't much on what she was talking about,
and sort of as if, too, ma'am, she was frightened at herself
for coming. I guess she's kind of a lady, though, ma'am,"

ended Margaret, as if this were a matter at once dubious and palliative.

Angela remembered her servant's words a little while afterward, for they so perfectly described the woman who was occupying one of the drawing-room sofas with her and whose name had just been given, with a painful gasp of timidity, as Jane Heath.

She was thin and faded and scared-looking, now, but she had once been pretty, as her brow and chin yet showed, and there lurked just enough refinement in her rapid, alarmed speech to make you admit of her that she was not really *mal élevée*. She spoke with a slight lisp, which might have been fascinating before the lips whence it proceeded had got that rather sickly bluish tinge they now wore, and her dark eyes had a look which might have been caused by the shedding of many tears, and gave Angela an odd idea of black velvet faintly frosted by age and use.

" I've been thinking for whole days at a time," she told Angela, " as to whether I ought to come here—as to whether you wouldn't be furious when you found out who I am." (Her manner was that of the born prattler, and there now clung to it a feverish " do or die " kind of eagerness that her listener soon found infinitely pathetic.) " You've really seen me once before, you know ; still, you *don't* know, I'm sure. It was that day when I went to visit Mrs. Averill. I recollected you perfectly when I afterward saw you in court. I'd . . I'd (yes, I *will* say it !) hated you till then. After I heard of your marriage to *him* I almost went crazy. I'd believed he *would* pay me that atonement for the madness he had made me commit . . . Oh, I don't call myself blameless —far, far from *that !* But I was such a mere slip of a girl— only seventeen—and he so filled with worldly wisdom ! . . . But when we met in court it was all different with me. I saw in your face how you had suffered, and I heard it (oh, so clearly !) in what you said. You don't dream of how grand and simple and good you seemed to us all, that day. Julius

—that's my brother, Julius Bradbourne Heath, though *you* only knew him as Julius Bradbourne—had let me go down to L—— after it had been found out that *I* would not be called as a witness. So I was in the big crowd and saw you. Besides, I'd got to feel quite sure that you had never cared at all for *him*—that you hated him, in fact."

Angela had not dreamed of being angry at all this. It had somehow given her a thrill of vague, indefinable expectancy when she had learned who her visitor really was ; and now that Jane Heath had begun her swift, excited, impetuous monologue, the expectancy deepened. In afterward seeking to explain this feeling she decided that it was born merely of an inward mental revolt against the entire stagnation in which a certain affair was now sunk. They had let Hubert go free, and now they were beginning to forget that they had done so. But they had never forgotten, and never *would* forget that his name was smirched and stained and branded for life !

"Who told you that I hated my husband.?" Angela here asked. "Your brother?" The tones that she used were not only ireless but even kindly as well. They seemed to reassure Jane Heath, who now spoke with fewer gasps for breath and a decidedly less rattling speed.

"Well, yes, Julius *had* found that out. There was one day when he saw you talking to a gentleman on horseback, just outside the gate of your own house down at Ponchatuk. Do you remember? *Do* you? He told me he thought you had disliked him ever since. You recollect, then, that he afterward mentioned the meeting as if with a mischievous purpose of making trouble? That was done to satisfy him-self concerning your true feelings. I mean your true feel-ings about that gentleman, Mr. Throckmorton. He had read all those things in the newspapers when the quarrel occurred at Long Branch. He had some idea, had Julius. Ah, he had many ideas *then* that he never let me know about. He has talked with me more since his wretched sickness than he ever talked before. He knew that you once cared for Mr. Throckmorton, and were engaged to him; the newspaper stories had caused him to find it all out; they were so searching, they went so into the depths, you understand. It's horrible for me to say such a thing, but I've come here to make a clean breast of all I'm aware of, so I must confess to you that he had not yet decided *what* sort of a revenge he would take, and that there were times when he had even made up his mind that he would somehow strike his blow through *you.* He listened afterward to the talk between Bleak—between your husband and yourself. You never suspected it, perhaps, but he was somewhere outside of the room, listening. He was very weak, was Julius, and very bad, too, in his vengeful desires. He's just like me, in the way of feebleness; I think we're both very weak about anything that requires firm and positive behavior. You see, he was almost wild when he came home from Australia and found me . . what I was. I shall never forget his rage, at first. I thought he would kill me; I had to send the child away and have her kept out of his sight; there were times when I dreaded that he would kill *her.* What saved me in his eyes (that and that alone!) was my having lived a decent life after my shame fell on me. He used to kiss me in a wild way one minute and then push me from him the next, crying out terrible things that were full of our poor dead father's name and of the horror father would have felt if he could only have known! . . . But when Julius went to live at *his* house and be his servant, I never knew where he had gone. He simply left me and said that business matters I could not understand would take him a good distance off. But he went away to . . to *punish* . . your husband. He admits that now; you know what he openly said in court. Still, as you also know, he hesitated; he never carried out his project, whatever it was . . . You saw how sick a man he looked and acted like at the trial? But oh, he has been much worse ever since. A few days after we both

got home again from L—— he was at death's door. The
doctors said that it meant nervous prostration. There have
been days when he would lie perfectly silent, with his eyes
closed, and never speak at all. Then he would change quite
suddenly, and act almost like his old self. But these alter-
ations in him would never last more than a day or two at a
time. Afterward he would droop again, and more dreadfully than before. Sometimes it seemed to me as if he were
in a kind of living death. His lips would often move,
though; he would whisper to himself with his eyes shut and
his face *so* thin and chalky! It has been horrible . . horrible!"

She stopped speaking, here, and wiped away the gathering
tears with her handkerchief. While she did this, Angela
said:

"Have you ever caught any of those words that he whispered to himself?"

She nodded almost violently; her emotion prevented any
answer for a little space, and then she resumed, with the
manner of one who has mastered hysteria yet is not quite
secure as to just how completely:

"Oh, yes . . . There was your husband's name, now and
then, and yours, and . . and Mr. Throckmorton's, and . . .
But it was very hard to overhear anything, for he would
start and open his eyes whenever I drew close to his bedside, no matter how carefully I did it. Not that I have ever
wanted to play the spy upon him; but it had filled me with
such anxiety to feel that he was lying there with all kinds of
wretched thoughts passing through his brain. Still, I never
believed his brain was affected until, a fortnight ago and
more, he began to get stronger in body, and care for his
food, and occasionally take a little stroll out-of-doors. But
I'm not by any means certain that his mind isn't all right
still. His general health is better; that I'm sure of. But
he has long fits of brooding, and sometimes he will wake up,
as it were, after one of them, and speak to me. What he

says is always the same thing. And it's *because* of what he
says, and of the mysterious doubt which will visit me regarding his sanity, that I've determined to come here and . .
and talk with you." Here she laughed a desolate little
laugh, checking it midway, and looking at Angela as if she
had committed an unpardonable error in giving it vent even
for such a brief instant. "Oh," she went on, " I've been an
awfully long time in . . in coming to the point, as they say :
haven't I ? "

Angela tried to smile, though she did not feel at all like
it. Still, the aim to encourage was uppermost. Evidently
something noteworthy and salient had yet to be told, and she
wished that it should be told with all attainable clearness
and coherence.

"And are you really just coming to the point ? " she said.
"Has your brother imparted anything to you which you've
grown convinced that I ought to hear ? "

"Oh, yes ! " cried Jane Heath, with a little impulsive
movement in Angela's direction that she immediately repressed. "You *ought* to hear it ! I'm sure you'll agree
with me that you ought, when I've made it known . . .
Julius is . . is filled with a plan. It frightened me almost
to death when he first confided it to me."

"A plan ? " questioned Angela.

"Yes. He . . he wants to get into your country-house at
Ponchatuk—Pineland you call it, do you not? He wants
to get into the house while you are away from it, and find
something, recover something."

"Find something? Recover something?" Angela repeated, feeling her heart begin to throb, she knew not why.

"He is convinced that your country house has been kept
closed since you went away from it—that no one ever lives
in it during the winter months."

"That is true. The gardener has a dwelling near by, but
there is never anyone in the house itself until the warmer
season comes on."

"That is just what my brother says. He heard it while he was there, and has not forgotten it. His one ruling idea is to enter the house without being seen—oh, I may as well call things by their names, madam—to enter it like a thief in the night! He doesn't want a living soul except myself to even dream that he has been there."

"Except yourself?"

"Yes. I alone, of the whole world, may share this part of his secret. It would almost madden him with horror, I think, if he knew that I was telling it to you. But I've reached that state when not telling it almost maddens *me*. And you, of all others, are the one to whom I feel that it should be made known. Of course he'd never let me have the dimmest suspicion of what his purpose really was, if he could only manage to do without me. But he can't; he must have some one near him whose help he can count on when his weak and giddy turns come over him. And for this reason he talks with me by the hour about it, his language being at times so full of strange repetitions that I get to doubting his sanity, and have creeping chills, and am afraid to stop with him like that while no one else is near. He'll take my hand in his own thin, wasted one, and he'll devour my face with his eyes, that seem so much larger and are so much brighter than they used to be, as they burn out above his sunken cheeks. 'I must spend a certain space of time, Jane, inside that house,' he will say, 'and no one must see me, no one except you must have the faintest idea that I'm there. And not *even* you, Jane, must know what I've gone there to do. You must keep watch while I'm doing it. You'll be in the big hall. You'll never know; remember that, Jane, *never*. But you'll serve me all the same, will you not? . . now, let us see.' . . . And then he will begin to count upon his fingers the different preparations we ought to make. There are two things that always perplex him greatly: one is where we can lodge without creating comment, and the other is how to procure a

false key that will admit us into the house when our time
for entering it arrives. 'But there must be a way . . there
must be a way,' he will mutter again and again. And in
the meanwhile I am growing so dreadfully nervous over it
all! And for days I've been tossed about between the
longing to let you know everything and the fear lest you
might be very severe with my brother. But lately a different
feeling has taken hold of me. I've become certain that
I ought to disclose it all because . ." Here the speaker
became abruptly silent and turned her dark, faded eyes full
upon Angela.

"Because?" came the gently demanding response.

"Oh," cried Jane Heath, with great abandonment and
impulsiveness of manner, while she seemed to struggle once
more against the tears that she had already controlled, "because I think . . I imagine . . I—I've got some sort of
fancy, that there's evidence of—of guilt hidden in your Long
Island house. And if that is true I should never forgive
myself for not having put every means in your power to . .
to take away all blemish from the name of Mr. Throckmorton!"

Here she sprang to her feet and reached out both hands
in a supplicating gesture. Angela gravely watched her for
a moment, and soon slowly rose also. Then, with a swift
movement, she caught each of the extended hands and held
them tightly, drawing them both toward her. But before
she could pronounce a word, her visitor gasped forth, with
an agitation that showed itself in the throbs of her stretched
throat as she leaned her head backward and at the same
time strove to loosen this unexpected clasp.

"No, no! It isn't right that you—*you* should treat me
this way! Think what I am—*who* I am! I—I should not
have come here at all. You are *his* widow. *Think!* And
I! . . "

"Never mind," Angela said. "I know what he was.
Then, too, I married him—while you . . . Well," she ended,

with a swift, bitter smile that meant for her hearer a token
of priceless indulgence and tolerance, "I don't know which
of us was worse. I was, no doubt. . . ."

"Oh, don't say that!" exclaimed Jane Heath, with the
tears visibly brimming her eyes and a smile of unmistakable
joy beaming so warm and sweet from her lips that it made
Angela realize just how pretty she must have been when a
certain dastardly deed wrecked all her trusting youth. "You
fill me with *such* gratitude, though! Ah! you can't conceive
what it is! To have a good woman like you take my hand!
It's . . . it's . . . well, it's just *heaven* to me!"

"I'm not a good woman," Angela returned, still retaining
the hands that she had seized. "I am very far from good.
. . . . But never mind all that, now. If you thought I
would not take your hand because you had done something
very sinful, you did not know my nature—that is all. . . .
There have been times when I have yearned to go and
find just such women as you are—women who have erred,
who have behaved unwisely, madly, recklessly, *yet who are
regretful.* Ah, there's the point! There is something that
so commands a woman's best sympathy in the repentance—the
honest repentance of a wrong done as you did yours. . . .
Besides, I knew *him* . . . I knew and know just what
the sin must have been, on either side—just how infamous a
pressure of temptation such a man as he was may have brought
to bear upon you, and just how your youth and purity may have
struggled against it. . . . Ah, I'm not so generous as your tear-
ful eyes try to tell me ! I'm human, and I'm . . a woman like
yourself. Then, too, recollect that I'd heard about all this before. It came to me through a friend of Mr. Throckmorton—
a very dear and noble friend of his. And then there's your
personality, your face, your look, your sorrow. . . . These
could not escape me. I put the deepest faith in you, and I
thank you with all my heart for coming here. . . . This may
sound strange to you," Angela hurried on—"that I should
thank you. And why do I thank you? I see your eyes ask-

ing me why. . . But you've said some very peculiar words
to me—words that fill my heart with a passionate and thrilling hope. I'm afraid you don't understand just *how much*
hope you've wakened in me ! *To take away all blemish from
the name of Mr. Throckmorton !* Do you realize what that
means ?. . Come, now, explain to me just what it does mean
in your own conception of the words you've used."

But Jane Heath only shook her head negatively ; and while
the tears flowed faster from her eyes, and the look of devoted
thankfulness toward Angela grew still more fervent than it
had already shone, she tremulously faltered :

"Oh, I'm in doubt if I meant anything ! . . . . You're *so*
good, so good ! I ought not to have said it. There was
nothing behind it. How could there be ? Julius has never
given me a clew. If he had, I would have told you. I'd have
told you even if I'd thought you would have rearrested him. . .
No, no—not that ! And yet it was . . it was conscience ! yes,
it was conscience that brought me to you this day !—that and
only that ! I knew you loved Mr. Throckmorton, and I felt
that there might be a chance of . . of . . what is the word ?
. . I don't remember it . . . I'm not educated like you,
though I'm . . well, not *ignorant*, as you see. I—"

"A chance of exonerating him ?" replied Angela, while
she watched Jane's perturbed face intently.

"Yes—yes," came the answer, in a voice of fervent acquiescence.

Angela dropped the hands that she had taken. A look of
mournful distrust had overspread her face.

"How *can* Hubert Throckmorton be exonerated ? " she
exclaimed, drawing several paces backward from the guest
whom she had a brief while before treated with so opposite
an ardor. "The law declares that Hubert Throckmorton
shot Bleakly Voght by accident."

"By accident," Jane Heath iterated, with drooped head.
"I recall perfectly. That was the verdict." Angela darted

toward her and grasped her arm. "Is there any other verdict possible?"

"I—I don't know."

"You don't know! Do you. . do you even *dream* that any other could be possible?"

"Yes." ·

"You do? Tell me, then, what it is! Tell me!—tell me!"

"I—I cannot!"

"And yet you speak as you have done!"

"I speak of what . . of what seems to me like guilt in my brother. . . "

"But this guilt—what was it? Can you give a name for it?"

"No."

"Then why did you mention it? . . Because you have seen him tormented by a curious fear?"

"Yes."

"And you think that curious fear might lead to. . . ?"

"I don't know what it might lead to. I've seen it. It is fear. It's like the fear of a man who has done a . . a crime."

"A crime!" Angela echoed. "But there was *only one shot fired*. You know that as well as I do. *Don't* you know it?"

She leaned close to Jane Heath and put a hand on each of the woman's rather frail shoulders.

Jane Heath met her vividly searching eyes. "Yes, yes. But let my brother go to that place of yours . . . Pineland," she said. "Let him go. Let me go with him. Find a way for both of us to get in at night when all is quite still—when he thinks there is no one on the watch. Do this. . will you do it? . or. . ?"

Jane's voice failed her, then. She might, however, have regained it a minute later, if Angela had not suddenly thrown both arms about her neck and said, with lips leaned close to her ear:

"I *will* do it! You shall have every means that you desire.

Thank God that you came! I don't know why I say that, but I say it! Thank God that you came!"

And she kissed Jane Heath, pressing her lips to the lips of the woman whom she knew to have once been betrayed by her husband. A little later she said : "We have more to talk about—more to arrange. Your brother and you shall go to a farmer's cottage that I know of, not far from Pineland. On a certain night he shall enter my house with a key that I will provide for him—through you. You will make everything seen plausible to him. It will not be hard—we will talk *that* over. . . And when he enters Pineland I will be there. I will be there, hidden, with witnesses. You understand ?"

"I understand," replied Jane Heath.

XVII.

"I THINK he is merely a madman," said O'Hara.

Angela laughed brokenly, and shrugged her shoulders in a way that might have had numberless meanings.

"Think as you please," she said. "It is all arranged."

It had indeed all been arranged, and most carefully. The words just recorded had passed between O'Hara and Angela in one of the lower rooms at Pineland. They had arrived at the old Voght homestead about an hour previously. Two sentinels were in ambush not far away. The time was now about nine o'clock in the evening. They were aware that for two days past Jane Heath and her invalid brother had been residents of a farm-house located within a quarter of a mile from Pineland.

Jane Heath had efficiently deceived her brother. She had been able to convince him by a certain tale the intricacy of whose deceptive falsehood need not concern us. She had procured a key wherewith to unlock the front-door of the house, and had made her brother believe that the locksmith who fashioned it had done so through the happy accident of having in his shop an old wax impression of a key with which he had supplied Mr. Voght during the previous year. Two dark-lanterns were also ready, one for Julius Heath and one for his sister. All day the invalid had been saving his strength for that quarter of a mile walk and the return. It affected Jane with a dreary sense of drollery when he said to her, that same afternoon :

"Are you sure these people in the house will not think it strange we should go out like this at night.'?

"Oh, I've prepared them for all that," replied Jane.

He started. It seemed to his sister, nowadays, as if he were always starting at something. With the excessive pallor of his cadaverous face, with his restless, vigilant, uneasy eyes, he looked like. a man tormented by one of two agencies, remorse or fear—or perhaps by both together.

"Prepared them?" he now echoed nervously. "How?"

"I said yesterday that you were apt to feel stronger at night, and that when the weather was fine your doctor thought there would be benefit to you in a long evening stroll. And to-night is almost perfect weather, you know."

This was true. The stars beamed lustrously from the April heavens, and the air had a chilly, bracing tingle in it. No least hint of leafage had yet appeared on any of the trees, but the glamour of the softly brilliant starlight robbed them of all gauntness. Underfoot the ground was firm and dry, without a trace of that March thaw which is so grim a foe to the country pedestrian.

Jane, a little while after they had begun their short journey, perceived that her brother already gave signs of exhaustion. Once or twice he leaned heavily on her arm, which he had taken. Still, he seemed upborne by a most vigorous determination. "Don't be afraid that my strength will give out," he said to his sister, after they had progressed about half the distance which they were to traverse. "It won't give out; I may seem a little feeble, but in reality I shall be quite tough enough to carry this little affair through. . . . I only hope," he went on, in a lingering, plaintive way, "that we may get across the lawn and into the house without being seen by a soul. If there's even a dog, it may ruin everything. You, Jane, who have been so clever, who have found out so many things, have made sure that the only people on the estate live a good distance off from the main building itself. That's what I was nearly certain of, as I told you; still, you've turned it into a real certainty. The house is empty. . . the house is empty. . . . I'm glad of that; I'm very, very glad of that!"

Jane's conscience was keenly smiting her, just now. This man was her brother, and had placed the most implicit trust in her devotion to his mysterious cause. She, herself, had been to blame for all that was disastrous in his present fate. But for her sin he would have returned from Australia to the enjoyment of a happy home with the sister for whose companionship he had so long yearned. She had been horribly, unspeakably at fault as regarded their previous relations, and now she was committing toward him an act of guile that would make him turn and curse her when the truth became plain.

Still, there was another side to the question, and when Jane allowed herself to regard this, an inspiriting glow dispelled her compunction. She had never forgotten Angela's entire presentment in court, that day—her face, her demeanor, her words. Until then Jane had hated her for being the wife of Bleakly Voght; but thenceforward a totally new feeling had supervened. It was not difficult for her to divine the whole truth, in a general if not a detailed sense. Angela had foolishly married one man, loving another, and that other was Hubert Throckmorton. Now Jane had read the newspapers both before and after Hubert's trial. Her heart—which was a very tender and womanly one—grew heavy in her breast as she realized the full darkness of that stigma which he must evermore bear. Then gradually rose within her the conviction that Julius might know of some reason why the stigma need not be borne at all. She pondered the potentiality of this fact until there were times when its vexing uncertainty seemed almost a threat to drive her mad. She had no friends outside of her brother, for there were not a few people who had turned from her in the wrath of offended righteousness when they learned that she had become an unwedded mother, and on this account she had never again sought any close human associations. A strong inward trust, therefore, that she was about to do something of secure moral worth blent with a sort of desperate eagerness for feminine counsel and aid. She had never once feared that she could possibly be jeopardizing her brother's life. Still, there were moments when she had sufficient force and nerve to tell herself that it was better for justice to be carried out where due than for disgrace to be inflicted where undeserved.

Angela and O'Hara were seated together in one of the back rooms of the homestead. The light had been cautiously turned rather low, but there was no danger of Julius Heath discerning it as he approached the house, since it could not by any chance be distinguished from the road which he and Jane would be sure to take. Such a system of signalling had become pre-arranged between the two ambuscaded men that Angela felt quite sure of prompt notification as soon as Julius and his sister appeared.

"You're skeptical," she said to O'Hara, as they sat and faced one another in the dimness. " You're skeptical, and I don't blame you for being so. I suppose I'm *really* that way myself."

" Upon my word," softly laughed O'Hara, "there seems so little to be skeptical or otherwise *about!*"

" You're right," said Angela. She turned and stared for a moment at the somewhat feebly-glimmering lamp. " *That* looks so theatrical, doesn't it?" she added. "I was reading, the other day, something that one of the 'naturalistic' novel-writers had asserted in high scorn of his more romantically inclined brethren. Good heavens! as if life were not both ordinary and extraordinary, prosy and fantastic, humdrum and spectacular! This little episode in which we're about to take part . . isn't it like the last act of a drama, and rather a lurid one as well?"

" I hope there will be a truly dramatic end to it," smiled O'Hara, "and not a farcical one."

" It may be farcical," admitted Angela, with a very serious pressing together of the lips. Then a sudden light seemed to sweep across her face in the dimness. "Oh, but if only I could gain some sort of priceless knowledge that would wipe away the blot from *his* life! If only I could! what a glorious gift it would be to him from *me!* From *me*, who once gave him so bitterly different a gift in other days. . . There, you've that pitying look again, as though you thought me almost as crazy as you believe Julius Heath. . . . Well, this is a crazy thing for me to do, surely! coming down here, I mean, with no one but yourself and those men. Suppose we failed to catch the last train for town!" She rose abruptly, and lifted her clasped hands in a dismayed manner. "I have brought no servants with me; I am quite alone except for you . . . and it could never be held a pardonable thing if it were known that I . . ." She paused, and O'Hara saw the color steal into her face.

"You never thought, did you?" he said, with a gentle accent of courtesy that she instantly appreciated. "But I thought—I remembered. If you *were* detained, Mrs. Voght, there is the gardener's wife (a friend of mine, by the way, good old Mrs. Malley) whom I could get to come over and play duenna for you in no time at all."

"And you thought of that!" she exclaimed, stretching forth both her hands to him. "Oh, how kind of you! How like you! You see, my mind has been so occupied, so perplexed!"

O'Hara drooped his eyes for a moment, and shook his handsome curled head. "Don't thank *me*," came his response. "Hubert recollected, and reminded me this very afternoon."

"Hubert! But you told me that he so strongly disapproved this whole idea!"

"He did disapprove it. But nevertheless he felt convinced of your resolute obstinacy in carrying it out."

Just then a soft yet very clear knock sounded at one of the doors.

"Hark," murmured Angela. "It's the sign that they are here." She hurried toward the door with silent speed, while O'Hara followed her.

One of their sentries had come to tell them that Julius and his sister had arrived and were entering the house.

16

XVIII

THE key which Julius carried (and which he insisted on using himself, although his hand shook most feebly while he did so) opened the big front door of Pineland as soon as it was turned in the lock.

Presently Heath whispered to his sister, after they had found their way into the dark, still hall :

"Now stand just here. Don't move. Wait for me. You've your lantern. You needn't let its light shine a bit. No matter how long I'm away, wait for me. I may not be gone very long. I don't think I shall go upstairs. I may, but I don't think I shall. You understand me, Jane, don't you ? "

" Yes," she whispered back.

She watched his dim figure, seen inky-black behind the cylindrical shaft of light that his own lantern emitted, until he had disappeared into what seemed a room opening off from the same hall where she herself yet remained immovably stationed.

Heath had crossed the threshold of an apartment which he well remembered. In Bleakly Voght's earlier days of sportmanship he had been wont to keep all guns and fishing-tackle here, and even now there were proofs of this past occupancy in some dingy covered baskets that may once have held scores of rosy-gilled Long Island trout, or in big coils of trolling-line, with their oval "squids" of lead and that dark latent hook, curving at the end of each, which had made many a blue-fish writhe. The room itself was rather shabbily furnished than otherwise; Voght had once said of it that every old bit of furniture used to be put there after it became unfit to keep anywhere else, and this was

certainly true of a huge hair-cloth sofa with bird-claws of
tarnished gilt, a monstrous mahogany bureau with a pro-
fusion of small glass knobs, and a few other like objects, as
antique as they were uncouth.

It was in a certain large closet of this room that Julius
had found the two guns which he and Voght had taken
with them on their momentous trip. He now went directly
to this closet, but soon saw that neither gun was there.

He then swept the light of his lantern eagerly, ransack-
ingly about the room. On a sudden he uttered a short,
glad cry. He had seen a weapon of the sort that he
searched for, leaning against the opposite wall.

His tremulous hand set down the lantern on a table close
beside him. Then he darted forward, and seized the gun.

" It's mine—it's the one I had—what 'luck, what luck ! "
broke from him ; and while he framed these words he did
not know that he spoke at all.

In the steady stream of light he soon was holding the
piece, while he examined it with a scrutiny that swiftly told
him what he desired to know. It was now plain that he
had discovered one barrel to be empty and the other loaded.
With great softness he laid the gun on the table. After
doing so he began another search with his lantern. But it
was briefer than the last. Very near to the spot where the
gun had been discovered, he now came across the ammuni-
tion which he had carried on that fatal day. Evidently
someone had tossed it here beside the gun after thrusting
it all into this game-bag which he recollected also to have.
taken with him. Yes, everything that he needed was here!
He brought the bag back with him to the table, placed the
lantern beside it, and took up the gun once more. The
glare on his face gave it. an unearthly lividness, ghastly and
worn as it had been for weeks past. But the wild, triumphant smile that parted his lips added a demoniac element
to his elfin weirdness, and made him look like some hellish
minion of crime and horror while he stood there with

skinny hands clutching what he had so long and so avidly craved. Again his lips opened and his voice sounded; but he did not know this time that he spoke, any more than he had known it previously.

"Better load it than drop it down *there!* Better load it and leave it . . . load it and leave it . . . that's far the best way! If I took it out in the hall Jane might easily see what it was while I-passed her! . . . Load it and leave it . . . load it and leave it . . . There's no better way than just that."

His fingers trembled so that there seemed, at first, little chance of his being able to load the weapon. But by the time that he had really succeeded in commencing to load it, something occurred which made a great cry burst from him.

Two men had slipped into the room like phantoms. One held a big lighted lamp, which he instantly deposited somewhere, while it filled the room with its rays. The other glided straight up to Heath and snatched the gun from his hands.

"You needn't load that gun, Mr. Heath," he said quietly. "I want it, sir, just as it is."

Heath dropped into a chair, gasping. "Spies on me!" were the first words that left him.

"You're right, there," said the man who had brought in the lamp and who was not so civil as he who had seized the gun. "What did you want to put the load back for? Eh? What made you say it was luck for you to get that gun instead of some other? That was yours—the one you carried the day Mr. Voght was shot. Oh, you needn't shake your head; *it was.* And how is it you're found sneaking into this house with a false key, after dark, for no purpose under heaven but to re-load that gun? Why did you talk about loading it and leaving it, and say that to do this was better than to drop it *down there?* Down where? What's the meaning of this mystery? You've got to answer some time or other, and you may as well do it now."

"I'll never do it," Heath muttered, as if through his meeting teeth. "Nobody can tell my reason for coming here. Even my sister Jane (who must have betrayed me in the meanest way!) cannot tell it. I'll keep the secret, such as it is . . . I'll keep the secret till I die!"

But a voice full of deep vibrations now spoke. It was a woman's voice, and Heath recognized it instantly, with a choked, shivering moan. The door on whose threshold Angela and O'Hara had been standing, was bathed in shadow. They had heard nearly all that had passed since the entrance of the two men. A few seconds before Heath finished speaking, Angela had felt what she believed the whole explanatory truth dart through her astonished mind.

"You cannot keep the secret, Bradbourne," she said. "No, for I have guessed it if the others here have not. *You fired at the same second of time that Mr. Throckmorton did, and so the report seemed like a single one.* You fired, meaning to kill Mr. Voght. Then you found out what had accidentally occurred to the gun of Mr. Throckmorton. This accounts for all your strange behavior after the dreadful affair took place. It accounts for your desire to come here without having a soul except your sister know that you had come. It accounts for everything—everything!" . . . Her eyes were flaming, her bosom was in a tumult of pulsation, as she now turned toward O'Hara. "Am I not right?" she cried. "It *must* have been that! I remember, years ago, hearing my father, who was once a confirmed sportsman, tell some story of two reports, both produced at the same moment, sounding exactly like one, and deceiving all who were within earshot. I —"

"Good God!" struck in O'Hara. He caught one of her hands, and stooping down, impetuously kissed it. "You've guessed what the cleverest lawyers in the country failed to dream of—what these detectives and I, even after the developments we've witnessed, would doubtless never have hit upon ! This is like. . . well, by Jove, it's like the purest inspiration and nothing a whit less ! "

She smiled, letting him hold her hand, and saying quite low and with great speed: "*Call* it that ! I shall like to believe it *was* that ! I shall always like to believe it the inspiration, the intuition, of my love—my devoted, repentant love !"

Heath did not catch these words, but he had caught O'Hara's, and they were now producing a terrible effect upon him. He strove to rise from the chair into which he had sunk, but failed; and then, in tones husky, defiant, fraught with the most rebellious and hysteric challenge, he shouted:

"It's . . it's no inspiration—it's falsehood—nothing but falsehood ! I—I did not come here to re-load that gun. I saw it while—while I was searching for something else. For something else, do you hear ? I—I happened to notice that one barrel had been discharged since—since I took it with me that day. This was all—this explains my attempt to re-load the gun. . . Ah, you are so clever, Mrs. Voght ! But you are *too* clever, just at present ! You've hated me for a good while past ! You . . ." His further articulation became a mere pell-mell incoherence. He tried once more to rise from his chair, and then, failing a second time, dropped backward. His head fell on one side ; he looked as though he had been smitten by death.

" Oh, if it *should* be ! " Angela faltered, while she busied herself with his resuscitation as best she could. Jane had appeared, but was almost incapable, through extreme dismay and alarm, of doing anything except stare helplessly at her brother's white, spectral face. •

"It is not death," O'Hara soon whispered to Angela. "He is a miserably weak and shattered man, but he may have months of life yet before him. If he has, we must use every means toward obtaining a full confession of his crime. But even if none should come, the testimony of these two men—both bearing flawless reputations—will be sufficient to cleanse Hubert's name. That, and your wonderful solution of the enigma ;—for such it undoubtedly is, and as such it will be accepted."

But Angela shook her head with sad incredulity. " Nothing will be accepted," she replied, except this man's complete and lucid confession, made before the most disinterested witnesses. Unless we obtain that, it will be said that we have sought to exculpate Hubert by an artful *ruse.* Ah, you know the world as well as I do ! It believes the worst about anyone whom it has condemned until every vestige of compromising statement has been rendered null ! "

Heath did not positively recover consciousness that night, nor for several days afterward. He was carried into one of the upstairs chambers at Pineland, and lay there, visited by two or three competent physicians and most carefully nursed by Angela and his sister. A severe stroke of paralysis had befallen him, and the first glimmers of reason that manifested themselves gave slight hope of his brain ever regaining its natural equipoise.

After about a fortnight of semi-stupor, however, he surprised his watchers by becoming thoroughly clear-headed once more. But he was awakening only to die of another trouble—a heart complaint which at intervals caused him acute suffering and made him clearly realize that his end was imminent. This realization altered the entire trend of his former secretive resolve. On first recovering consciousness he had upbraided his sister bitterly for her treachery. Afterward, in his weakness and pain, he had pardoned her. Angela had spent hours at his bedside, praying him to do so, and at last she had succeeded. But she also succeeded in another far more vitally important matter. She and death together unlocked at last the stubborn mood of his silence. One afternoon, propped up by pillows and in the company of certain auditors who had been hastily summoned to hear him, he declared himself the murderer of Bleakly Voght.

Angela had been right. Just at the same instant that
Hubert's gun was discharged by accident, Heath had deliberately fired upon Voght. A hundred times the man had
made up his mind, before then, to kill the wronger of his
sister, and a hundred times he had left such design unac-
complished. But Hubert's own angry reference to the
shame inflicted upon Jane had suddenly nerved him into
homicidal action, standing as he did stand there among the
obscuring trees. He had not stopped to think of the consequences his act would entail—he had stopped for that
only too often already . . . When, a brief while later, he
had seen Hubert kneeling beside the fallen man and accusing himself of being the author of Voght's death, then a
temptation had swept through Heath to escape by deceitful
means. He alone, in the whole world, knew of those
strangely simultaneous shots, one of which had passed without harm by Voght, and the other of which had dealt a
deadly intended wound. Later he had striven, as we have
seen, partially to shield Hubert by inducing the latter to
say nothing on the subject of his own presence so near the
scene of the shooting, and hence to suppress all that damning record of a previous quarrel between the two men. Not
succeeding in this plan, he had entrenched himself behind
his apparently impregnable innocence. But months afterward his guilty fears had begun morbidly to prey upon him.
He remembered his own foolish omission to re-load the
empty barrel of that gun. True, no one had ever thought
to inquire concerning it; it had been as little in the minds
of lawyers, of judge, or of jury as the gun carried by O'Hara
or Voght himself. *Yet there it remained*, in some one of the
many rooms of Pineland. Might it not be eventually examined and its condition commented upon? In vain he sought
to lull this insidious and augmenting fear. It haunted
and teased him as a gadfly might haunt and tease a bound
captive. While he grew more ill in body his mind grew
more susceptible to its grim and shrewd visitations. Finally

he had felt inaction an unendurable torture. He must return to Pineland, and either make way with the gun by dropping it into an old well not far from the house itself, or else reload its tell-tale empty barrel ! . . .

His confession was made public, and its delivery had been attended by circumstances of such strong credibility that in a few more days Hubert Throckmorton found himself overwhelmed by legions of congratulations. No doubt was possible any longer. His hottest newspaper foes were forced to make open retraction of their charges. He stood before the world as a man with a character all the more spotless because of that dark brand which had been removed from it.

Heath's death occurred on the day that succeeded his most fateful deposition, and was held to have been accelerated by the intense excitement which that event produced.

Only now did Hubert dare trust himself to meet Angela, and now he appeared before her, burning to express his devoted thanks. O'Hara had told him of how it had been she who had really reinstated him in the old place of honor among his fellow-men. But for her the secret of Heath might forever have remained undivulged, needing that one decisive mental leap toward its solution which mathematicians tell us it has been the higher gift of their ruling geniuses at rare intervals to take.

Hubert made some reference of this sort during his first happy interview with Angela. But she tossed her head a little, and somewhat brusquely answered :

"It wasn't more than ordinarily bright of me, after all. I merely shine in a relative way. You know the French saying : '*Dans le pays des aveugles*,' etc. All those wiseacre lawyers were so ridiculously dull about it ; they needed a bit of feminine common-sense to open their sleepy eyes."

"Ah," said Hubert, "they had none of them your sweet talisman of discovery ! "

She sighed and trembled as his arms clasped her. "Hubert," she murmured, "at last I've redeemed all the bitterness of those yesterdays? Tell me that I have!"

"You have more than done so," he answered; and then he put his lips to hers, and a little later she heard him whisper, "My love, my one inalienable love!—my wife that soon shall be!" . . .

But before they were married Angela insisted on signing away every dollar of her dead husband's fortune to a few of his nearest relatives.

"I come to you, Hubert," she said, "just as I would have come in those other times. I was a poor girl then, you know. I would have brought you nothing then; I bring you nothing now."

"You bring me everything now," he answered, "and you are all the dearer because of destiny's trying delays!"

END.

www.ingramcontent.com/pod-product-compliance
Lightning Source LLC
Chambersburg PA
CBHW020853270326
41928CB00006B/677